THE STORY OF WRITING

D1069582

THE STORY OF WRITING

with over 355 illustrations, 50 in colour

NEW EDITION

Andrew Robinson

Thames & Hudson

I dedicate this book to my mother, who encouraged me to read

Author's note

Brian Lapping, an innovative television producer, enabled me to undertake a period of research into writing systems in 1989–90. I am duly grateful.

No one person could be an expert on all the writing systems discussed in this book. I cannot claim to be an expert in any one of them. I have therefore relied on the work of genuine experts, none of whom will be fully satisfied with my summaries of what are extremely complex and subtle issues. I have tried to take account of their knowledgeable criticisms but hasten to add – more forcefully than usual for an author – that any errors are my sole responsibility.

I offer sincere thanks to John Chadwick (*The Decipherment of Linear B*), Michael Coe (*Breaking the Maya Code*), John DeFrancis (*The Chinese Language* and *Visible Speech*), Asko Parpola (*Deciphering the Indus Script*) and J. Marshall Unger (*The Fifth Generation Fallacy*) for their detailed comments and their encouragement. I also thank Irving Finkel, and Carol Andrews, Simon Martin and Nicholas Postgate; and Emmett Bennett, Ann Brown, Stephen Houston, Mogens Trolle Larsen, Iravatham Mahadevan, David Parsons and John Ray for providing source material.

For Japanese, Tetsuo Amaya was unfailingly helpful and imaginative; he also provided several examples of Japanese script. Krishna Dutta provided a sample of Bengali script.

Concerning Michael Ventris and the decipherment of Linear B, I thank Patrick Hunter, former classics master of Ventris who witnessed the beginning of Ventris' obsession in 1936; Prudence Smith, BBC radio producer who witnessed Ventris' moment of breakthrough in 1952; and Oliver Cox, friend and fellow architect of Ventris. Patrick Hunter kindly gave me a few personal items in the handwriting of Ventris which I shall always value. While writing this book, I like to think that I have been inspired, to the best of my ability, by the open-minded and generous intellectual spirit of Ventris.

Half-title Lady with a codex. Wall painting from Pompeii, before AD 79. Museo Archeologico Nazionale, Naples.
Photo Scala Florence.
Frontispiece Detail from an Egyptian wall painting.
Photo John Ross.

First published in the United Kingdom in 1995 by
Thames & Hudson Ltd, 181A High Holborn, London WC1V 7QX

The Story of Writing © 1995 and 2007 Thames & Hudson Ltd, London

New edition 2007
Reprinted 2016

All Rights Reserved. No part of this publication may be reproduced or transmitted in any form or by any means, electronic or mechanical, including photocopy, recording or any other information storage and retrieval system, without prior permission in writing from the publisher.

British Library Cataloguing-in-Publication Data
A catalogue record for this book is available from the British Library

ISBN 978-0-500-28660-9

Printed and bound in China by Everbest Printing Co. Ltd

To find out about all our publications, please visit
www.thamesandhudson.com. There you can subscribe to our e-newsletter, browse or download our current catalogue, and buy any titles that are in print.

CONTENTS

INTRODUCTION

Writing is among the greatest inventions in human history, perhaps *the* greatest invention, since it made history possible. Yet it is a skill most writers take for granted. We learn it at school, building on the alphabet, or (if we live in China or Japan) the Chinese characters. As adults we seldom stop to think about the mental-cum-physical process that turns our thoughts into symbols on a piece of paper or on a video screen, or bytes of information in a computer disc. Few of us have any clear recollection of how we learnt to write.

A page of text in a foreign script, totally incomprehensible to us, reminds us forcibly of the nature of our achievement. An extinct script, such as Egyptian hieroglyphs or cuneiform from the ancient Near East, strikes us as little short of miraculous. By what means did these pioneering writers of 4000–5000 years ago learn to write? How did their symbols encode their speech and thought? How do we decipher (or attempt to decipher) the symbols after centuries of silence? Do today's writing systems work in a completely different way from the ancient scripts? What about the Chinese and Japanese scripts – are they like ancient hieroglyphs? Do hieroglyphs have any advantages over alphabets? Finally, what kind of people were the early writers – and what kind of information, ideas and feelings did they make permanent?

This book tries to answer these questions. It encompasses many cultures, many languages and almost all periods of human development; it draws upon ideas and information from a range of disciplines, including anthropology, archaeology, art history, economics, linguistics, mathematics, political and social history, psychology and theology; and it touches on literature, medieval and Renaissance manuscripts, calligraphy, typography and printing. But though its canvas is a broad one – so influential has writing been – it is not a historical portrait. It does not trace the development of writing from earliest times to the present day; nor does it mention every significant script, past and present (there are far too many). It is, rather, an account of the scripts used in the major civilizations of the ancient world, of the major scripts we use today, and of the underlying principles that unite the two. For the ancient scripts turn out not to be dead letters, not just esoteric curiosities. Fundamentally, the way we write at the start of the 3rd millennium AD is not different from the way that the ancient Egyptians wrote. That is the simple, if surprising, idea behind this book.

Without writing there would be no history. In all civilizations, scribes have been the transmitters of culture, the first historians. The Buddhist scribes seen here in a 10th-century AD wall painting from the monastery at Karashahr, China, were as important to Chinese civilization as the monks of medieval Europe or the scribes of ancient Egypt.

Writing as propaganda. On the eve of the battle of Kadesh, *c.* 1285 BC, the Egyptian pharaoh Ramesses II discusses the plan of attack against the Hittites. According to Ramesses, there was a great Egyptian victory; but according to a Hittite inscription, the Hittites were the victors.

The Function of Writing

Writing and literacy are generally seen as forces for good. It hardly needs saying that a person who can read and write has greater opportunities for fulfilment than one who is illiterate. But there is also a dark side to the spread of writing that is present throughout its history, if somewhat less obvious. Writing has been used to tell lies as well as truth, to bamboozle and exploit as well as to educate, to make minds lazy as well as to stretch them.

Socrates pinpointed our ambivalence towards writing in his story of the Egyptian god Thoth, the inventor of writing, who came to see the king seeking royal blessing on his enlightening invention. The king told Thoth: 'You, who are the father of letters, have been led by your affection to ascribe to them a power the opposite of that which they really possess . . . You have invented an elixir not of memory, but of reminding; and you offer your pupils the appearance of wisdom, not true wisdom, for they will read many things without instruction and will therefore seem to know many things, when they are for the most part ignorant.' In a 21st-century world drenched with written information and surrounded by information technologies of astonishing speed, convenience and power, these words spoken in antiquity have a distinctly contemporary ring.

Political leaders have always used writing for propaganda purposes. Nearly 4000 years and a totally different script separated the famous black basalt law code of Hammurabi of Babylon from the slogans and billboards of 1990s Iraq – but the message is similar. Hammurabi called himself 'mighty King, King of

Babylon, King of the whole country of Amurru, King of Sumer and Akkad, King of the Four Quarters of the World'; and he promised that if his laws were obeyed, then all his people would benefit. 'Writing', wrote H. G. Wells in his *Short History of the World*, 'put agreements, laws, commandments on record. It made the growth of states larger than the old city states possible. … The command of the priest or king and his seal could go far beyond his sight and voice and could survive his death.'

Yes, regrettably, Babylonian and Assyrian cuneiform, Egyptian hieroglyphs and the Mayan glyphs of Central America, carved on palace and temple walls, were used much as Stalin used posters about Lenin in the Soviet Union: to remind the people who was the boss, how great were his triumphs, how firmly based in the most high was his authority. At Karnak, in Egypt, on the outer wall of a temple, there are carved representations of the battle at Kadesh fought by Ramesses II against the Hittites, around 1285 BC. Hieroglyphs recount a peace treaty between the pharaoh and the Hittite king, and celebrate a great Egyptian victory. But another version of the same treaty found at the Hittite capital Boghazköy turns the battle into a win for the Hittites!

The urge for immortality has always been of the first importance to writers. Most of the thousands of known fragments written by the Etruscans, for instance, are funerary inscriptions. We can read the name, date and place of death because they are written in an adaptation of the Greek alphabet; but that is the level of our knowledge of the enigmatic language of this important people, who borrowed the alphabet from Greece, handed it on to the Romans, who in turn gave it to the rest of Europe. Decipherment of the Etruscan language is like trying to learn English by reading nothing but gravestones.

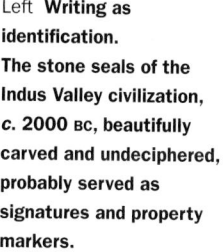

Writing as prognostication. The earliest Chinese inscriptions are the 'oracle bones', dating from the Shang dynasty, *c.* 1200 BC. The symbols were the precursors of some Chinese characters.

Another purpose for writing was to predict the future. All ancient societies were obsessed with what was to come. Writing allowed them to codify their worries. Among the Maya it took the form of bark-paper books elaborately painted in colour and bound in jaguar skin; the prognostications were based on a written calendrical system so

Left **Writing as identification. The stone seals of the Indus Valley civilization, *c.* 2000 BC, beautifully carved and undeciphered, probably served as signatures and property markers.**

sophisticated it extended as far back as 5 billion years ago, more than our present scientifically estimated age for the earth. In China, on the other hand, during the Bronze Age Shang dynasty, questions about the future were written on turtle shells and ox bones, so-called 'oracle bones'. The bone was heated with a brand until it cracked, the meaning of the shape of the crack was divined, and the answer to the question was inscribed. Later, what actually transpired might be added to the bone.

But of course most writing was comparatively mundane. It provided, for instance, the equivalent of an ancient identity card or a property marker. The cartouche enclosing the name of Tutankhamun was found on objects throughout his tomb, from the grandest of thrones to the smallest of boxes. Anyone who was anyone among ancient rulers required a personal seal for signing clay tablets and other inscriptions. So did any merchant or other person of substance. (Today in Japan, a seal, rather than a western-style signature, is standard practice for signing business and legal documents.) Such name-tagging has been found as far apart as Mesopotamia, China and Central America. The stone seals from the Indus Valley civilization, which flourished around 2000 BC, are especially interesting: not only are they exquisitely carved – depicting, among other motifs, a mysterious unicorn (see p. 144) – the symbols written on them are undeciphered. Unlike the script of Babylonia, the Indus Valley writing does not appear on walls as public inscriptions. Instead the seals have been found scattered around the houses and streets of the 'capital' city. They were probably worn on a cord or thong and used as a personal 'signature' or to indicate a person's office or the social or professional group to which he or she belonged.

Writing as accountancy. In the late 8th century BC, two Assyrian warriors greet each other after a battle, two scribes record the number slain. The scribe in the foreground writes in imperial Aramaic, an alphabetic script, using a brush on papyrus. His bearded colleague writes in the traditional cuneiform script on a clay or wax-covered tablet.

Writing used for accountancy was much commoner than that on seals and tags. The earliest writing of all, on Sumerian clay tablets from Mesopotamia, concerns lists of raw materials and products, such as barley and beer, lists of labourers and their tasks, lists of field areas and their owners, the income and outgoings of temples, and so forth – all with calculations concerning production levels, delivery dates, locations and debts. And the same is true, generally speaking, of the earliest deciphered European writing, tablets from pre-Homeric Greece and Crete written in Linear B script. The tablet that clinched the decipherment of Linear B in 1953 was simply an inventory of tripod cauldrons (one of them with its legs burnt off), and of goblets of varying sizes and numbers of handles.

The Origin(s) of Writing

Most scholars now accept that writing began with accountancy, even though accountancy is little in evidence in the surviving writing of ancient Egypt, China and Central America. To quote an expert on early Sumerian tablets, writing developed 'as a direct consequence of the compelling demands of an expanding economy'. In other words, some time in the late 4th millennium BC, the complexity of trade and administration in the early cities of Mesopotamia reached a point at which it outstripped the power of memory of the governing élite. To record transactions in a dependable, permanent form became essential. Administrators and merchants could then say the Sumerian equivalents of 'I shall put it in writing' and 'Can I have this in writing?'

But this does not explain how writing actually emerged out of no-writing. Divine origin, in favour until the Enlightenment in the 18th century, has given way to the theory of a pictographic origin. The first written symbols are generally thought to have been pictograms, pictorial representations of concrete objects. Some scholars believe that writing was the result of a conscious search by an unknown Sumerian individual in the city of Uruk (biblical Erech), in about 3300 BC. Others believe it was the work of a group, presumably of clever administrators and merchants. Still others think it was not an invention at all, but an accidental discovery. Many regard it as the result of evolution over a long period, rather than a flash of inspiration. One particularly well-aired theory holds that writing grew out of a long-standing counting system of clay 'tokens' (such 'tokens', exact purpose unknown, have been found in many Middle Eastern archaeological sites):

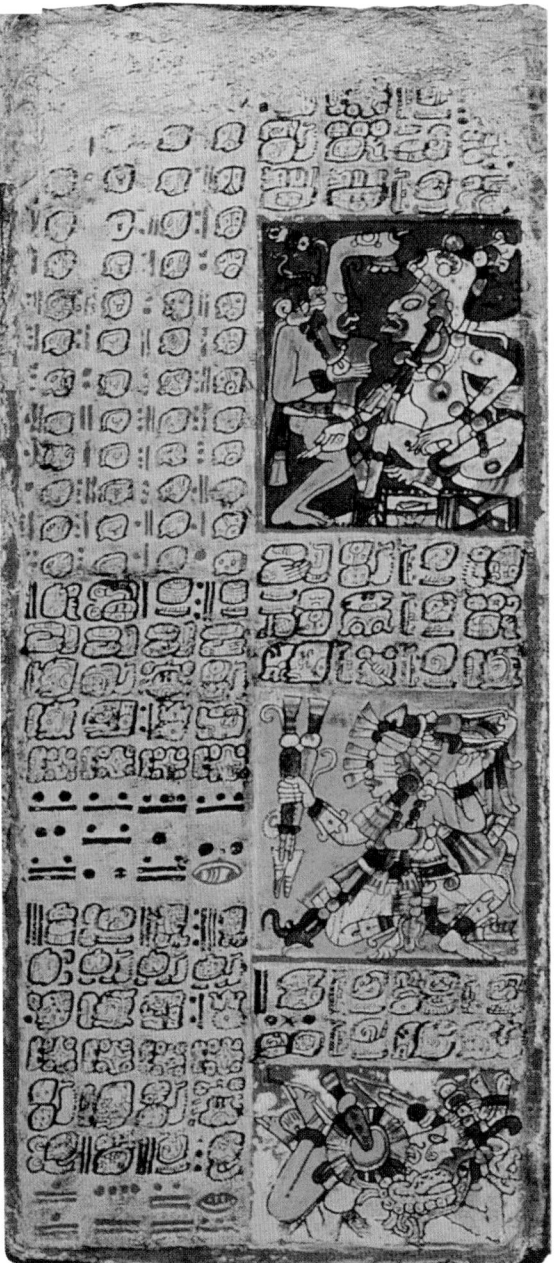

Writing as an almanac. This page of the Dresden Codex, *c.* 15th century AD, contains Maya dates. The Maya used a sophisticated calendrical system.

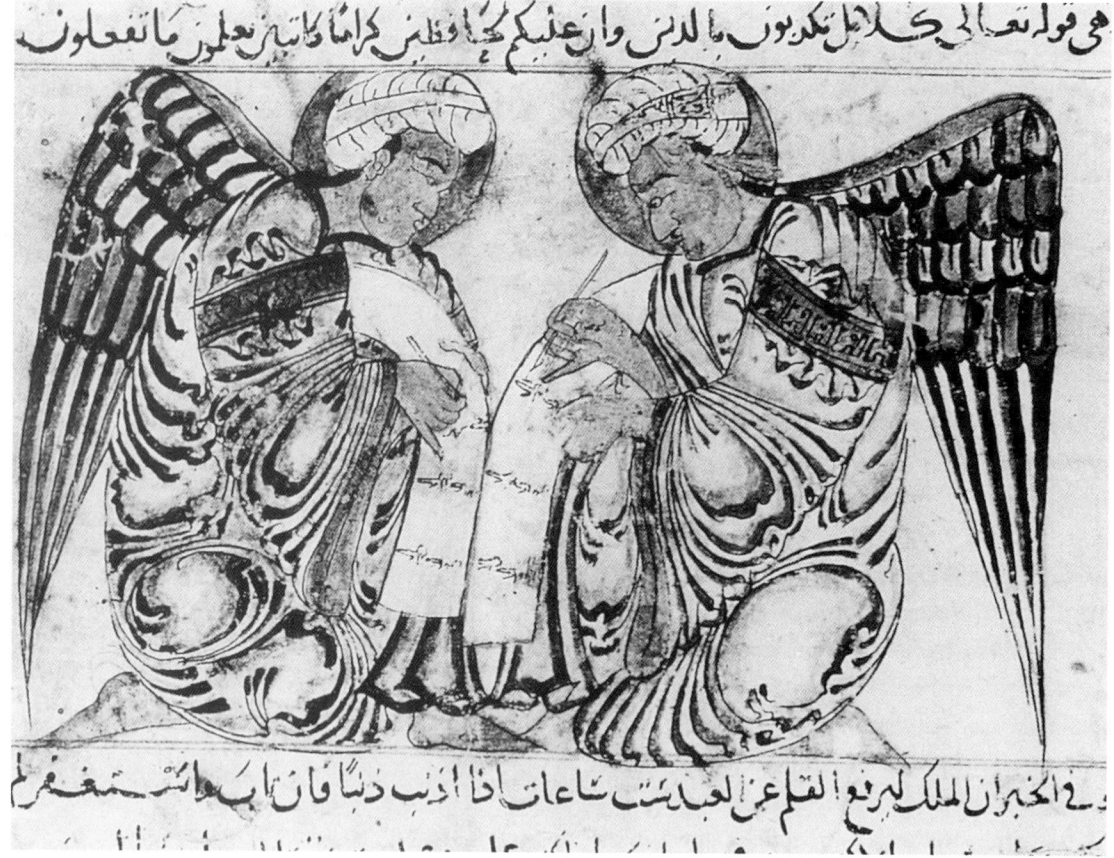

 في قوله تعالى كلا بل تكذبون ما الدين وان عليكم كرام كاتبين يعلمون ما تفعلون

في الخبران الملك ليرفع القلم عن العبد ست ساعات اذا اذنب ذنبا فان استغفر

the substitution of two-dimensional signs for these tokens, with the signs resembling the shapes of the tokens, was a first step towards writing, according to this theory.

In any case, essential to the development of full writing, as opposed to the limited, purely pictographic writing of North American Indians and others, was the discovery of the rebus principle. This was the radical idea that a pictographic symbol could be used for its phonetic value. Thus a drawing of an owl in Egyptian hieroglyphs could represent a consonantal sound with an inherent *m*; and in English a picture of a bee with a picture of a leaf might (if one were so minded) represent the word belief.

Sacred writing. Angels record the good and bad deeds of humanity in an illuminated manuscript by al-Qazwini, 1280. The Arabic script is revered in Islam, since the Koran is regarded as the word of God.

The Development of Writing

Once invented, accidentally discovered or evolved – take your pick – did writing then diffuse throughout the globe from Mesopotamia? The earliest Egyptian writing dates from 3100 BC, that of the Indus Valley from 2500 BC, that of Crete from 1900 BC, that of China from 1200 BC, that of Central America from 600 BC (all dates are approximate). On this basis, it seems reasonable that the idea of writing, but not the particular symbols of a script, did spread gradually from culture to distant culture. It took 600 or 700 years for the idea of printing to reach Europe from China, and even longer for the idea of paper: why should writing not have reached China from Mesopotamia over an even longer period?

Nevertheless, in the absence of solid evidence for transmission of the idea (even in the case of the much nearer civilizations of Mesopotamia and Egypt), a majority of scholars prefer to think that writing developed independently in the major civilizations of the ancient world. The optimist, or at any rate the anti-imperialist, will prefer to emphasize the intelligence and inventiveness of human societies; the pessimist, who takes a more conservative view of history, will tend to assume that humans prefer to copy what already exists, as faithfully as they can, restricting their innovations to cases of absolute necessity. The latter is the preferred explanation for how the Greeks borrowed the alphabet from the Phoenicians, adding in the process the vowels not expressed in the Phoenician script.

There can be no doubt about certain script borrowings, such as the Romans taking the Etruscan script, the Japanese taking the Chinese characters and, in our own time, the Turks (under Kemal Atatürk) abandoning the Arabic script in favour of the Latin script. Changes are made to a borrowed script because the new language has sounds in it that are not found in the language for which the script was being used (hence the umlaut on the 'u' of Atatürk). This idea is easy enough to grasp when the two languages are similar, but it can be extremely awkward to follow when the two languages differ vastly, as Japanese does from Chinese. In order to cope with the differences, the Japanese script has *two* entirely distinct sets of symbols: Chinese characters (thousands), and Japanese syllabic signs (about 50) that symbolize the basic sounds of Japanese speech. A Japanese sentence therefore mixes Chinese characters and Japanese syllabic signs in what is generally regarded as the most complicated system of writing in the world.

Script, Speech and Language

Europeans and Americans of ordinary literacy must recognize and write around 52 alphabetic signs, and sundry other symbols, such as numerals, punctuation marks and 'whole-word' semantic symbols, for example +, &, £, $, 2, which are sometimes called logograms. Their Japanese counterparts, by contrast, are supposed to know and be able to write some 2000 symbols, and, if they are highly educated, must recognize 5000 symbols or more. The two situations, in Europe/America and in Japan, appear to be poles apart. But in fact, the positions resemble each other more than appears.

Borrowing a script. Scripts have been borrowed by languages throughout history. In Turkey Kemal Atatürk replaced the Arabic script with the Roman script in 1928. Here he teaches the new script.

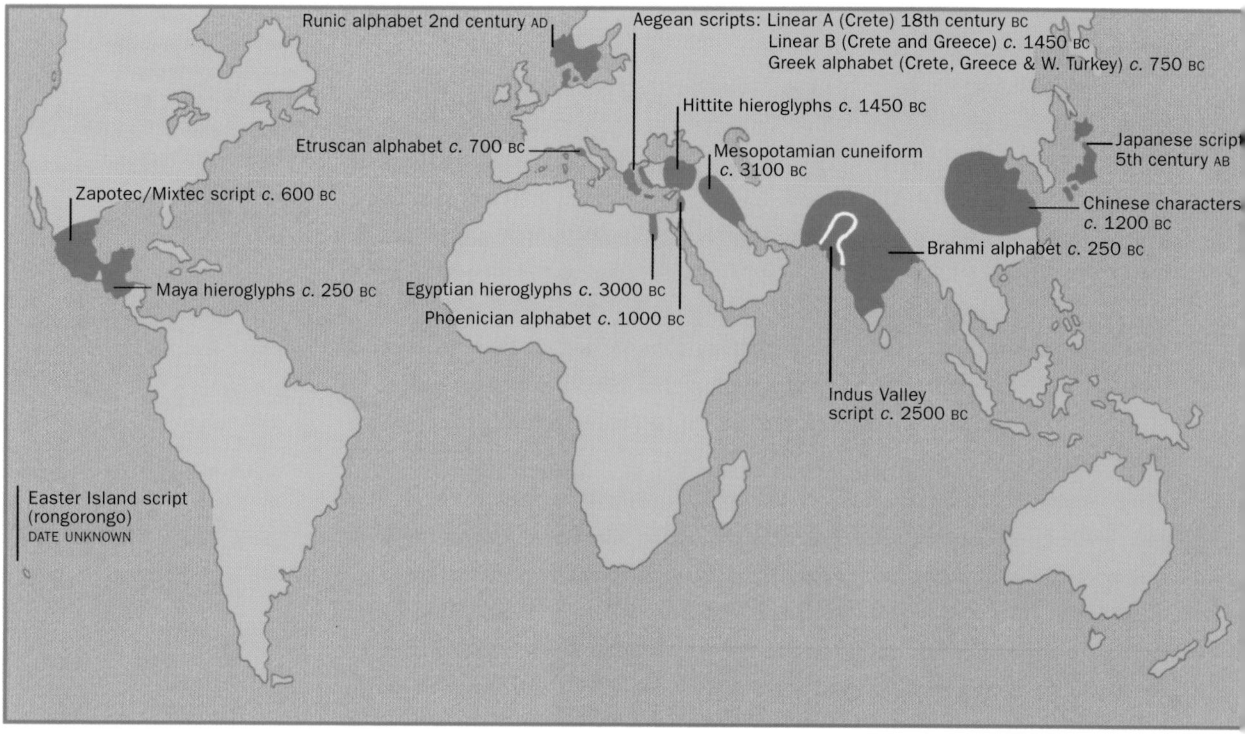

Runic alphabet 2nd century AD

Aegean scripts: Linear A (Crete) 18th century BC
Linear B (Crete and Greece) *c.* 1450 BC
Greek alphabet (Crete, Greece & W. Turkey) *c.* 750 BC

Hittite hieroglyphs *c.* 1450 BC

Etruscan alphabet *c.* 700 BC

Mesopotamian cuneiform *c.* 3100 BC

Japanese script 5th century AB

Zapotec/Mixtec script *c.* 600 BC

Chinese characters *c.* 1200 BC

Brahmi alphabet *c.* 250 BC

Maya hieroglyphs *c.* 250 BC

Egyptian hieroglyphs *c.* 3000 BC

Phoenician alphabet *c.* 1000 BC

Indus Valley script *c.* 2500 BC

Easter Island script (rongorongo)
DATE UNKNOWN

All scripts that are full writing – that is, a 'system of graphic symbols that can be used to convey any and all thought' (to quote John DeFrancis, a distinguished American student of Chinese) – operate on one basic principle, contrary to what most people think, some scholars included. Both alphabets and the Chinese and Japanese scripts use symbols to represent sounds (i.e. phonetic signs); and all writing systems use a mixture of phonetic and semantic signs. What differs – apart from the outward forms of the symbols, of course – is the *proportion* of phonetic to semantic signs. The higher the proportion, the easier it is to guess the pronunciation of a word. In English the proportion is high, in Chinese it is low. Thus English spelling represents English speech sound by sound more accurately than Chinese characters represent Mandarin speech; but Finnish spelling represents the Finnish language better than either of them. The Finnish script is highly efficient phonetically, while the Chinese (and Japanese) script is phonetically seriously deficient.

Above **The beginnings of writing.**

Below **Written versus spoken language (from DeFrancis and Unger). Writing systems are shown on a theoretical continuum of writing between pure phonography and pure logography, with Finnish script as the most phonetically efficient and Chinese script the least.**

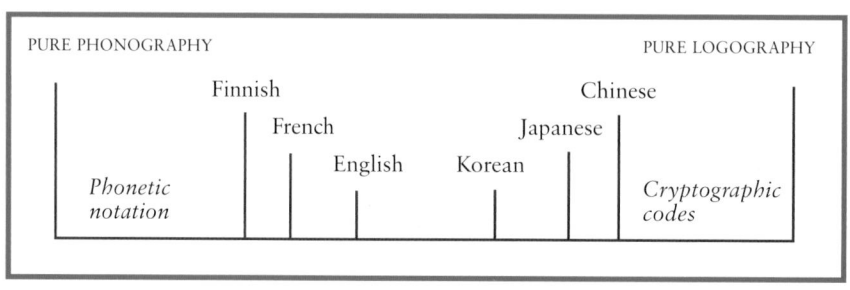

PURE PHONOGRAPHY						PURE LOGOGRAPHY
		Finnish		Chinese		
		French			Japanese	
			English	Korean		
Phonetic notation						*Cryptographic codes*

The difficulty of learning the Chinese and Japanese scripts cannot be denied. In Japan, in the mid-1950s, a peak in teenage suicides seems to have been connected with the expansion of mass education post-war, using the full-blown Japanese script with its several thousand characters. It takes a Chinese or Japanese person several years longer than a western counterpart to achieve fluency in reading.

That said, there are many millions of westerners who have failed to learn to read and write. The level of literacy in Japan is higher than in the West (though probably not as high as is claimed). The intricacy of the Japanese script has not stopped the Japanese from becoming a great economic power; nor has it caused them to abandon their use of Chinese characters in favour of a much smaller set of signs based on their already-existing syllabic signs – a theoretically feasible move.

Cultural Revolution, China, mid-1960s. Mao Zedong maintained that, ideally, he would sweep away the Chinese characters altogether, so that millions of illiterate Chinese could become literate in the Latin script. But conservative opposition was too strong, and during the Cultural Revolution Red Guards destroyed examples of the Latin script.

WRITING: A CHRONICLE

Ice Ages (after 25,000 BC)	Proto-writing, i.e. pictographic communication, in use
8000 BC onwards	Clay 'tokens' in use as counters, Middle East
3300 BC	Sumerian clay tablets with writing, Uruk, Iraq
3100 BC	Cuneiform inscriptions begin, Mesopotamia
3100–3000 BC	Hieroglyphic inscriptions begin, Egypt
2500 BC	Indus script begins, Pakistan/N.W. India
18th cent. BC	Cretan Linear A inscriptions begin
1792–1750 BC	Hammurabi, king of Babylon, reigns; inscribes law code on stela
17th–16th cent. BC	First known alphabet, Palestine
1450 BC	Cretan Linear B inscriptions begin
14th cent. BC	Alphabetic cuneiform inscriptions, Ugarit, Syria
1361–1352 BC	Tutankhamun reigns, Egypt
c. 1285 BC	Battle of Kadesh celebrated by both Ramesses II and Hittites
1200 BC	Oracle bone inscriptions in Chinese characters begin
1000 BC	Phoenician alphabetic inscriptions begin, Mediterranean area
730 BC	Greek alphabetic inscriptions begin
c. 8th cent. BC	Etruscan alphabet appears, northern Italy
650 BC	Demotic inscriptions, derived from hieroglyphs, begin, Egypt
c. 600 BC	Glyphic inscriptions begin, Mesoamerica
521–486 BC	Darius, king of the Persians, reigns; creates Behistun inscription (key to decipherment of cuneiform)
400 BC	Ionian alphabet becomes standard Greek alphabet
c. 270–c. 232 BC	Ashoka creates rock edicts in Brahmi and Kharosthi script, northern India
221 BC	Qin dynasty reforms Chinese character spelling
c. 2nd cent. BC	Paper invented, China
1st cent. AD	Dead Sea Scrolls written in Aramaic/Hebrew script
75 AD	Last inscription written in cuneiform
2nd cent.	Runic inscriptions begin, northern Europe
394	Last inscription written in Egyptian hieroglyphs
615–683	Pacal, Classic Maya ruler of Palenque, Mexico
712	*Kojiki*, earliest work of Japanese literature (in Chinese characters)
Before 800	Printing invented, China
9th cent.	Cyrillic alphabet invented, Russia
1418–1450	Sejong, king of Korea, reigns; invents Hangul alphabet
15th cent.	Movable type invented, Europe
1560s	Diego de Landa records Mayan 'alphabet', Yucatán
1799	Rosetta stone discovered, Egypt
1821	Cherokee 'alphabet' invented by Sequoya, USA
1823	Egyptian hieroglyphs deciphered by Champollion
1840s onwards	Mesopotamian cuneiform deciphered by Rawlinson, Hincks and others
1867	Typewriter invented
1899	Oracle bone inscriptions discovered, China
1900	Knossos discovered by Evans, who identifies Cretan Linear A and B
1905	Proto-Sinaitic inscriptions discovered by Petrie, Serabit el-Khadim, Sinai
1920s	Indus civilization discovered
1940s	Electronic computers invented
1948	Hebrew becomes a national language in Israel
1952	Linear B deciphered by Ventris
1950s onwards	Mayan glyphs deciphered by Knorosov and others
1958	Pinyin spelling introduced in China
1980s	Wordprocessors invented; writing becomes electronic
1990s	World Wide Web (www) introduced; revolutionizes information retrieval

Modern 'Hieroglyphs'

Are the huge claims made for the efficiency of the alphabet then perhaps misguided? Maybe writing and reading would work best if alphabetic scripts contained more logograms standing for whole words, as in Chinese and Japanese writing and (less so) in Egyptian hieroglyphs? Why is it necessarily desirable to have a *sound*-based script? What, after all, has sound got to do with the actual process of writing and reading?

We have only to look around us to see that 'hieroglyphs' are striking back – beside highways, at airports, on maps, in weather forecasts, on clothes labels, on computer screens and on electronic goods including the keyboard of one's word processor. Instead of 'move cursor to right', there is a simple ⇨. The hieroglyphs tell us where we must not overtake, where the nearest telephone is, which road is a motorway, whether it is likely to rain tomorrow, how we should (and should not) clean a garment, and how we should rewind a tape. Some people, beginning with the philosopher and mathematician Leibniz in the 17th century, even like to imagine that we can invent an entire written language for universal communication. It would aim to be independent of any of the spoken languages of the world, dependent only upon the concepts essential to high-level philosophical, political and scientific communication. If music and mathematics can achieve it, so the thought goes – why not more generally?

This book shows why that dream, appealing as it is, can never become a reality. Writing and reading are intimately and inextricably bound to speech, whether or not we move our lips. Chinese characters do *not* speak directly to the mind without the intervention of sound, despite centuries of claims to the contrary by the Chinese and by many western scholars. Nor do Egyptian hieroglyphs, notwithstanding the beauty of their symbols and the fact that we can recognize people, animals, objects and the natural world depicted in them.

Aristotle called the basic unit of language – by which he meant both spoken *and* written language – 'gramma'. Ferdinand de Saussure, the founder of modern linguistics, said of language that it might be compared to a sheet of paper. 'Thought is one side of the sheet and sound the reverse side. Just as it is impossible to take a pair of scissors and cut one side of the paper without at the same time cutting the other, so it is impossible in a language to isolate sound from thought, or thought from sound.' We have just begun to understand the mental processes in speaking, we understand still less about those in reading and writing, but we may be sure of this: full writing cannot be divorced from speech; words, and the scripts that employ words, involve both sounds *and* signs.

HOW WRITING

Above **Ceramic vase from Yaloch, Guatemala, depicting a mythological scene.**

Below **Box in the shape of a cartouche from the treasures of Tutankhamun.**

I

Two hundred years ago, no one knew how to read Egyptian hieroglyphs, Mesopotamian cuneiform or Mayan glyphs. Most scholars in fact doubted whether these scripts *could* be read in the same way as alphabetic writing. The assumption was that their exotic symbols represented ideas and thoughts, probably exalted and mystical, not the sounds of a once-living language.

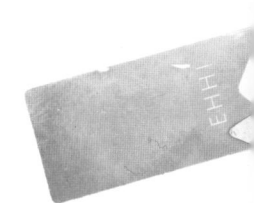

WORKS

Today we can read many of the glyphs on this exquisite ceramic pot, painted with weird and wonderful mythological scenes of the ancient Maya, and each ebony and tinted ivory hieroglyph on this box of Tutankhamun. And we know that, strange as it may seem, both these samples of ancient writing resemble our alphabet in their fundamental principles of operation.

To understand how this can be, we need to grasp how our own scripts represent sound and meaning. We do not generally use symbols that are recognizably pictorial, unlike Egyptian hieroglyphs, the symbols on Sumerian clay tablets, or the ambiguous signs which accompany the cave paintings of Ice Age Europe. What role do pictures play in the evolution of writing? Can the earliest known symbols be regarded as writing? How, precisely, is writing defined?

Chapter 1

Reading the Rosetta Stone

**The Rosetta Stone,
key to the decipherment
of Egyptian hieroglyphs.**

The Classical Image of Egypt

The Rosetta Stone is probably the most famous inscription in the world. Its discovery in Egypt in 1799 permitted Egyptian hieroglyphs to be read. Perhaps the best way to understand how hieroglyphs and alphabets both resemble and differ from each other is to follow the decipherment of the Rosetta Stone.

Let us go back 2000 years and more, to the Greeks and Romans and the eclipse of ancient Egypt after 3000 years of civilization. The Romans and especially the Greeks regarded ancient Egypt with a paradoxical mixture of contempt for its 'barbarism' and reverence for its wisdom and antiquity. Its obelisks were taken to Rome and became symbols of prestige; even today, thirteen obelisks stand in Rome, while only four remain in Egypt.

The classical authors generally credited Egypt with the invention of writing (though Pliny attributed it to the inventors of cuneiform). But no classical authors were able to read the hieroglyphs in the way they read Greek and Latin. They believed rather, as Diodorus Siculus said, that the Egyptian writing 'does not express the intended concept by means of syllables joined one to another, but by means of the significance of the objects which have been copied'. Thus, a picture of a hawk signified anything that happened swiftly, a crocodile signified all that was evil.

The Hieroglyphs of Horapollo

By far the most important authority was an Egyptian named Horapollo from Nilopolis. His treatise was probably composed in Greek, during the 4th century AD or later, and then lost until a manuscript was discovered on a Greek island in about 1419. Published in 1505, it went through 30 editions, one of them illustrated by Albrecht Dürer. Horapollo's readings of hieroglyphs were a combination of the (mainly) fictitious and the genuine. For instance, 'when they wish to indicate a sacred scribe, or a prophet, or an embalmer, or the spleen, or odour, or laughter, or sneezing, or rule, or a judge, they draw a dog.' Or consider Horapollo's 'What they mean by a vulture':

When they mean a mother, sight, or boundaries, or foreknowledge . . . they draw a vulture. A mother, since there is no male in this species of animal . . . the vulture stands for sight since of all other animals the vulture has the keenest vision . . . It means boundaries, because when a war is about to break out, it limits the place in which the battle will occur, hovering over it for seven days. Foreknowledge, because of what has been said above and because it looks forward to the amount of corpses which the slaughter will provide it for food . . .

This was sheer fantasy – except for 'mother': the hieroglyph for mother is indeed a vulture.

Cynocephalus, inspired by Horapollo. Many Renaissance artists drew hieroglyphs based on the descriptions of Horapollo. Top by Albrecht Dürer, middle from a French edition of Horapollo, bottom from an Italian edition.

The Wisdom of the Hieroglyphs

With the Renaissance revival of classical learning went a revival of the Greek and Roman belief in Egyptian hieroglyphic wisdom. In Rome, between 1582 and 1589, six ancient Egyptian obelisks were either re-sited or re-erected. One of the city's main attractions was moved from the church of San Lorenzo to the Capitol. It was an ancient temple-frieze, not Egyptian but supposedly representing hieroglyphs. So valuable a relic was it thought to be, that nearly all the important artists copied it in their sketchbooks.

The first of many scholars in the modern world to write a book on hieroglyphs was a Venetian, Pierius Valerianus. His book was published in 1556. Taking his cue from Horapollo, he illustrated his readings with delightfully fantastic 'Renaissance' hieroglyphs.

Early 'Hieroglyphers'

The most famous (not to say notorious) of these early interpreters was the Jesuit priest Athanasius Kircher. In the mid-17th century, he was Rome's accepted pundit on ancient Egypt. But his voluminous writings took him far beyond 'Egyptology'; he was among the last scholars to attempt to combine the totality of human knowledge. The result was a mixture of brilliance and fallacy – much more of the latter than the former – from which Kircher's reputation never recovered.

In 1666 he was entrusted with the publication of a hieroglyphic inscription on an obelisk in Rome's Piazza della Minerva (*above left*; Kircher's drawing, *left*). This had been erected on the orders of Pope

Top **'Wisdom'. The hieroglyphic sceptre sign presumably began as a walking-stick, which was then animated** (middle). **It acquired a further meaning 'well-being over mischief', the ancient Egyptian word for 'sceptre' meaning also 'well-being', and the word for 'simple stake' meaning also 'mischief'.**

Bottom **Pierius Valerianus chose to view the animated sign as a stork, symbol of filial piety, over the claws of a hippopotamus, symbol of injustice and ingratitude. He therefore 'translated' this hieroglyph as 'Impietati praelata Pietas' (Devotion over Selfishness).**

Above left **6th-century-BC Egyptian obelisk, erected in Rome's Piazza della Minerva in 1667.**

Below left **Drawing of the Minervan obelisk by Athanasius Kircher, 1666.**

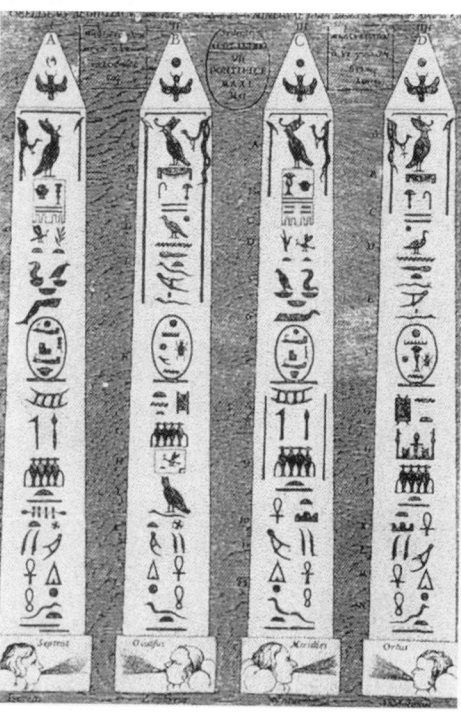

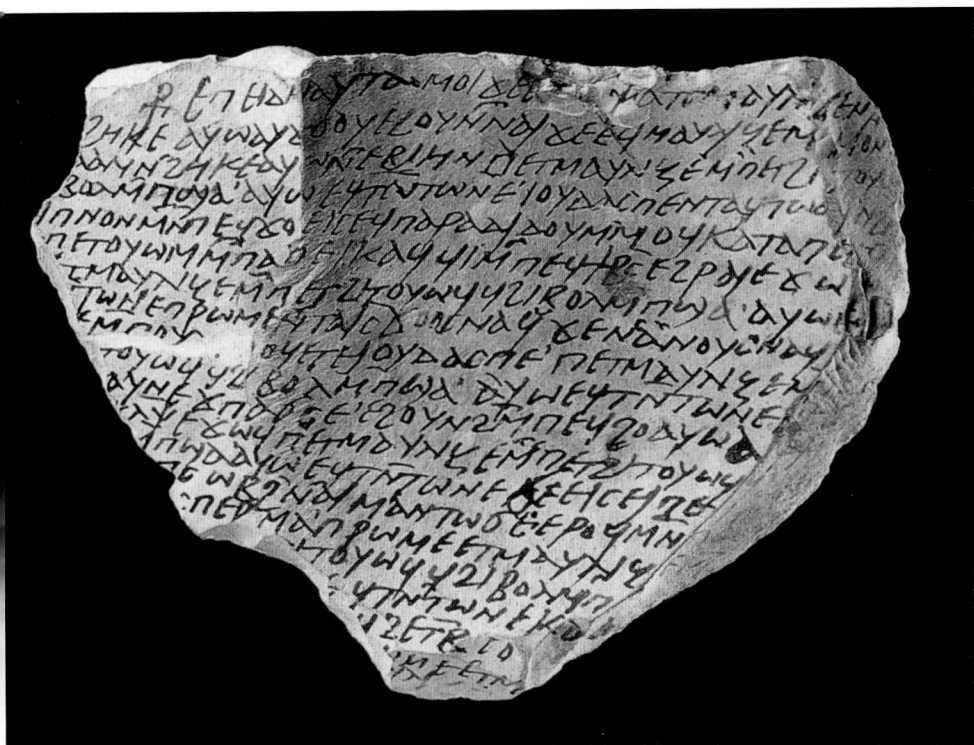

Left **Coptic ostracon. This is a pastoral letter from a bishop written in the 6th century AD. Coptic survived (marginally) as a spoken language until almost the present day; its written form is still used in some sacred texts of the Coptic church.**

Below **The Coptic alphabet. In its standard form (Sahidic), it consists of the 24 Greek letters plus 6 signs borrowed from the old Egyptian script (demotic not hieroglyphic form), that stand for Coptic sounds not symbolized in Greek.**

Coptic	name	Phonetic value
ⲁ	alpha	*a*
ⲃ	vita	*v (b)*
ⲅ	gamma	*g*
ⲇ	delta	*d*
ⲉ	epsilon	*e*
ⲍ	zita	*z*
ⲏ	ita	*i, e*
ⲑ	tita	*t*
ⲓ	iota	*i*
ⲕ	kappa	*k*
ⲗ	laula	*l*
ⲙ	mi	*m*
ⲛ	ni	*n*
ⲝ	xi	*x*
ⲟ	omicron	*o*
ⲡ	pi	*p*
ⲣ	ro	*r*
ⲥ	sima	*s*
ⲧ	tau	*t*
ⲩ	ypsilon	*y, u*
ⲫ	phi	*ph*
ⲭ	khi	*ch, kh*
ⲯ	psi	*ps*
ⲱ	omega	*o*
ⲩ̈	shei	*s*
ϥ	fai	*f*
ⳓ	hori	*h*
ⳉ	djandja	*g*
ϭ	chima	*c*
ϯ	ti	*ti*

Alexander VII to a design by Bernini (it stands to this day). Kircher gave his reading of a cartouche, i.e. a small group of hieroglyphs in the inscription enclosed in an oval outline, as follows:

The protection of Osiris against the violence of Typho must be elicited according to the proper rites and ceremonies by sacrifices and by appeal to the tutelary Genii of the triple world in order to ensure the enjoyment of the prosperity customarily given by the Nile against the violence of the enemy Typho.

Today's accepted reading is simply the name of a pharaoh, Wahibre (Apries), of the 26th dynasty!

By contrast, Kircher genuinely assisted in the rescue of Coptic, the language of the last phase of ancient Egypt. The word Copt is derived from the Arabic 'gubti', which is itself a corruption of Greek 'Aiguptos' (Egypt). The Coptic language dates from Christian times and was the official language of the Egyptian church, but lost ground to Arabic and by the late 17th century was headed for extinction. During the next century, however, several scholars acquired a knowledge of Coptic that would later prove essential in the decipherment of the hieroglyphs.

They also, under the influence of the Enlightenment, began to question the classical view of the hieroglyphs. William Warburton, the future bishop of Gloucester, was the first to suggest that all writing, hieroglyphs included, might have evolved from pictures. The Abbé Barthélemy, an admirer of Warburton's, guessed that cartouches might contain the names of kings or gods.

A Danish scholar, Zoëga, writing just before 1800, hazarded that some hieroglyphs might be, in some measure at least, 'phonetic signs'; Zoëga coined the phrase 'notae phoneticae'. The path towards decipherment of the hieroglyphs was being prepared.

The Discovery of the Rosetta Stone

The word cartouche was coined by French soldiers in Egypt who were part of Napoleon's invasion force in 1798. The ovals enclosing groups of hieroglyphs within an inscription reminded them of the cartridges ('cartouches') in their guns.

Fortunately, the expedition was almost as interested in culture as in conquest. A party of French savants accompanied the military men and remained in Egypt for some three years. There were also many artists, chief of whom was Domenique Vivant Denon (*above*). Between 1809 and 1813, he illustrated *La Description de L'Egypte*, and the whole of Europe was astonished by the marvels of ancient Egypt. This drawing shows the city of Thebes, with the columns of the temple of Luxor behind and highly inscribed obelisks in the foreground. The carved scenes depict the charge of chariot-borne archers under the command of Ramesses II against the Hittites in the battle of Kadesh. Napoleon's army was so struck by this spectacle that, according to a witness, 'it halted of itself and, by one spontaneous impulse, grounded its arms'.

A demolition squad of soldiers discovered the Rosetta Stone in mid-July 1799, probably built into a very old wall in the village of Rashid (Rosetta), on a branch of the Nile just a few miles from the sea. Recognizing its importance, the officer in charge had the Stone moved immediately to Cairo. Copies were made and distributed to the scholars of Europe during 1800. In 1801, the Stone was moved to Alexandria in an attempt to avoid its capture by British forces. But it was eventually handed over, taken to Britain, and displayed in the British Museum, where it has remained ever since.

The Decipherment Begins

The Rosetta Stone is a slab of compact granitic stone weighing some three quarters of a ton and measuring just 3 ft 9 in (114 cm) in height, 2 ft 4½ in (72 cm) in width and 11 in (28 cm) in thickness.

From the moment of discovery, it was clear that the inscription on the stone was written in three different scripts, the bottom one being Greek and the top one (which was badly damaged) Egyptian hieroglyphs with visible cartouches. In between was a script about which little was known. It clearly did not resemble Greek script, but it seemed to bear some resemblance to the hieroglyphic script above it, without having cartouches. Today we know it to be a cursive form of the hieroglyphic script, known as demotic.

The first step was obviously to translate the Greek inscription. It turned out to be a decree passed by a general council of priests from all parts of Egypt which assembled at Memphis on the first anniversary of the coronation of Ptolemy V Epiphanes, king of all Egypt, on 27 March 196 BC. It was written in Greek because the rulers of Egypt were by then not Egyptians but Macedonian Greeks, descendants of a general of Alexander the Great. The names Ptolemy, Alexander, Alexandria, among others, occurred in the inscription.

Then scholars turned their attention to the demotic script. (The hieroglyphic section was too damaged to appear promising.) They knew from a statement in the Greek text that the three inscriptions were equivalent in meaning, even if not 'word for word' translations. So they searched for a name such as Ptolemy, by isolating repeated groups of demotic symbols located in roughly the same position as the known occurrences of Ptolemy in the Greek inscription. Having found these groups, they noticed that the names in demotic seemed to be written alphabetically, as in the Greek inscription. They were able to draw up a tentative demotic alphabet. Certain other demotic words, such as 'Greek', 'Egypt', 'temple', could now be identified using this demotic alphabet. It looked as though the entire demotic script might be alphabetic.

Unfortunately it was not. The first scholars could proceed no further, because they could not get rid of their idea that the demotic inscription was an alphabet – in contrast to the hieroglyphic inscription, which they took to be wholly non-phonetic, its symbols expressing ideas in the manner of Horapollo. The difference in appearance between the hieroglyphic and demotic signs, and the weight of Renaissance tradition concerning Egyptian hieroglyphs, convinced scholars that the invisible principles of operation of the two scripts, hieroglyphic and demotic, were wholly different.

Thomas Young's Breakthrough

The person who broke this mould was the Englishman Thomas Young. A remarkable man – linguist, physician and physicist, who is still remembered for his wave theory of light – Young began work on the Rosetta Stone in 1814. He noted what he called 'a striking resemblance' between some demotic symbols and 'the corresponding hieroglyphs' and remarked that 'none of these characters [i.e. the hieroglyphs] could be reconciled, without inconceivable violence, to the forms

Thomas Young (1773–1829), Fellow of the Royal Society, linguist, physician, physicist and major contributor to the decipherment of Egyptian hieroglyphs.

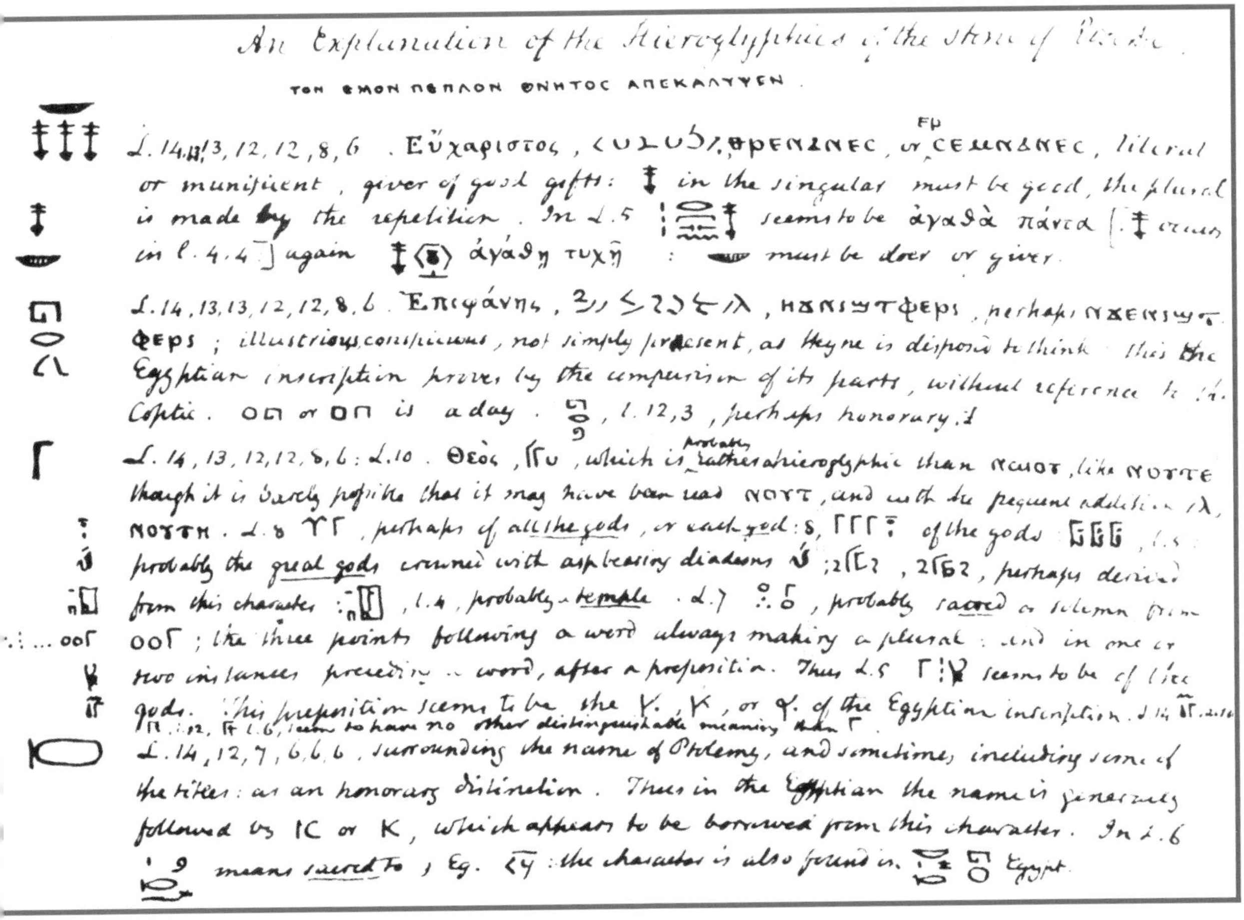

An Explanation of the Hieroglyphics of the Stone of ...

ΤΟΝ ΕΜΟΝ ΠΕΠΛΟΝ ΘΝΗΤΟΣ ΑΠΕΚΑΛΥΨΕΝ.

[A page of handwritten notes by Thomas Young, comprising Greek, Coptic and hieroglyphic transcriptions with English annotations, largely illegible. Legible fragments include:]

∠. 14, 13, 12, 12, 8, 6. Εὐχάριστος, ... literal or munificent, giver of good gifts ... in the singular must be good, the plural is made by the repetition. In ∠.5 ... seems to be ἀγαθὰ πάντα ... again ... ἀγάθη τύχη ... must be doer or giver.

∠. 14, 13, 13, 12, 12, 8, 6. Ἐπιφάνης ... perhaps ... illustrious conspicuous, not simply present, as they are disposed to think. This the Egyptian inscription proves, by the comparison of its parts, without reference to the Coptic. ... is a day. ... l. 12, 3, perhaps honorary.

∠. 14, 13, 12, 12, 8, 6: ∠.10. Θεός, ... which is rather a hieroglyphic than ... like ... though it is barely possible that it may have been read ... and with the frequent addition of ... ∠.8 ... perhaps of all the gods, or each god: S ... of the gods ... probably the great gods crowned with asp-bearing diadems ... perhaps derived from this character ... l.4, probably a temple ... l.7 ... probably sacred or solemn from ... the three points following a word always making a plural; and in one or two instances preceding a word, after a preposition. Thus ∠.5 ... seems to be of the gods. This preposition seems to be the ... or ... of the Egyptian inscription ... to have no other distinguishable meaning than ...

∠. 14, 12, 7, 6, 6, 6. surrounding the name of Ptolemy, and sometimes including some of the titles; as an honorary distinction. Thus in the Egyptian the name is generally followed by IC or K, which appears to be borrowed from this character. In ∠.6 ... means sacred to, Eg. ... the character is also found in ... Egypt.

of any imaginable alphabet'. He therefore concluded that the demotic script was a *mixture* of alphabetic signs and other, hieroglyphic-type signs.

And he went further. He acted on the suggestion made by earlier scholars that the cartouches contained royal or religious names. There were six cartouches in the Rosetta Stone's hieroglyphic inscription, which clearly had to contain the name Ptolemy. Young now assumed that Ptolemy, though written in hieroglyphs, was spelt alphabetically. His reason was that Ptolemy was a foreign name, non-Egyptian, and therefore could not be spelt non-phonetically as a native Egyptian name would be. He cited an analogy, the Chinese script, in which western names were spelt in Chinese characters but with the addition of an appropriate mark to render the characters simply phonetic. By matching up the hieroglyphs in the cartouche with the letters of the Greek spelling of Ptolemy, Young assigned sound values (*p, t, m*, etc.) to various hieroglyphs. Many were correct.

Here, however, Young came unstuck. The spell of Horapollo was a strong one. While Young could accept that the hieroglyphic script used an alphabet to spell foreign names, he was convinced that the *remaining* hieroglyphs, the part used to write the Egyptian language (rather than words borrowed from Greek), were *non*-phonetic. His 'hieroglyphic alphabet' would therefore not apply to the bulk of the hieroglyphic script. Young had taken a vital step towards the decipherment of hieroglyphs, but he would not be the person to break the code.

A page from the Egyptian research papers of Thomas Young. His basic insight – that the Egyptian script contained both phonetic and non-phonetic elements – was correct, but his specific results were sometimes incorrect.

Champollion Breaks the Egyptian Code

The full decipherment of Egyptian hieroglyphs is the work of Jean-François Champollion, who announced it in 1823. Born in 1790 during the French Revolution, he was unable to attend early school. Instead, he received private tuition in Greek and Latin, and by the age of nine, it is said, he could read Homer and Virgil. Moving to Grenoble to attend the Lycée, he came into contact with the mathematician and physicist Fourier, who had been secretary of Napoleon's Egyptian mission. It was Fourier who launched the young Champollion into Egyptology. In 1807, aged not yet seventeen, Champollion presented a paper on the Coptic etymology of Egyptian place-names preserved in the works of Greek and Latin authors. Three years later, after studying oriental languages in Paris in addition to Coptic, Champollion returned to Grenoble and began serious study of Pharaonic Egypt.

In 1819, Thomas Young published his ideas on the Egyptian script in a *Supplement to the Encyclopaedia Britannica* (4th edition). He had already communicated them by letter to Champollion. But Champollion at first ignored them and continued to believe that the hieroglyphs were entirely *non*-phonetic; in 1821 he published an article to this effect. He and Young were undoubtedly rivals, and there is still doubt as to how much Champollion was influenced by Young's work; he certainly took pains to dismiss it in his chief book on Egyptian writing. However, there can be no question about Champollion's originality and rigour, which was based on a knowledge of Egypt and its languages far superior to Young's.

This obelisk was excavated at Philae by William Bankes, who took it back home to Britain, where it now stands at Kingston Lacy in Dorset. In 1822, it provided Champollion with a crucial clue.

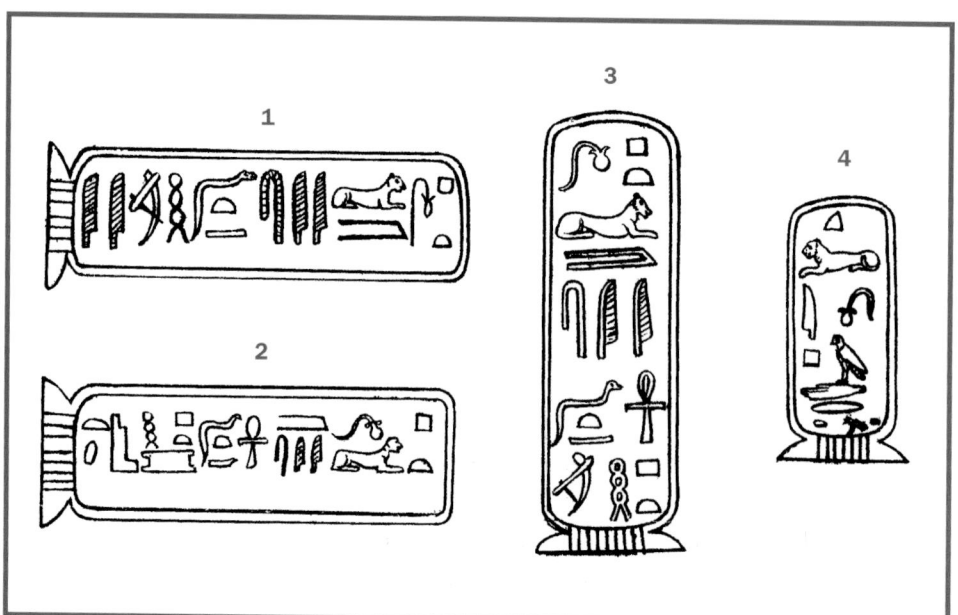

Four cartouches drawn by Champollion:
(1) Ptolemy (Rosetta Stone);
(2) Ptolemy with royal title (Rosetta Stone);
(3) Ptolemy (Philae obelisk);
(4) Cleopatra (Philae obelisk).

There was also a shorter version of the Ptolemy cartouche on the Rosetta Stone:

Left **Jean-François Champollion (1790–1832), decipherer of Egyptian hieroglyphs. The portrait shows him holding his 'Tableau des Signes Phonétiques' (see p. 31), in 1823, the year of his breakthrough.**

Champollion decided that the shorter version spelt Ptolemy, while the longer (Rosetta) cartouche must involve some royal title, tacked onto Ptolemy's name. Following Young, he now assumed that Ptolemy was spelt alphabetically. He proceeded to guess the sound values of the hieroglyphs of the second cartouche on the Philae obelisk:

The Philae Obelisk

The key to further progress was a copy of a bilingual obelisk inscription sent to Paris by William Bankes around January 1822. It came from Britain, where the obelisk had been dispatched after its excavation at Philae. The base block inscription was in Greek, the column inscription in hieroglyphic script. In the Greek the names of Ptolemy and Cleopatra were mentioned, in the hieroglyphs only two cartouches occurred – presumably representing the same two names as on the base. One of the cartouches was almost identical to one form of the cartouche of Ptolemy on the Rosetta Stone:

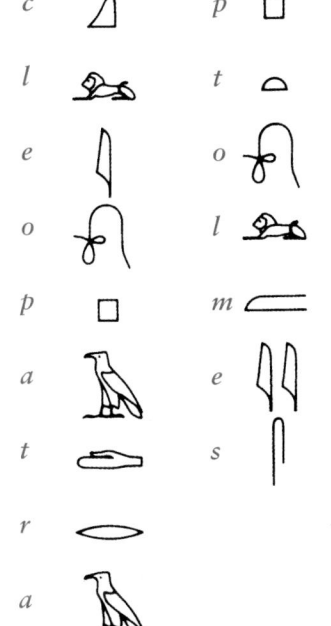

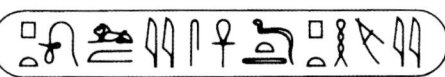

Rosetta Stone

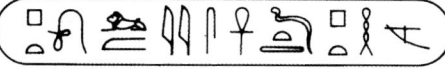

Philae obelisk

There were four signs in common, those with the values *l*, *e*, *o*, *p*, but the sound value *t* was represented differently. Champollion deduced correctly that the two signs for *t* were homophones, i.e. different signs with the same sound value (compare in English Jill and Gill, practice and practise).

Alexander and Caesar in Hieroglyphs

The real test, however, was whether the new sound values when applied to other inscriptions, would produce sensible names. Champollion tried the following cartouche:

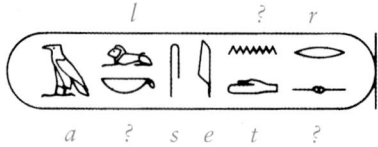

Substituting sound values produced *Al?se?tr?*. Champollion guessed Alksentrs = Greek Alexandros (Alexander) – again the two signs for *k/c* (and) are homophonous, as are the two signs for *s* (and).

He went on to identify the cartouches of other rulers of non-Egyptian origin, such as Queen Berenice (already identified by Young) and Caesar, and a title of the Roman emperors, Autocrator:

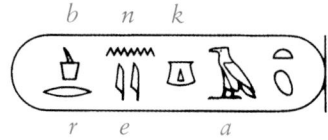

Berenice

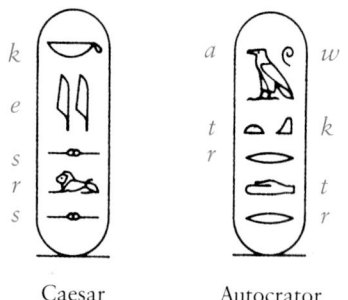

Caesar   Autocrator

These early efforts of Champollion in 1822 were based on the premise that *non-Egyptian* names and words in both demotic and hieroglyphic were spelt alphabetically. This was how he worked out his table of phonetic signs, reproduced on the opposite page. He did not initially expect this

Left **This relief from the 1st century BC at the temple of Hathor at Dendera depicts Cleopatra and her son Caesarion. Between their headdresses are two cartouches, those of Cleopatra and Ptolemy.**

alphabet to apply to the names of pharaohs, which he persisted in thinking would be spelt non-phonetically. Even less did he expect his 'decipherment' to apply to the entire hieroglyphic system. The hoary idea, dating from classical times, that Egyptian hieroglyphs for the most part expressed *only* ideas, rather than sounds *and* ideas, still possessed Champollion's mind, as it had Thomas Young's. Not until April 1823 did Champollion announce that he understood the principles of the hieroglyphs as a whole.

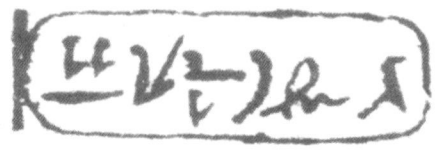

The first fruits of decipherment. This table of demotic and hieroglyphic signs with their Greek equivalents was drawn up in October 1822, to accompany Champollion's first printed announcement of the decipherment, his famous *Lettre à M. Dacier*. Note the extensive homophony, e.g. three different signs with the value b. Champollion revised this table extensively, as his decipherment proceeded in the 1820s. His own name appears in demotic script at the bottom, enclosed in a cartouche (omitted from his later, more dignified version of the table). It has been magnified on the left.

Pl. IV.

Tableau des Signes Phonétiques
des Écritures Hiéroglyphique et Démotique des anciens Égyptiens

Lettres Grecques	Signes Démotiques	Signes Hiéroglyphiques
A		
B		
Γ		
Δ		
E		
Z		
H		
Θ		
I		
K		
Λ		
M		
N		
Ξ		
O		
Π		
P		
Σ		
T		
Υ		
Φ		
Ψ		
X		
Ω		
ΤΟ. ΤΩ.		

Ramesses II's greatest monument, the huge temple at Abu Simbel (inaugurated in 1256 BC), carved out of a sandstone cliff.

Reading Ramesses the Great

The shift in Champollion's conception of the hieroglyphs had started when he received copies of various reliefs and inscriptions from ancient Egyptian temples in September 1822. One of them, from the temple of Abu Simbel in Nubia, contained intriguing cartouches. They appeared to write the same name in a variety of ways, the simplest being:

Champollion wondered if his new alphabet, derived from much later Graeco-Roman inscriptions, might apply to this set of purely Egyptian inscriptions. The last two signs were familiar to him, having the phonetic value *s*. Using his knowledge of Coptic, he guessed that the first sign had the value *re*, which was the Coptic word for 'sun' – the object apparently symbolized by the sign. Did an ancient Egyptian ruler with a name

that resembled *R(e)?ss* exist? Champollion immediately thought of Ramesses, a king of the 19th dynasty mentioned in a well-known Greek history of Egypt written by a Ptolemaic historian, Manetho. If this was correct, then the sign must have the sound value *m*.

Encouragement came from a second inscription:

Two of these signs were 'known'; the first, an ibis, was a symbol of the god Thoth. Then the name had to be Thothmes, a king of the 18th dynasty also mentioned by Manetho. The Rosetta Stone appeared to confirm the value of . The sign occurred there, again with , as part of a group of hieroglyphs with the Greek translation 'genethlia', 'birth day'. Champollion was at once reminded of the Coptic for 'give birth', 'mīse'.

Ptolemy and his Title

Champollion was only half right about the spelling of Ramesses: 𓄟 does not have the value *m*, as he thought, it has the biconsonantal value *ms* (as implied by the Coptic 'mīse'). Champollion was as yet unaware of this complexity. For some months after his success in deciphering Ramesses and other pharaonic names, he resisted the idea that the *entire* hieroglyphic system had phonetic elements. He never said what finally changed his mind but it was probably a combination of factors. For one thing, he learnt with surprise from a French scholar of Chinese that there were phonetic elements even in the indigenous spellings of the Chinese script with its thousands of characters. For another, it struck him that there were only 66 different signs among the 1,419 hieroglyphic signs on the Rosetta Stone; if the hieroglyphs truly were purely semantic symbols, then many more than 66 different signs would have been expected, each one representing a different word – that is, they would have been logograms.

Once he had accepted that the hieroglyphs were a mixture of phonetic and semantic signs, Champollion could decipher the second half of the long cartouche of Ptolemy on the Philae obelisk. That is:

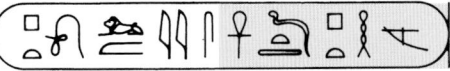

According to the Greek inscription, the entire cartouche meant 'Ptolemy living for ever, beloved of Ptah' (Ptah was the creator god of Memphis). In Coptic, the word for 'life' or 'living' was 'onkh'; this was thought to be derived from an ancient Egyptian word 'ankh' represented by the sign 𓋹 (i.e. a logogram). Presumably the next signs 𓏏𓐰 meant 'ever' and contained a *t* sound, given that the sign 𓏏 was now known to have the

phonetic value *t*. With help from Greek and Coptic, the 𓆓 could be assigned the phonetic value *dj*, giving a rough ancient Egyptian pronunciation *djet*, meaning 'for ever'. (The other sign ▬ was silent, a kind of classificatory logogram called a determinative; it symbolized 'flat land'.)

Of the remaining signs 𓊪𓏏𓎛 the first was now known to stand for *p* and the second for *t* – the first two sounds of Ptah; and so the third sign could be given the approximate phonetic value *h*. The fourth sign – another logogram – was therefore assumed to mean 'beloved'. Coptic once more came in useful to assign a pronunciation: the Coptic word for 'love' was known to be 'mere', and so the pronunciation of the fourth sign was thought to be *mer*. So, in sum, Champollion arrived at the rough pronunciation of the famous cartouche: *Ptolmes ankh djet Ptah mer* (Ptolemy living for ever, beloved of Ptah).

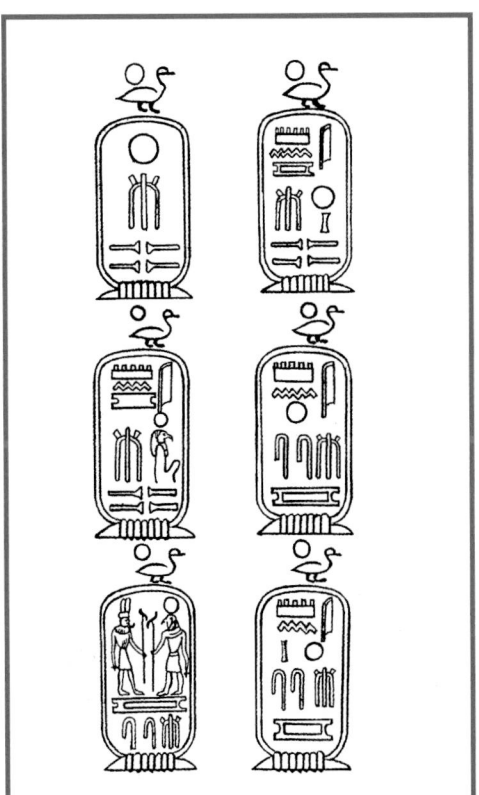

Six cartouches of Ramesses II, drawn by Champollion. Three of them spell the name in the way described in the text, the other three substitute an alternative sign for *s*, ▬. Compare the two homophonous signs for *s* in the hieroglyphs for Alexander on p. 30. The other signs, mostly phonetic too, are titles.

The Essence of Egyptian Hieroglyphs

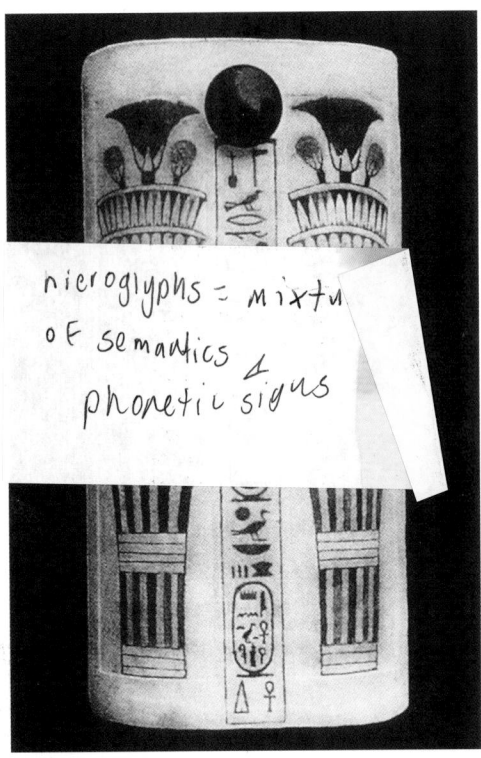

hieroglyphs = mixtu
of semantics &
phonetic signs

SUREI

Far left **The lid of Tutankhamun's alabaster chest, which contained two locks of hair wrapped in linen. The inscription reads: 'The good god great of victories, great of monuments, lord of ritual, Nebkheperure, son of the sun, lord of crowns, Tutankhamun, lord of Thebes, given life.'**

Left **Miniature coffin made of gold, for the protection of Tutankhamun's intestines. The hieroglyphs read: 'Words to be spoken by Selket: I have placed my two arms upon the one who is in me that I may secure the protection of Kebehsennef who is in me: the Kebehsennef of Osiris King Nebkheperure, true of voice.'**

The fundamentals of Egyptian hieroglyphs, first discovered by Champollion, may be summarized. The writing system is a mixture of semantic symbols, i.e. symbols that stand for words and ideas, also known as logograms, and phonetic signs, phonograms, that represent one or more sounds (alphabetic or poly-consonantal). Some hieroglyphs are recognizable pictures of objects, such as a bird or snake, i.e. they are pictograms, but the picture does *not* necessarily give the meaning of the sign. For example, the 'hand' sign in the cartouche of Cleopatra has nothing to do with the meaning 'hand'; it is a phonogram with value *t*. Thus a pictogram may function as a phonogram and as a logogram, depending on its context.

In other words, a given sign in Egyptian hieroglyphs can have more than one function.

The cartouche of Tutankhamun on the right, which is the upper part of an inlaid box found in his tomb, demonstrates these fundamentals. Let us read it from the top.

The single reed is an alphabetic phonogram with the approximate value *i*.

The game board with playing pieces is a phonogram with the biconsonantal value *mn*.

Water is an alphabetic phonogram with the value *n*. Functioning (as here) as a 'phonetic complement', it reinforces the sound of the *n* in *mn*.

These three signs are therefore read *imn*, which is normally pronounced *imen* or, more commonly, *amon* or *amun*. (Vowels were mostly absent in hieroglyphic spelling, as we shall see.) Amun was the god of Luxor, regarded as the king of the gods during the New Kingdom. Out of respect, his name is placed first.

The half circle (familiar from the cartouche for Ptolemy) is an alphabetic phonogram with the value *t*. It appears twice in the cartouche.

The chick is a phonogram with the value *w*, a weak consonant similar to the vowel *u*.

This is the triconsonantal 'ankh' sign already seen in the cartouche of Ptolemy, meaning 'life' or 'living' (which later became the 'handled or eyed' cross, 'crux ansata', of the Coptic church).

These four signs therefore read 'tutankh'.

The shepherd's crook is a logogram meaning 'ruler'.

The column is a logogram for Heliopolis, a city near Cairo.

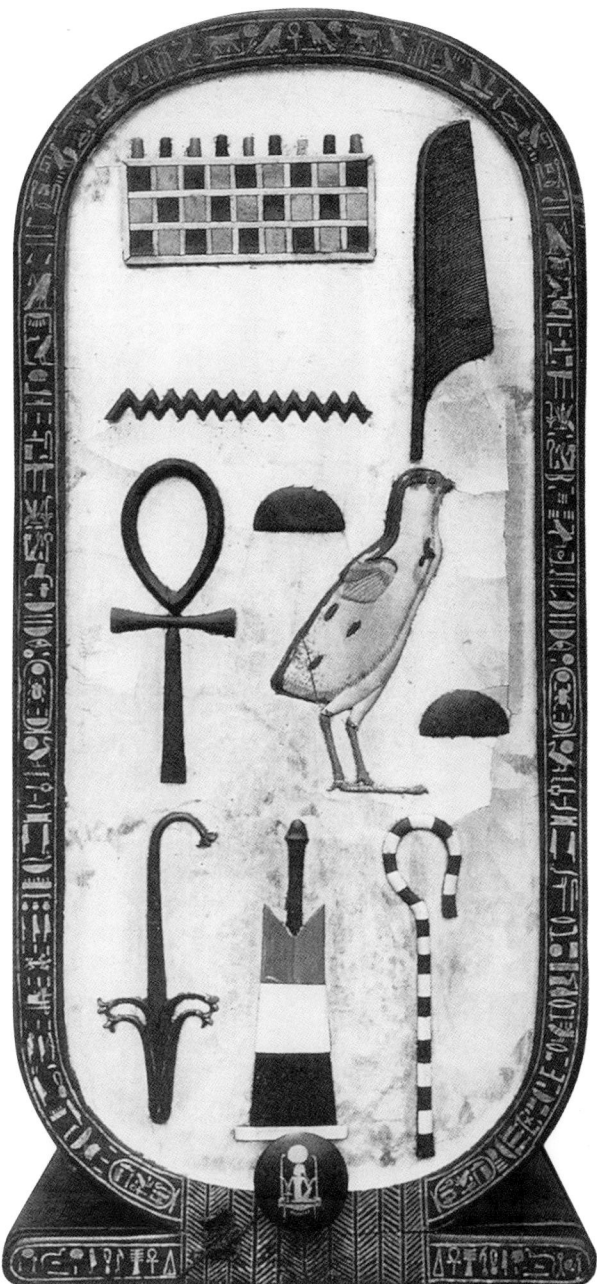

This is the heraldic plant of Upper Egypt. It is a logogram for Upper Egypt.

'Heliopolis of Upper Egypt' is another name for the city of Thebes. So the complete cartouche reads:
'Tutankhamun, Ruler of Thebes'.

Chapter 2 Sound, Symbol and Script

Scripts represent sounds with varying degrees of accuracy. Ten scripts have been used to write 'four score and seven years ago' (the opening words of Abraham Lincoln's Gettysburg Address). At the top is the acoustic wave graph of the particular speaker (a Chinese-American linguist). This is followed by (1), the transcription in the International Phonetic Alphabet; (2), the English spelling; (3), the Russian alphabetic transcription; (4), the Bengali alphabetic version, with transcription; (5), the Korean Hangul version, with transcription; (6), the Egyptian hieroglyphic version (Ptolemaic period), with transcription; (7), the Arabic consonantal version, with transcription; (8), the Japanese syllabic version, with transcription; (9), the cuneiform syllabic version, with transcription; (10), the Chinese syllabic version, with Pinyin transcription. (After DeFrancis, 1989)

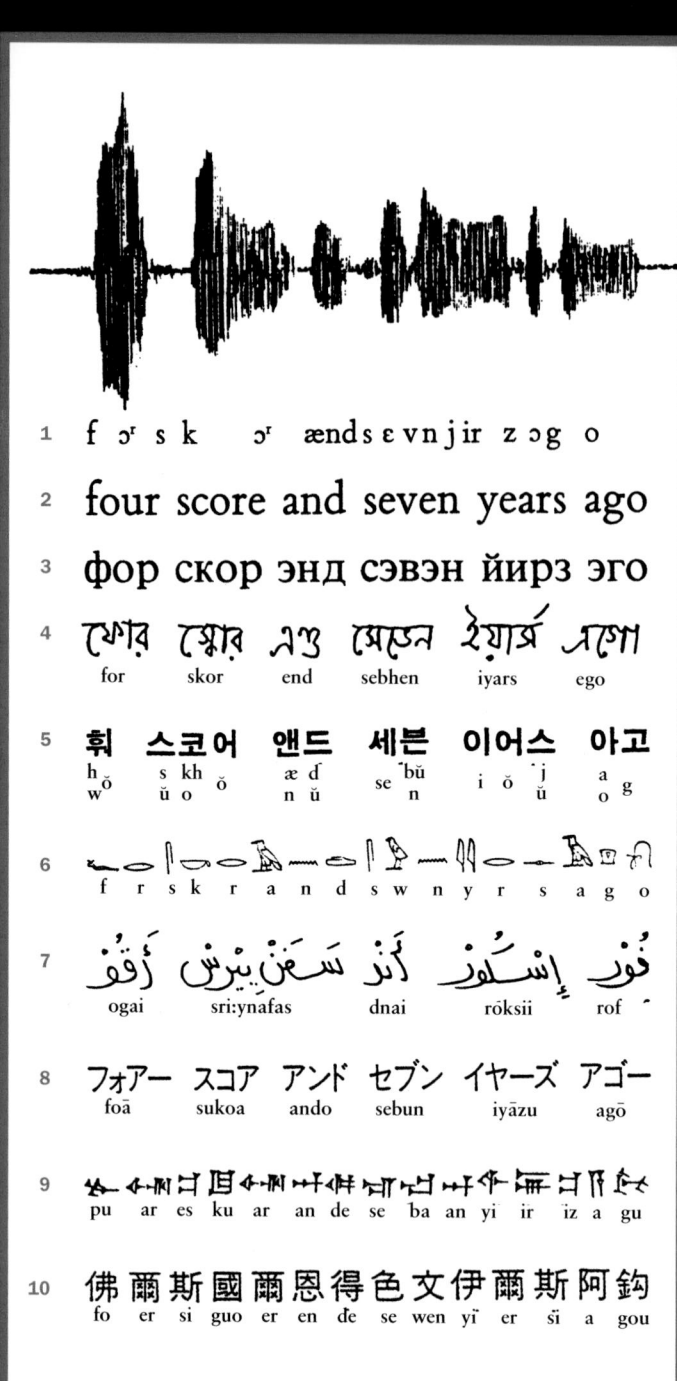

Visible and Invisible Speech

What are the key differences between written and spoken language – apart from the self-evident fact that writing is visible and speech invisible? The most important is that a passage of writing naturally breaks down into its constituent symbols, be they letters of an alphabet, Chinese characters or Egyptian hieroglyphs, whereas a passage of

If we were to splice a tape of someone saying 'cat' into its two constituent consonants and one vowel (as near as can be done), and then reverse them, we would not hear 'tac' but something unintelligible. Over half the words we use in normal conversation we cannot recognize if they are replayed in isolation, because they are so rapidly and informally articulated.

Issue of the phonetic journal *Le Maître Phonétique*, published in 1914; after 1970 the journal opted for a standard orthography, because readers found the phonetic orthography too demanding. The masthead reads:
'Le Maître Phonétique, organ de l'association phonétique international, vingt-neuvième année – janvier–février 1914'

le

mɛːtrə fɔnetik

ɔrgan

de l asɔsjɑːsjɔ̃ fɔnetik ɛ̃tɛrnasjɔnal

vɛ̃tnœvjɛm anc. — ʒɑ̃ːvje-fevrie 1914

speech does not. Of course we do often divide speech into consonants, vowels and syllables, and linguists create many other categories of spoken 'atoms and molecules'. But these divisions are always artificial and never entirely free from overlap.

'Speech is a river of breath, bent into hisses and hums by the soft flesh of the mouth and throat', wrote the linguistic scientist Steven Pinker. There are no spaces between words in normal speech, as there are white spaces between words in most of today's writing systems. We may imagine that there are such gaps, but when we listen to speech in a foreign language, our delusion is exposed. Speech is a flow, constantly changing in frequencies, loudness and pitch.

Each spoken language has its own gamut of sounds, drawn from a literally infinite range of possible sounds. Its writing system represents some of this gamut – the proportion varies with the system – leaving readers to guess the rest. The divergence between sound and script is greatest with foreign words and names. Each script opposite does the job differently and with differing degrees of accuracy. The phonetic alphabet is so accurate that it represents even the accent of the original speaker (if he were British or French, the symbols would be different); but this gain is offset by a consequent lack of readability. All scripts must strike a compromise between accuracy to the mouth and intelligibility to the mind.

Sign Language

Sign language is not 'writing in the air'; nor, clearly, is it speech, yet it resembles both speech and writing in certain crucial ways. There are three common misconceptions about the established systems of sign language. First, the vast majority of signs are *not* iconic like the signs used in shadow plays, 'rabbit', 'duck', 'snake' and so on – 'manual pictograms', so to speak; they are abstract in conception, like the letters of an alphabet. Second, they are *not* independent of speech; every successful system, such as American Sign Language (ASL), shown in the photographs (*right*), is based on a spoken language. (Thus an ASL user cannot communicate with a Chinese Sign Language user.) Third, sign languages are *not* primitive; a fluent signer can maintain a conversational rate comparable to that of speech, and many of the signs express meaning far more succinctly than the corresponding spoken language. In this last respect, signs resemble logograms that in some contexts may communicate more efficiently than alphabetic letters.

It is extremely difficult to grasp how sign language works when we speakers and writers first encounter it. This is because we are so thoroughly immersed in the expressive techniques of speech and writing. For instance, we may use tenses to express time past, present and future; sign language uses space. Gestures made well in front of the person refer to the future, while those made well behind refer to the past. Furthermore, sign language expresses meaning using both the hands and the face. As the photographs suggest, this can permit remarkable complexity and richness.

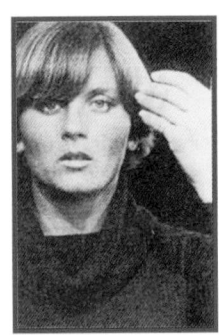

'The woman forgot the purse.' The sequence of signs 'woman – forget – purse' is used as a statement.

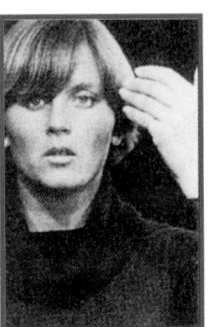

'Did the woman forget the purse?' The same sign sequence, but with a forward movement of head and shoulders and eyebrows raised.

'The woman who forgot the purse . . .' The relative clause is indicated by raising the brow and upper lip and tilting the head back.

American Sign Language.

Theories of Reading

The majority of experienced readers have had the disconcerting experience of looking at a familiar word, correctly spelt, and thinking: 'that doesn't look right'. We resort to the dictionary, atomize the word into its constituent letters, see that each is correct – and yet we may still feel that the word looks somehow unfamiliar.

Reading is undoubtedly a complex process, witness the complex process of learning to read. No simple theory can account for it. Both vision and sound, the eye and the ear (so to speak), are intimately implicated. We may like to imagine that the words on a page become meaningful in our minds 'directly', but as soon as we enquire within ourselves what that meaning is, 'internal speech' becomes necessary.

Experimental evidence supports both the 'eye' and the 'ear' theory. To take the 'eye' evidence first, consider homophones like 'read' and 'reed', 'write' and 'right': the mind is not at all confused by them. Moreover, it chooses the meaning of 'bow' in 'he bowed down' and 'she bowed the violin', *before* deciding the pronunciation of 'bow'. Also, in brief exposure experiments, subjects identify whole words more quickly than isolated letters. For instance, in the group RED, ERD, E, they perform best with RED. The 'eye' theory also allows for the performance of 'speed readers', who read more than 500 words per minute – a rate too great for letter-by-letter reading by 'ear'. But the 'ear' theory gains support from letter recognition speeds, about 10–20 milliseconds per letter, which correlate with average speeds for reading aloud (around 250 words per

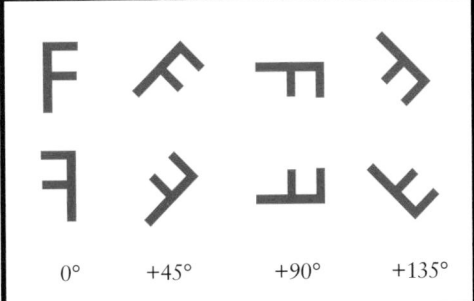

minute), and which are similar for both silent and oral reading. Also, significantly, when reading difficult material, people often move their lips and sometimes read a sentence to themselves aloud, in order, it would seem, to aid comprehension. What is more, they cope quite easily with a wide range of typefaces and handwriting, contrary to the expectations of the 'eye' theory.

Images or Words?

The underlying issue is whether our thoughts are in images or words or in some other form that has been called 'mentalese'. The importance of words, as opposed to images, is suggested by a simple test. Shut your eyes and imagine following a familiar route, say to get to a shopping centre, as if you were driving along in a car. Images, largely independent of language, will come to your mind. Now imagine, without actually speaking aloud, that you need to explain to someone else how to get to the same place. Immediately you will switch into a linguistic mode to describe the same scenes, ineffective though this may be for the purpose in hand. (You might also draw a map, but words will always be essential.)

Experiments with reflected and rotated letters prove that the mind thinks partly in images. A subject was momentarily shown images of an alphabetic letter on a screen and was asked if the letter was normal or a mirror image of itself. In order to probe the mental process, the letter had been rotated – through angles up to 180 degrees – requiring the subject mentally to rotate it back to its upright position. It was found that the further round the letter had to rotate, the longer the subject took to answer. The letter was estimated to rotate at 56 revolutions per minute within the mind.

Sound and Spelling

Just as we can read a wide variety of handwriting, so we are also able to understand a wide range of spoken accents. New York pronunciation of English differs vastly from Queen's English, but with a little practice, any native-speaker of English can recognize that two different sounds actually share the same spoken 'element'.

Phonetics is the study of all spoken sounds, regardless of whether they determine meaning. Phonology studies the order in this phonetic chaos: how the speakers of a language select from all possible sounds in order to construct a system that communicates meaning. Thus in phonetics a vowel is a sound made by little or no constriction of the vocal tract, and a consonant is a sound made by narrowing or stopping the vocal tract. In phonology, by contrast, a vowel (V) is defined as the unit that typically occurs at the centre of a syllable, while a consonant (C) belongs typically to the margin of a syllable. Often a syllable, e.g. 'cat', is represented by the structure CVC.

This leads us to the phoneme, an important concept in phonology. The phoneme has been defined as 'the smallest contrastive unit in the sound system of a language'. Unlike an alphabetic letter, the phoneme has no existence independent of a particular language; it is not a real but an invented sound, the underlying spoken 'element' mentioned above. For that reason, phonemes are written between slanted lines. Examples of vowel phonemes in English are /e/ and /a/ in the words set and sat, while consonantal phonemes include /b/ and /p/ in

the words bat and pat. A phoneme in one language may not be a phoneme in another. For example, there is only one phoneme involved in the 'l' sounds of 'leaf' and 'pool', even though they are pronounced in two distinct ways in English (feel the position of your tongue); but in Russian these sounds would involve two completely different phonemes.

Ideally, alphabetic spelling should represent the phonemes of a language. The reality is much more arbitrary, at least in English. English is full of homophony, where one sound is spelt in several different ways, e.g. *o* in the vowel in the words so, sow, sew, oh, owe, dough, doe, beau, soak, soul. There is also polyphony, in which one letter represents many different sounds, e.g. the words so, to, on, honey, horse, woman, borough. In Hebrew and Arabic, on the other hand, the vowels are not normally represented in the script at all; the reader is expected to supply them from the context. nglsh cn b rd wtht vwls, bt thr r cnsdrbl dffclts.

George Bernard Shaw (1856–1950), not only a playwright of world renown, but also a famous critic of English spelling; he himself wrote in Pitman's shorthand. Shaw left money in his will to encourage the design of a rational alphabet of at least 40 letters (see Kingsley Read's Shaw alphabet, below). There are four types of letter: talls, deeps, shorts and compounds. The name of the letter is given beneath it, and its sound is printed in bold type.

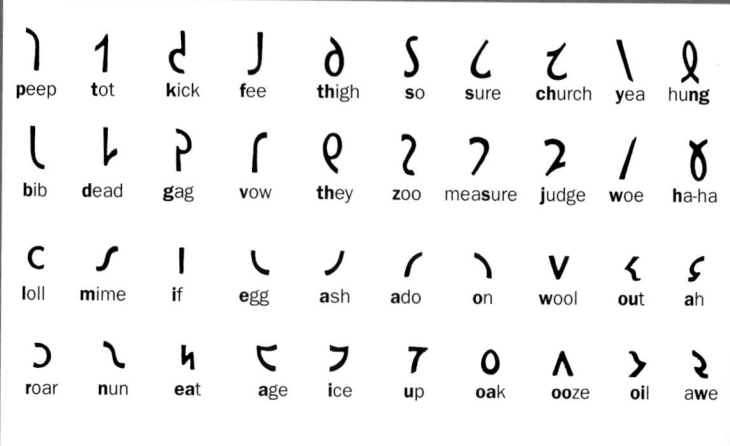

peep	tot	kick	fee	thigh	so	sure	church	yea	hung
bib	dead	gag	vow	they	zoo	measure	judge	woe	ha-ha
loll	mime	if	egg	ash	ado	on	wool	out	ah
roar	nun	eat	age	ice	up	oak	ooze	oil	awe

Conveying Meaning in Writing

- the concept '10', 'ten' in English, 'dix' in French, 'shí' in Chinese, etc.
- the 24th item in a sequence of 26 letters derived from the Latin alphabet
- an unknown quantity, as in $x^2 + 2x = 3$, and 'Mr X'
- 'times', i.e. multiplied by, as in $3 \times 5 = 15$
- a negative command, e.g. a sign depicting a camera crossed out, meaning 'no photography'
- a wrong answer, as in an examination paper
- pornographic, as in X-rated movies
- the location of an object, e.g. a buried treasure
- the signature of an illiterate
- a vote cast on a voting paper
- a kiss

So there are other examples of logograms in ordinary written English – more than one may think – besides the familiar ones, such as £, $, &, %, !, †, and mathematical symbols.

Even high-level mathematics is not purely logographic; words are required to link equations. If they are not always seen on mathematicians' blackboards, it is because mathematicians have supplied the explanations orally, while calculating, either to themselves or to their listeners.

The letters of the English alphabet are phonetic symbols, phonograms. Generally speaking, they are without meaning; meaning derives from their combination into words. But 'a' can also be a semantic symbol, a logogram, when it stands for the indefinite article next to a noun ('a dog', for example); and it can be encircled to make @, creating the meaning 'at the rate of'. 'x/X' is still more ambidextrous. As a phonetic symbol, it can stand for *z* in 'xenophobia', *ks* in 'excel', *gz* in 'exist', *kris* in 'Xmas', *cross* in Xing, *ten* in 'Xth' (or *dix* in French X^e = 'dixième'). As a semantic symbol, x/X has a wide range of meanings; some are listed above.

The electric field **E** is also a function of the particle configuration and so we ought to be able to express U as a function of **E**. To explore this possibility we consider the function
$$U_T = \tfrac{1}{2}\int \varepsilon_0 E^2 \mathrm{d}^3\mathbf{R}.$$
If we write $\mathbf{E} = -\nabla\varphi\,(\mathbf{R})$ where

$$\phi(\mathbf{R}) = \sum_m \frac{q(m)}{4\pi\varepsilon_0|\mathbf{R} - \mathbf{r}(m)|}$$

with

$$\nabla^2\phi(\mathbf{R}) = -\frac{1}{\varepsilon_0}\sum_m q(m)\delta(\mathbf{r}(m) - \mathbf{R}),$$

we can express U_T as
$$U_T = \tfrac{1}{2}\varepsilon_0 \int(\nabla\varphi)^2 \mathrm{d}^3\mathbf{R} = -\tfrac{1}{2}\varepsilon_0 \int \varphi\,\nabla^2\varphi\,\mathrm{d}^3\mathbf{R} + \tfrac{1}{2}\varepsilon_0 \int \varphi\,{}^{\partial\varphi}\!/_{\partial n}\,\mathrm{d}S,$$
in which the surface integral at infinity can be discarded.

Rebuses

'The man loves cats.' It is easy enough to 'read' this sentence. One might be tempted to think that the method can be developed to express more complex ideas. But a moment's reflection reveals almost insuperable hurdles. It would be fairly easy to write 'the man loves his cat', 'his old cat', even 'Sarah's cat' – but what about 'the man used to love cats', and 'the man will always love cats'?

A purely pictographic system fails at the outset to express some elementary spoken concepts. However it can be transformed with an ingenious idea: the rebus. This pictographic symbol represents not the idea it depicts but the sound associated with that idea. With the rebus principle, sounds could be made visible in a systematic way, and abstract concepts symbolized. Egyptian hieroglyphs are full of rebuses, for example the 'sun' sign, $\odot$ *R(e)*, that forms the first symbol in the hieroglyphic spelling of Ramesses. In a Sumerian tablet of an early period we find the word reimburse, which cannot easily be symbolized pictographically, shown by a reed, because 'reimburse' and 'reed' shared the same sound *gi* in Sumerian.

Rebus writing by Giovanbattista Palatino, *c.* 1540. The verse reads:

Dove son gli occhi, et la serena forma,
del santo alegro, et amoroso aspetto?
dov'e la man eburna ov'e 'l bel petto,
Ch'appensarvi hor' in fonte mi transforma?

(Where are those eyes, the serene form,
Of your blessed, happy and loving face?
The ivory hand, the beautiful breast,
Which when I think of them, make me as a fountain?)

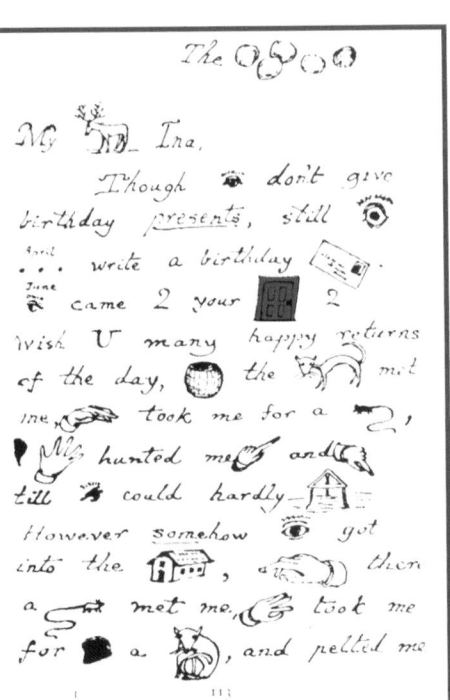

Rebus letter written to a girl by Lewis Carroll, author of *Alice's Adventures in Wonderland*, from a house called The Chestnuts, *c.* 1869.

Far left **A Sumerian rebus, *c.* 3000 BC.** The 'reed' in the top left hand corner is a rebus for 'reimburse'.

Shorthand

Over 400 shorthand systems for writing the English language have been devised. Some use abbreviations of conventional spelling; others represent the sounds of speech; yet others require the learning of a list of arbitrary symbols; and some approaches combine these different principles.

The best known was invented by Sir Isaac Pitman in the 19th century. Its basic principle is phonetic, which makes it relatively easy to adapt for writing languages other than English. Some 65 letters are used, consisting of 25 single consonants, 24 double consonants and 16 vowel sounds. However most vowels are omitted, though they may be indicated by the positioning of a word above, on or below the line. The signs are a mixture of straight lines, curves, dots and dashes, as well as a contrast in positioning and shading. They relate to the sound system; for example, straight lines are used for all stop consonants (such as *p*), and signs for all labial consonants (such as *f*) slope backwards. The thickness of a line indicates whether a sound is voiceless or voiced.

The shorthand used by Samuel Pepys for writing his famous diary from 1660 to 1669 was much less sophisticated. Invented by Thomas Shelton in the 1620s, in some ways it resembled an ancient writing system, such as Babylonian cuneiform. Although many of the signs were simply reduced forms of letters and abbreviations for words, there

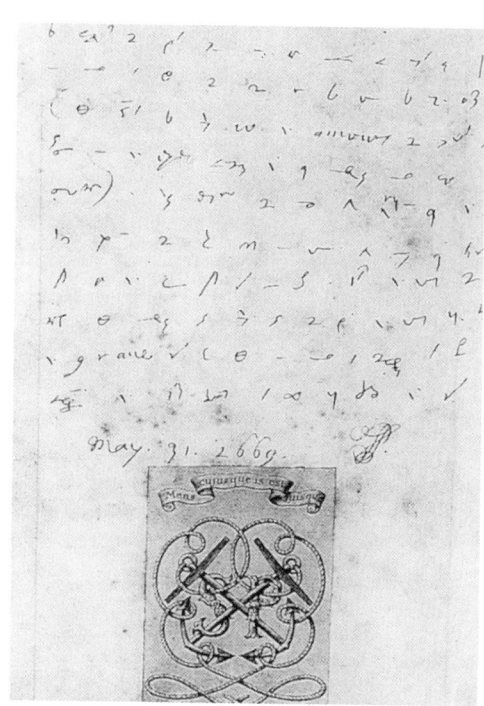

were nearly 300 invented symbols, mainly arbitrary logograms, such as 2 for 'to', a larger 2 for 'two', 5 for 'because', 6 for 'us'. (Several of these symbols were 'empty', presumably to foster the secrecy of the work.) Initial vowels were symbolized; medial vowels were indicated by placing the consonant following the vowel in five positions on, below or to the side of the preceding consonant; and final vowels were shown by dots, arranged similarly. Overall, the system was quasi-phonetic. Despite its drawbacks, it was popular in its day for reporting sermons and speeches, perhaps as fast as a hundred words per minute.

Samuel Pepys, diarist (1633–1703).

Left **The last page of Samuel Pepys' celebrated diary, which he gave up in 1669 when he was (mistakenly) convinced he was going blind, 'being not able to do it any longer, having done now so long as to undo my eyes almost every time I take a pen in my hand . . . And so I do betake myself to that course, which is almost as much as to see myself go into my grave: for which, and all the discomforts that will accompany my being blind, the good God prepare me!'**

Left **Pitman's shorthand and** (right) **Speedwriting: 'Since the dawn of history man has strived to communicate with his fellows and to record experiences that would otherwise be forgotten.'**

Classification of Writing Systems

This tree divides writing systems according to their nature, not according to their age; it does *not* show how one writing system may have given rise to another historically. (The dashed lines indicate possible influences of one system upon another.) How best to classify writing systems is a controversial matter. For instance, some scholars deny the existence of alphabets prior to the Greek alphabet, on the grounds that the Phoenician script marked only consonants, no vowels (like today's Arabic script). The root of the problem of classification is that there is no such thing as a 'pure' writing system – i.e. a system that expresses meaning entirely through syllabic signs or alphabetic letters or logograms – because *all* full writing systems are a mixture of phonetic and semantic symbols. Nevertheless, labels are useful to remind one of the predominant nature of different systems. The labels used here, e.g. logophonemic, are necessarily a little complicated: their meaning will become clearer as we encounter each writing system in some detail.

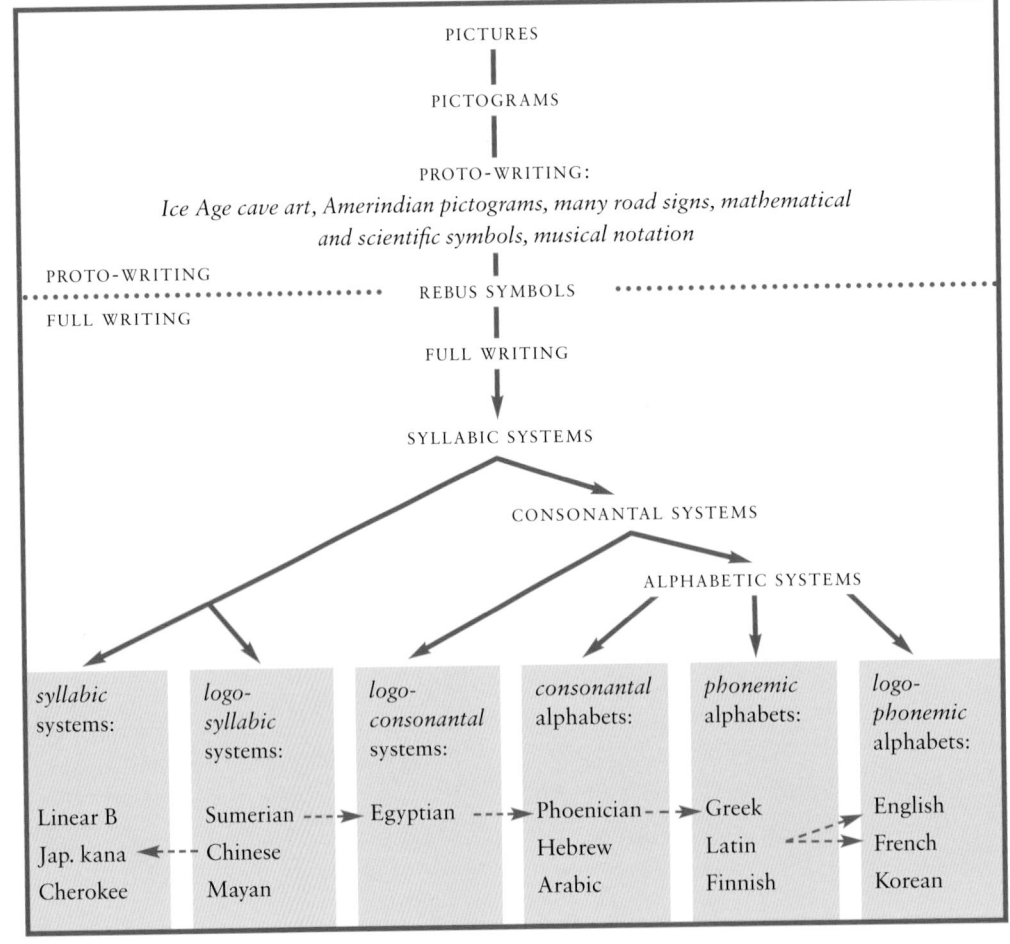

Language and Script

Language and script are so closely entwined in our minds we forget that English, French or German, say, theoretically could be written in almost any script. We would suffer a severe handicap if we decided to write English entirely in the Arabic script or in Japanese 'kana', because there are many sounds in English not represented in these scripts. But in principle a script used for writing one language can be adapted to write another.

This has happened throughout history. The Akkadians, who ruled Mesopotamia after the Sumerians, took over the Sumerian cuneiform script, even though Akkadian and Sumerian were dissimilar languages. The Japanese imported the Chinese characters, despite the great disparity between the two languages. And the Greeks took their alphabet most probably from the Phoenicians, modifying the Semitic script and extending it with vowel signs.

Borrowed Scripts Today

The process continues. In China, since 1958, the Pinyin system has permitted the Chinese language to be written in romanized form. In Malta, the Maltese language, though a form of Arabic, is written in the Roman alphabet – the only form of Arabic to be written in this way. And in Turkey, an Arabic script used by the Ottoman Turks was officially abandoned in 1928 by Kemal Atatürk, and a Roman script substituted. The Turkish language is structurally entirely unrelated to Arabic, despite Arabic loan-words and a strong cultural link with Islam. To cope with Turkish phonemes not represented by 26 alphabetic letters, several diacritics were required, for example ğ (soft /g/y/), ö and ü (as in German), ş (/sh/).

There are obvious political overtones to such decisions. In 1960, newly independent Somalia was faced with the question of deciding on a script for the Somali language. Islam is the official religion of Somalia, and Arabic is an official language along with Somali; however Italian and English are widely spoken. A government committee considered 18 suggested scripts: eleven 'Somali', four Arabic, and three Roman. The leading 'Somali' contender was the Osmanian alphabet, named after its inventor Osman Yusuf. He blended ideas from Italian, Arabic and Ethiopic scripts. The use of distinct signs for consonants and vowels and the direction of writing came from Italian. The order of the letters and the way of representing the long vowels was based on the Arabic alphabet. The general look of the letters showed Ethiopic influence.

In 1961, two alphabets were officially selected, the Osmanian and a Roman alphabet. In 1969, there was a coup with one of its stated aims the resolution of the debate over the country's writing system. In 1973, the Osmanian system was abandoned and the official script of Somalia became a Roman script.

JOE'S TV SERVICE
TISWIJIET fuq kull marka ta' TVs u monitors. Servizz fil-pront u efficjenti. Ċemplu 434212, 444264.

Maltese is the only form of Arabic to be written in a Roman alphabet. Note the addition of a letter, and a diacritic above some consonants.

Below **The Osmanian alphabet, invented by Osman Yusuf during the 20th century, for writing the Somali language. It was abandoned in 1973.**

The Prestige of a Script

MCMXCV

Tradition is extremely important in the history of scripts. Often it takes precedence over convenience. Egyptian hieroglyphs and Mesopotamian cuneiform survived for many centuries after alphabets became widespread. In Japan today, partly for reasons of tradition, no well-educated person can contemplate radical change to the writing system based on Chinese characters, despite its daunting complexity. In China and Japan, Chinese characters are revered, as witness the rubbing of a commemorative inscription written by Mao Zedong around 1953.

In Israel, since 1948, a unique situation has arisen: a colloquial language has been moulded around an ancient written language. Before 1948, for centuries, both the language and script of Hebrew had been confined largely to religious literature. With the founding of the state of Israel, Hebrew became a national language and a national script – its lack of vowel signs and consequent difficulty of reading notwithstanding.

It is almost as if spoken Latin had been resurrected and used for daily conversation, instead of being retained only for religious and ceremonial purposes. Some forms from *written* Latin, on the other hand, have survived in common use, particularly Roman numerals. The latter appear on coinage, on clock faces, on certain public inscriptions,

on the bindings of some learned journals, and even on the credits for television programmes made by the BBC. It would be quite unacceptable to write Louis 16 or Queen Elizabeth 2 (except on a ship), or that Big Ben should display ordinary Arabic numerals. Clumsy though they are, Roman numerals retain a prestige not accorded to Arabic numerals. And the same is true, to a lesser extent, of 'black-letter' or Gothic script, the standard handwriting of European Christendom for about 500 years until the Renaissance. Subsequently, Roman

Above right **German black-letter script.**

Right **Sumerian–Akkadian bilingual, *c.* 1750 BC. The Sumerian text on the left is translated into Akkadian on the right. The smaller signs beneath each line of Sumerian indicate its pronunciation.**

Far right **Reverence for Chinese characters. A rubbing of a commemorative inscription written by Mao Zedong, *c.* 1953.**

Below left **By the time Darius I (521–486 BC) erected a statue of himself to celebrate a victory over the Egyptians, the official hand of the Persian empire was the alphabetic Aramaic script. But the statue's inscriptions are in cuneiform and Egyptian hieroglyphs, the scripts hallowed for celebrating victories. The first four cuneiform lines (turning the photo 90 degrees anticlockwise) are written in Old Persian, the next three lines in Elamite, and the last three, in shadow, are in Akkadian.**

Below right **Crowd awaiting the arrival of the Jewish Commission, Mount of Olives, Jerusalem, April 1918. The making of modern Hebrew began long before the founding of the state of Israel. The revival of the ancient script brought a renewed sense of unity.**

rankfurter

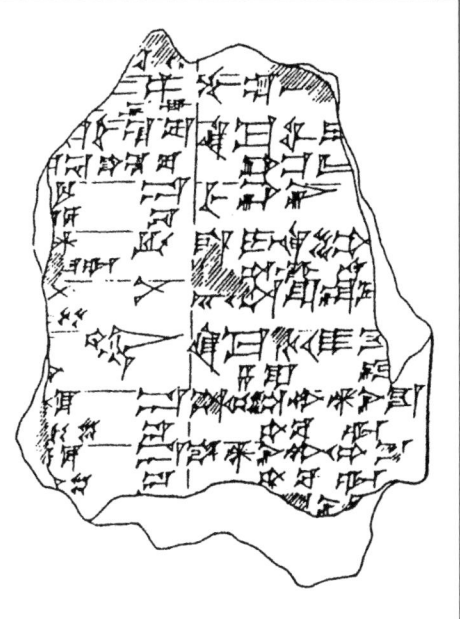

script superseded it, being considered more suitable by humanists, except in Germany, where black-letter script persisted until 1940, when Adolf Hitler banned it on the grounds of its 'Jewish' origin.

In general scripts change much more gradually than speech. Western writers still pay tribute to Roman scripts, Jewish writers to the ancient Hebrew script and Japanese writers to the Chinese characters; in India, millions write in the Devanagari script, the 'script of the city of the gods', evolved from the first script used to write Sanskrit. This literary conservatism goes right back to the beginning of writing. Two and a half millennia ago, we find Darius, king of the Persians, erecting cuneiform inscriptions in Akkadian, the language of earlier rulers. A millennium before him, scribes in Babylonia were busy compiling bilingual tablets to help students learn to write Sumerian in cuneiform. They are the clay equivalents of the Latin-English dictionaries of generations of western schoolchildren.

The Graphic Dimension

All scripts function through both phonetic and semantic signs, as we have seen. They also communicate graphically, through the shapes of their signs. Alphabet users tend to neglect the graphic dimension because they perceive no meaning in the individual letters of the alphabet, though they do regard different styles of letter as conveying meaning in different ways (hence the significance of typefaces such as Roman, Italic, Gothic). Users of Chinese characters, by contrast, tend to claim too much for their symbols because each character, unlike an alphabetic letter, *has* a meaning, and some of the characters seem visually to resemble their meanings. Writers of Chinese like to suggest that the characters somehow 'speak directly to the mind', without the intervention of sound.

While this is not true, there undoubtedly is an extra dimension of meaning in Chinese characters, and in Egyptian hieroglyphs. Both systems, when finely executed, yield writing that appears to have a life of its own. The giant character opposite means Buddha. It would be most unusual for a Christian today to pray before alphabetic letters: however beautifully illuminated by a medieval monk, alphabetic letters do not have the symbolic power and vitality of Chinese characters.

Very few characters are instantly recognizable. Yet foreigners often feel as if Chinese characters are appropriate to their meanings – once they have been told what they mean! Consequently, visual mnemonics for characters can be devised to help learn the characters and their meanings. But one should not fall into the trap of thinking that the mnemonics 'explain' the evolution of a character from the original image. A few Chinese characters *are* pictographic in origin – 'woman' and 'paddyfield' are two such – but the vast majority are not.

女 woman	𗷗 𗷘 𗷙 𗷚
子 child	𗷛 𗷜 𗷝 𗷞
田 paddyfield	𗷟
力 strength	𗷠 𗷡 力
男 male	𗷢

Five common Chinese characters and their visual mnemonics. The character for 'male' is supposed to represent 'strength in the paddyfields', reflecting the fact that until recently men's major occupation in China was rice cultivation. Below left **Nowadays, women too cultivate rice.**

Buddha carved on a boulder at Xiamen (Amoy) in the form of the characte 'fo'. This is one of the main Buddhist shrines in south China. The character was carved in 1905.

Pictography

Prehistoric rock carving, Camonica Valley, northern Italy.

Early Chinese pictogram for 'overhead' or 'sky, heaven'.

Drawing of a shaman, Tungus, Manchuria.

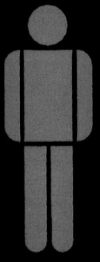

Modern symbol that could represent e.g. 'man' or 'stand' or 'men's WC'.

Common sense suggests that many written symbols began life as pictures, and a consensus among scholars supports this idea. What could be easier to 'read' than a pictogram of a person, a cow, a snake or a tree? In fact, pictograms are not as simple as they appear. Here are twelve early Chinese pictograms, dating to 1200–1045 BC, and eighteen Sumerian pictograms from *c.* 3000 BC. Try to guess their meanings before reading the answers below.

| tripod | elephant | sheep/ram | basket | pelt | woman |
| opening/mouth | fish | moon/month | horse | field | turtle |

hand	day	cow	eat	pot	date-palm
pig	orchard	bird	reed	donkey	ox
head	walk, stand	fish	barley	well	water

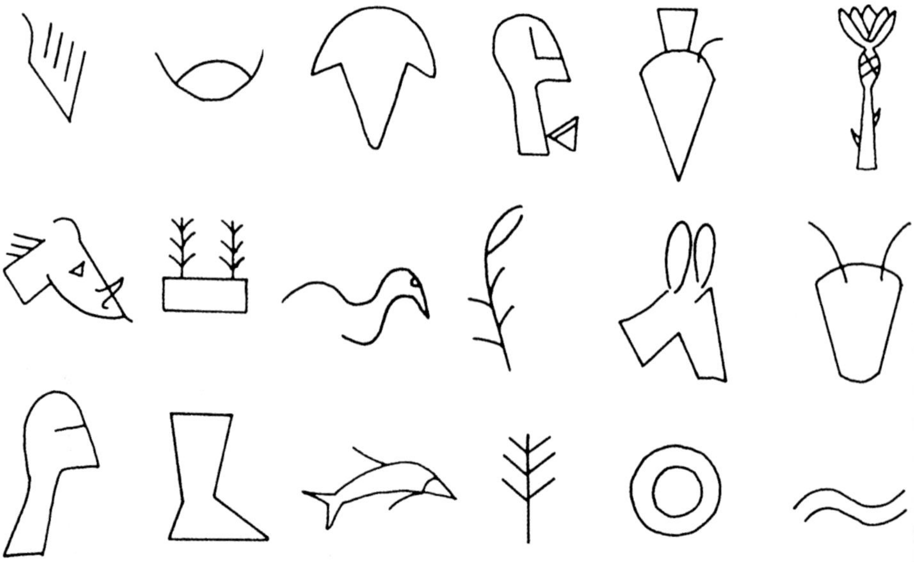

Two major practical difficulties arise with pictography. First, where on a scale does a symbol become a pictogram? Conversely, how abstract can a pictogram become, before it ceases to be one? The artist M. C. Escher turned this conundrum into fascinating works of art, such as the one reproduced above. The black shapes in the middle are clearly triangles, those on the right are clearly pictograms of birds. But what of the shapes between?

Second, at what point on a scale of generalization and association of ideas does the meaning of a pictogram fall? A standing male stick figure could mean, for example, anything from one individual to the totality of men; it could also symbolize 'stand', 'wait', 'alone', 'lonely' or indeed 'Men's WC'. Similarly, the Sumerian symbol for 'barley' could just as well mean any other kind of grain-producing plant, or indeed any plant. The situation is somewhat similar to that of children learning to talk. Having learnt that the family dog is called 'dog', they may overextend the word to other animals they see, such as cats – or they may use the word too narrowly, applying it only to one particular dog, their family dog.

Signs of Cultures

Pictograms are also fraught with difficulties of a cultural kind. There are dozens of designs for chairs, including bar stools, padded armchairs and bucket-shaped swivel chairs. None of these is likely to be found among the wicker stools in an African village. The cow is associated with milk and meat in the West; in India it has a hump, is holy to Hindus and may not be slaughtered by them. Pictograms of seating and cows are likely to differ both in appearance and in connotations from culture to culture.

Pictograms of advanced technology are relatively free of such ambiguities. Provided one is familiar with the devices concerned, pictograms work well in representing transistors, resistors, switches, capacitors, and so on. Circuit diagrams are highly effective examples of pictographic communication. Imagine trying to convey the same information in words. But circuit diagrams are also extremely specific in the type of information they can convey.

M. C. Escher,
Metamorphosis III,
1967–68.

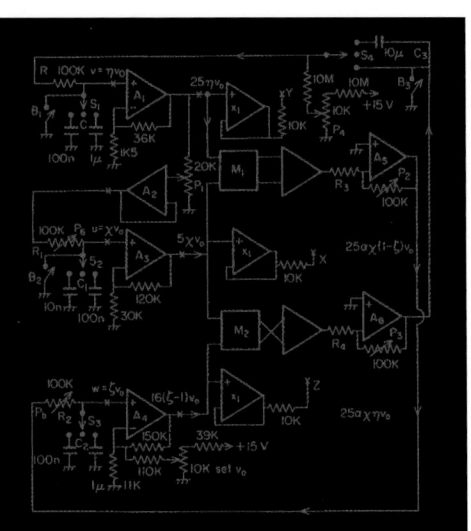

Electronic circuit diagrams
are a successful form of
pictographic communication.

Chapter 3   *Proto-Writing*

**Ice Age graffiti:
art or writing?**

Ice Age Symbols

Left **Bison bearing signs, from Marsoulas, southern France.**

Below **Engraved horse, over-engraved with a series of 'P' signs from Les Trois Frères, southern France. In an adjoining cave, Tuc d'Audoubert, hidden in a tiny recess, is another horse surrounded by more than 80 'P' signs, many clearly made with different tools. Perhaps, over time, it was an image of worship in the private ritual of some Ice Age individual?**

The stencilled hand and red dots on a boulder shown opposite are probably 20,000 years old. They were made in a cave at Pech Merle, in Lot, in southern France. What do these lively Ice Age graffiti mean? 'I was here, with my animals'? – or is the symbolism deeper? No one knows. Numerous examples of Ice Age painting and drawing – on cave walls and on objects – have turned up in southern France over the last century or so, some of which carry unexplained signs. There is the engraved profile of a stag's head with two lozenges from Lorthet, and a painted bison bearing signs from Marsoulas (*above*).

Is all this writing? If we mean – is it part of a 'system of graphic symbols that can be used to convey any and all thought' (to recall our earlier definition of writing) – then the answer is no. Credulity is stretched too far if we are asked to believe that Ice Age humans invented some kind of writing system,

perhaps even an alphabet, which was then completely lost; after all, we cannot be certain that the cave-painters could fully speak (though most scientists assume they could), let alone write. But equally hard to believe is that artists of such vitality and power were incapable of inventing a *limited* form of written communication. Let us call the Ice Age signs and other forms of partial writing 'proto-writing'. Endless varieties of proto-writing exist, coming from all periods, including our own age (for example circuit diagrams and road signs). Proto-writing long preceded the emergence of full writing in Sumer in about 3300 BC, and it will always exist alongside full writing.

*proto-writing —
forms of partial writing
that exist
alongside
full writing*

Tallies

According to Herodotus, the Greek historian, the Persian king Darius left a force of Greeks (his allies) to guard a strategic bridge at his rear during an expedition against the unruly Scythians. As he was about to leave, Darius gave the Greeks a thong with 60 knots in it and told them to untie one knot each day. If he had not returned by the time all the knots were undone, he said, they should take ship for home.

Tallies such as this are among the oldest types of proto-writing. Ice Age bones have been discovered bearing series of neat notches. Microscopic examination suggests the notches were made with various tools over a period of time. A plausible explanation is that the bones are lunar notations: by keeping track of the phases of the moon, Ice Age humans created useful calendars.

It is easy to assume that the use of tallies should die out with the spread of literacy in a society. In fact tallies can supplement literacy. A knot in a handkerchief can remind its illiterate owner to perform some task, but it can just as easily remind a *literate* person to (say) look up a fact in some library. The history of the British Treasury is inseparably connected with that of the tally; the Exchequer used tally sticks to record receipts from about 1100 until 1834, adding to the notches explanatory notes.

Left **Medieval customs officers collecting the duties on wine. One holds a purse, the other a pair of tallies, with a notching knife. From a 15th-century window in Tournai cathedral, Belgium.**

Below left **Engraved eagle bones from Le Placard, in Charente, western France, *c.* 13,500 BC. The notches may be a lunar notation.**

Below **Tally stick of the British Exchequer with explanatory notes. Such tallies were accepted until 1834. The larger the sum, the larger the amount of wood removed in the cutting process. £1000 was represented by cutting a straight indented notch the width of a man's hand (four inches); the groove for £1 would just take a ripe barley corn; a penny was simply a straight saw cut, a halfpenny merely a punched hole. Everybody, literate or not, was aware of these standard values.**

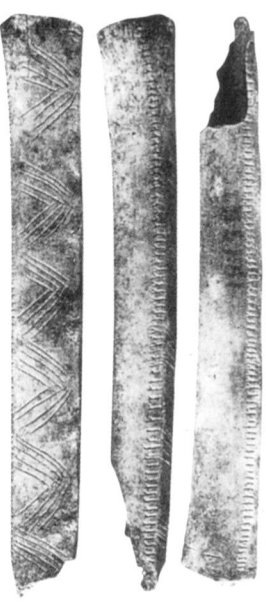

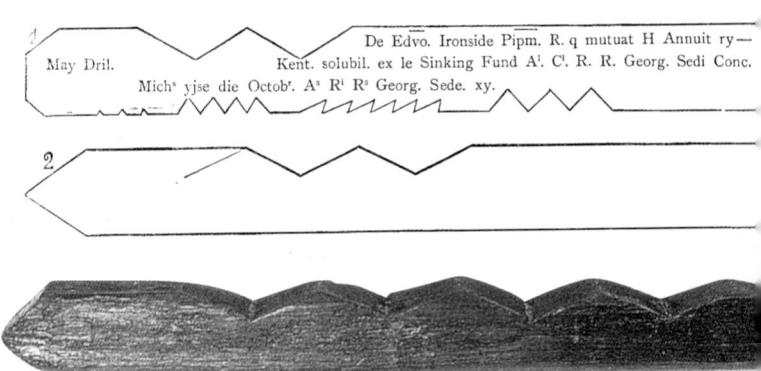

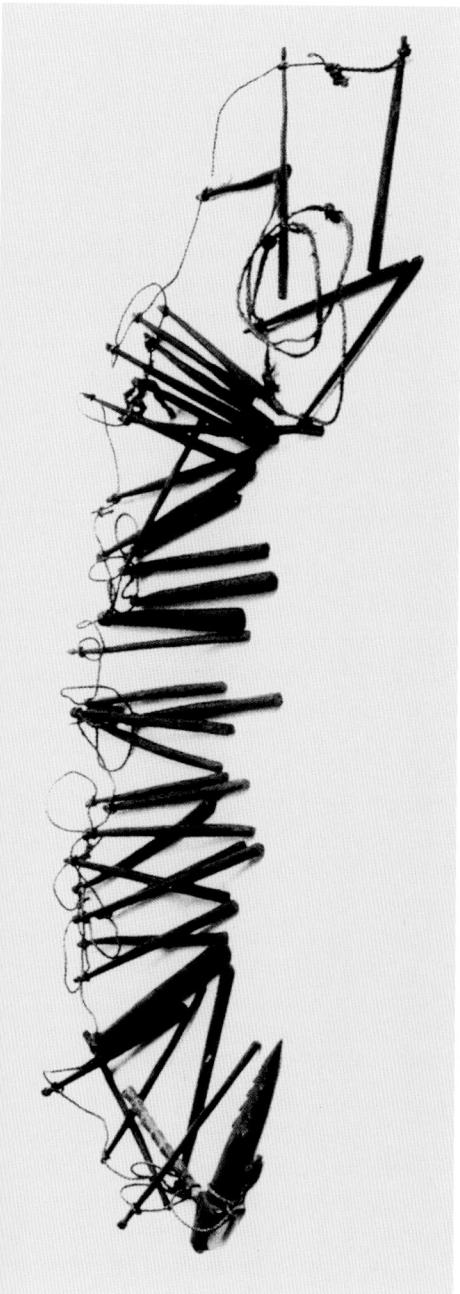

Left **Guaman Poma de Ayala's Inca imperial clerk with a quipu, *c.* 1613.**

Far left **Tally ('kupe') from the Torres Strait Islands.**

Bottom **Quipu from Peru. There were many types of knot in a quipu, each type representing a value in a decimal system; the absence of a knot denoted zero. For example, a string with two overhand knots above a group of four overhand knots surmounting a fivefold-long knot meant '245'. The value also varied according to the knot's position on the cord. In addition, summation cords were used to tie off bunches of strings.**

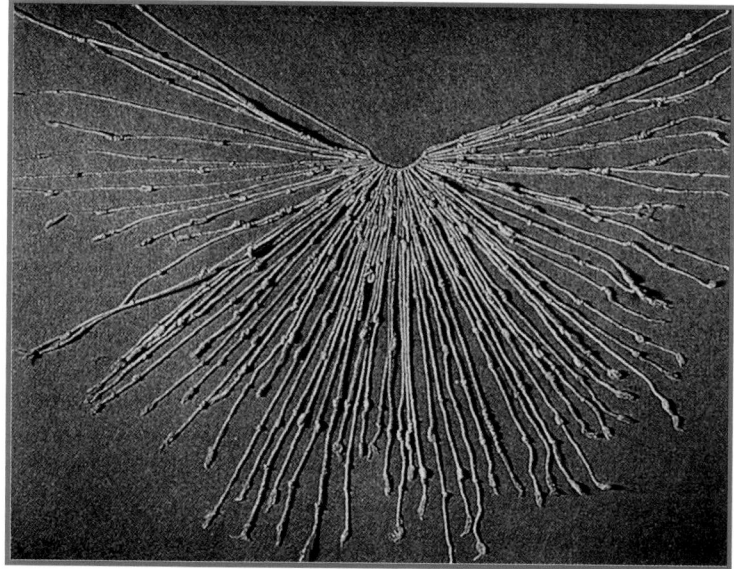

Inca Quipus

The Inca civilization is a celebrated exception to the general picture which emerges, of empires requiring writing. There is no script of the Incas (unlike the Aztecs and the Maya). Instead, a knotted arrangement of rope and cords called a 'quipu' kept track of the movement of goods in the Inca empire. Quipus were the sole bureaucratic recording device of the Incas; it was the job of the 'quipucamayocs', or knot keepers, in each town, to tie and interpret the knot records. The system worked well, and was retained for some time after the arrival of the Spanish 'conquistadores' in the 16th century.

Amerindian Pictograms

The best-known form of proto-writing is probably the pictography of the North American Indians. The pictograms are for the most part comparatively crude marks and symbols engraved or painted on walls and rocks. The commonest kind are usually known as petroglyphs. But some Amerindian pictograms are more sophisticated.

The above pictograms were 'written' in 1883 by the chief of the Oglala Sioux, at the behest of the US Indian agent in Dakota Territory. They list warriors (the red streaks on the faces indicate warriors). Their names are given by the signs above their heads, for instance, the-Bear-Spares-Him, Iron-Hawk (the colour blue signifies 'iron'), Red-Horn-Bull, Charging-Hawk, Wears-the-Feather and Red-Crow.

There are also a very few examples of pictographic 'letters' sent by American Indians. Quote marks around the word letter are necessary, because the 'letters' are not true letters: they are more like secret code letters that can be understood only by those 'in the know'.

Left **This letter was the work of a Cheyenne man called Turtle-Following-His-Wife and was addressed to his son Little-Man. It said that he was sending his son $53 (represented by 53 little circles) and asking him to return home. The letter was mailed by Turtle-Following-His-Wife, but the money was given to Agent Dyer with an explanation of the letter's meaning. Dyer sent the money and a covering explanation to Agent McGillycuddy, so that the agent was able to hand over the money to Little-Man on presentation of his father's letter. Presumably father and son had agreed on a letter in a similar style before the son had gone away from his father.**

A Siberian Love Letter

Another well known example of pictography is the so-called Yukaghir Love Letter. It was 'written' in about 1892 by a woman of the small and isolated Yukaghir tribe living in north-eastern Siberia, and published in 1895 by a Russian political exile, turned anthropologist, who had been banished to Siberia.

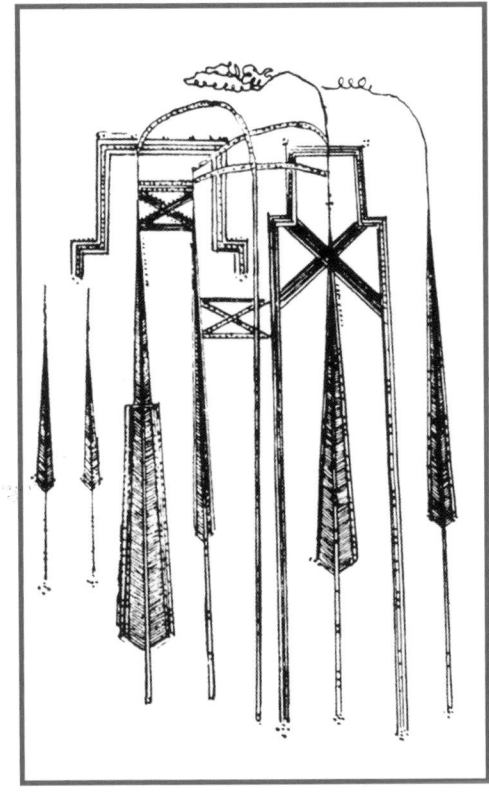

A glance tells us that we cannot make much sense of this document, simply by studying its constituent shapes and interrelationships. The explanation is (partly) as follows. The conifer-shaped objects represent people. Conifer **c** is the writer (female), conifer **b** the addressee (male), who was formerly the writer's lover but is now living with conifer **a**, a Russian woman, away from the Yukaghir village. This has naturally disrupted the relationship between the writer and the addressee, hence the line **x** from the head of the Russian woman which cuts through the line joining **b** and **c**. But the **a**–**b** menage is a stormy one (crossed lines between **a** and **b**), and the writer is unhappy alone in her house (crossed lines within rectangular enclosing structure); she is still thinking of the addressee (curly tendril reaching from **c** towards **b**).

On the other hand, she announces, the addressee should be aware of another young man in the village, conifer **d**, who is interested in the writer (curly tendril reaching from **d** towards **c**). If the addressee wants to act on the writer's message, he had better hurry, before his new household (incomplete structure) has children (two small conifers on far left).

It is a charming design, once explained, which has, not surprisingly, seduced many willing scholars into thinking it a true letter, an example of language-free pictographic communication. But this is a fallacy. Recent careful investigation of the original Russian sources has revealed that the 'letter' was really a sort of Yukhagir party game, cut into birchbark by a love-lorn girl. As she carved, other young Yukaghir would gather round, banter with her, and try to guess the meaning. This was made much easier by the fact that everyone knew each other. The 'letter' was never designed to be sent; its contents were conveyed orally to the addressee, either by the girl herself or by someone else.

Clay 'Tokens'

Excavations in the Middle East have yielded, besides clay tablets, large numbers of small, nondescript clay objects. According to the stratigraphy of the excavations, the objects date from 8000 BC to as late as 1500 BC, though the number of finds dated after 3000 BC tails off. The earlier objects are undecorated and geometrically shaped – spheres, discs, cones and so on, while the later ones are often incised and shaped in more complex ways.

No one knows their purpose for sure. The most probable explanation is that they were counting units in accountancy. Different shapes could have been used for different entities, such as a sheep from a flock, or a specified measure of a certain product, such as a bushel of grain. The number and variety of shapes could have been extended so that one object of a particular shape could stand for, say, ten sheep or a hundred sheep, or black sheep as opposed to white ones. This would have permitted large numbers and amounts to be manipulated arithmetically with comparatively small numbers of clay objects. It would also explain the noticeable trend towards greater complexity of object with time, as the ancient economies ramified.

On these assumptions, the objects are generally termed 'tokens', because they are thought to have represented ideas and quantities. According to one theory, this token system was pictographic writing in embryo; hence the decline in numbers of tokens with the growth of writing on clay tablets in the 3rd millennium BC. This theory is not widely accepted; we shall now see why.

Finds of clay 'tokens'. They occur widely from Palestine up through Anatolia and across Iraq to eastern Iran (though none has been found in Egypt); they are particularly plentiful in Babylonia. One major difficulty in compiling such a map is that excavators often discarded tokens; another is to decide whether a small clay object qualifies as a token or not. (After Schmandt-Besserat)

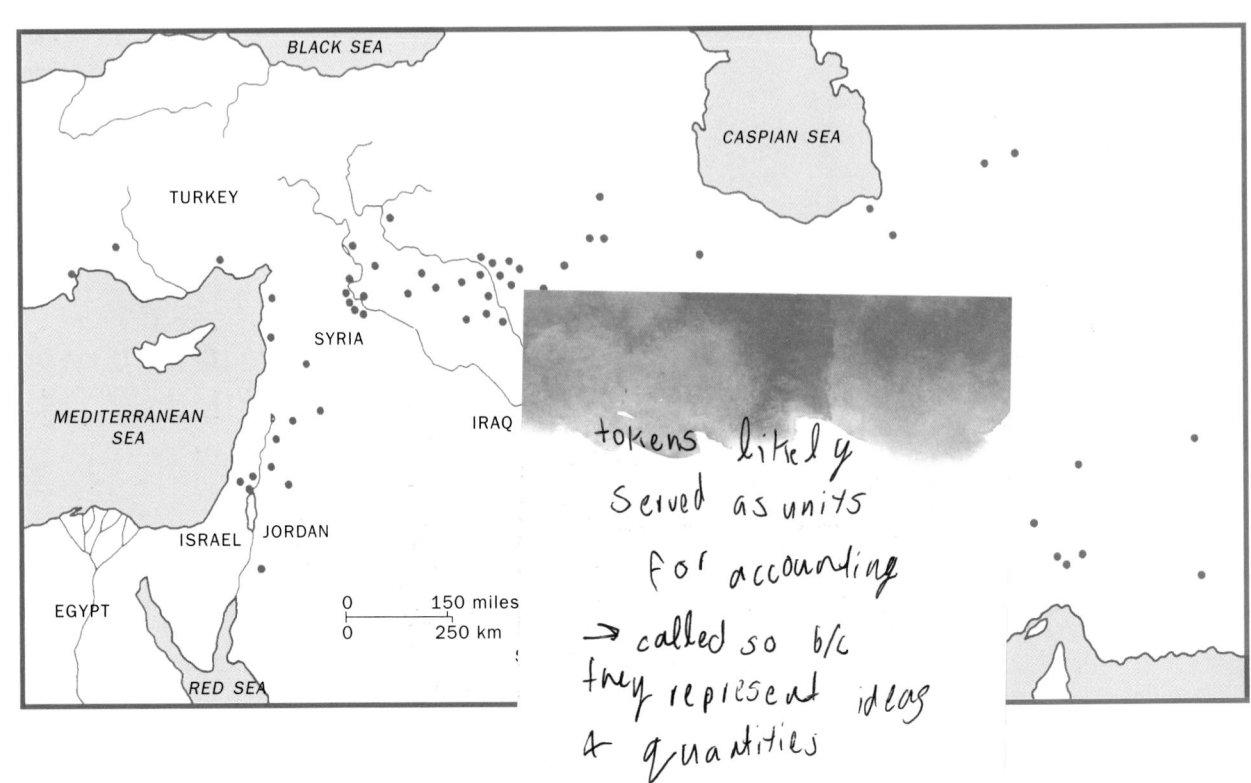

Above **Simple and complex 'tokens', dating from 8000 BC until the emergence of writing. The crossed token seems to have been used to record numbers of sheep.**

Left **Sir Leonard Woolley excavating at the ancient Sumerian city of Ur, 1920s. He and other early excavators discarded most tokens as worthless.**

Clay Envelopes

The most interesting finds of clay tokens are those in which the tokens have been enclosed in a clay envelope, generally shaped as a ball and known as a 'bulla', the outer surface has been sealed, and impressions have been made in its surface, which sometimes correspond to the contents. There are some 80 bullae known to exist with tokens intact: picked up and shaken, they rattle; X-rayed, they reveal the outlines of tokens within. A few bullae have been opened, while others have been found broken during excavation and the contents dispersed without proper records. But despite the limited evidence, certain conclusions can be drawn.

The purpose of a bulla was most probably to guarantee the accuracy and authenticity of stored tokens. Tokens kept on a string or in a bag could be tampered with; this was much less easy to do when the tokens were sealed away. If goods were being dispatched, a sealed bulla might have acted as a bill of lading. In the event of a dispute, the bulla could be broken and the contents checked against the merchandise.

By marking the outside of the clay, it would have been possible to check the contents without having to break the bulla (though of course such impressions would not have been as secure from tampering). But the evidence here is ambiguous. One would expect the number of exterior impressions to match the number of tokens. In some cases this is so, but not always. One might also expect a match between the shapes of the impressions and the shapes of the tokens. (Presumably, after the bulla was sealed, the impressions would be made with other tokens exactly like those hidden inside.) In fact, the correlation is patchy.

Many scholars (led by Denise Schmandt-Besserat) feel that these exterior marks on bullae were a step towards the marking of clay tablets with more complex signs, and the consequent emergence of writing. While this is reasonable, it seems over-complicated. Why should a sign on a clay tablet be considered a *more* advanced idea than an impression on a clay ball or, for that matter, than a clay token itself? If anything, the modelling of an engraved token seems to be more advanced than the scratching of a sign on a tablet. Compare the invention of coins, which postdated scratch marks and notches on a tally stick. Furthermore tokens and bullae continued to exist long after the emergence of cuneiform in about 3000 BC. Rather than giving rise to the idea of writing, as suggested, tokens and bullae probably acted as supplements to writing, like tallies. In other words, they did not precede writing but accompanied its development.

Below **Bulla with six tokens and six matching impressions on its surface.**

Left **Bulla with seven tokens and four impressions on its surface, probably made by some of the tokens;**
Below left **unique bulla from Nuzi with cuneiform inscription,** *c.* **1500 BC, describing 49 tokens (intact when excavated but now lost);**
Below right **sealed bulla with X-ray (tokens visible).**

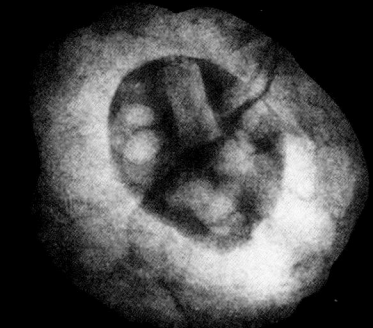

The First Clay Tablets

The earliest known clay tablets come from Uruk in Mesopotamia, were written by Sumerians and probably ~~from~~ about 3300 BC (all early tablet ~~uncertain). They are numerical ~~and cannot be thought of as showing ~~running~~: they solely concern calculations, and the signs consist of numerals and symbols that are pictographic or quasi-pictographic. We cannot be sure of their detailed meanings, though we can sometimes follow a calculation.

The numerals are impressed in ways that remained the same for many centuries, as cuneiform developed during the 3rd millennium BC. The round end of a reed stylus was either pressed vertically into the soft clay to make a circular hole, or it was pressed at an angle to make a fingernail-shaped depression (see p. 83) – or a combination of both impressions, superimposed, was used to express a larger numeral.

It is possible that the numerals developed out of the impressions made in the exterior of clay bullae. But it is equally possible that the numerals were developed separately, for use on tablets.

Probably the idea of tablets was the outcome of the increasing economic complexity of the Mesopotamian city states. Just as Ice Age humans turned to cave walls and bones to record what was important to them, the city dwellers of ancient Iraq turned to the most abundant natural material available in a land with little stone or wood. Clay was relatively easy to mark with a stylus, and also relatively easy to erase if a mistake was made; while when it had been

fired it left a more permanent record. In the early tablet pictured opposite, the commodity is known to be barley (used to brew beer), as indicated by a pictogram. Both the amounts recorded and the accounting period are known. The smallest unit ⌣ probably represented approximately 4.8 litres of barley. Each numeral sign is a multiple of the previous one, as follows:

▷	= 5	⌣	or about 24 litres
•	= 6	▷	or about 144 litres
●	= 10	•	or about 1,440 litres
▷	= 3	●	or about 4,320 litres
▶▷	= 10	▷	or about 43,200 litres

Left **Early clay tablet from Uruk, front** (above) **and back** (below). **The commodities are unknown, but the calculation can be summarized as follows:**

(front)   (back)
18 ▷ + 3 ● = 8 ▷ +4 ●
(if 1 ● = 10 ▷).

Right **Early clay tablet from Uruk used to record transaction involving barley, with transcription. The two signs in the bottom left hand corner occur on 18 tablets from this period and probably represent the name of the official responsible for this transaction (or they may denote the name of an institution or office). On the basis of the signs' resemblance to later signs of known phonetic value, the official's name may have been Kushim. Some other signs in the bottom right hand corner are less clear in meaning. Given the very large amount of barley and the long accounting period, the tablet appears to be a summary of a 'balance sheet'. (From Nissen, Damerow and Englund)**

earliest tablets = Uruk
numerical, result
of increasing
economic complexity

quantity of the product:

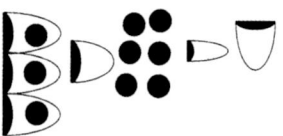

c. 135,000 litres

type of the product:

barley

accounting period:

37 months

name of the responsible official:

Kushim

function of the document (?):

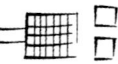

final account? (inscribed
over a partially erased sign)

use of barley (?):

exchange (?)

Counting in the Ancient Middle East

In one crucial respect, we still count in the way that the Sumerians counted five millennia ago. For marking time and angle, we use the sexagesimal system based on multiples of 60: there are 60 seconds in a minute, 60 minutes in an hour, 60 minutes in a degree and 360 degrees in a circle. In the Sumerian counting system, which included many subsystems, one important series of numerals was as follows:

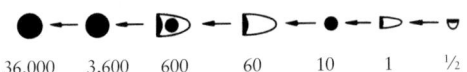

| 36,000 | 3,600 | 600 | 60 | 10 | 1 | ½ |

These particular numerals were used to count most discrete objects, for example humans and animals, dairy and textile products, fish, wooden and stone implements, and containers. A second series of numerals was probably a rationing system to count discrete grain products, cheese and fresh fish; and a third series was used to assess areas. Then there was a series used to note capacity measures of grain, in particular barley (we saw it on p. 63), a series used for germinated barley (malt), a series used for barley groats (hulled barley), and various other series. All this makes for considerable difficulties in interpreting the earliest tablets. Only the calendrical system is comparatively straightforward:

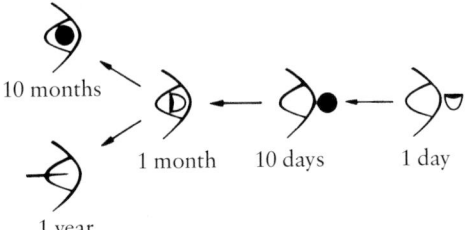

10 months

1 year

1 month   10 days   1 day

Left **Black obelisk, erected by the Assyrian king Shalmeneser III (858–824 BC) to celebrate his victories. The carvings show tribute being brought by his defeated enemies: the booty – gold, silver and other precious metals as well as raw materials such as grain and oil – gave the Assyrians an increasingly strong position as traders in the eastern Mediterranean. Numeral systems for calculation were consequently of great importance to the Assyrians, as they had been to the Babylonians and the Sumerians.**

Left **Rassam obelisk (detail) from Kalhu (Nimrud), showing tribute being weighed and measured before the Assyrian king Ashurnasirpal II (883–859 BC).**

Below **These Sumerian signs are not abstract numeral signs, but signs representing measures, e.g. 1 kg of malt, 10 kg of malt, that increase in size from right to left. We do not know the precise amount of the measure involved in each case,**
only the *ratios* between the measures.
NB The number of small incisions made in a given sign varies from tablet to tablet. (From Nissen et al)

The cardinal principle of our numeral system – that a numeral is an abstract entity that can be attached to anything from minutes to kilograms of cheese – had not been conceived by the earliest people to count. The resultant arithmetical ambiguity in their signs is disturbing to us modern counters. For instance, the numeral sign • can take the following values, depending on its context:

• =10 ▷ in context with sheep

• = 6 ▷ in context with barley

• =18 ▷ in context with fields.

Here are three of the numeral systems, some of the signs of which we shall use to understand the signs on a complex tablet about beer-making, on pp. 66–67. System 1 applies to measures of barley and to cereal products, system 2 to measures of malt, and system 3 to measures of barley groats (hulled barley).

System 1 Barley and cereal products

System 2 Malt

System 3 Barley groats

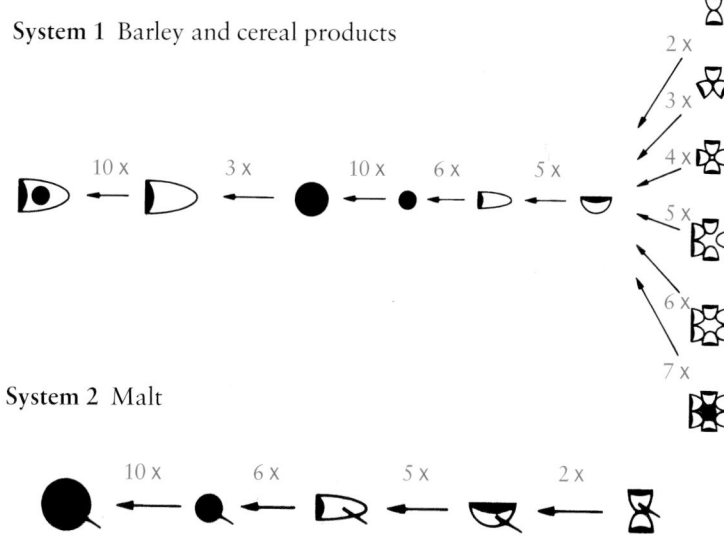

Archaic Book-keeping

The tablet on these pages is one of the most important early Sumerian tablets. Can we call its symbols writing? No, this is still proto-writing, concerned purely with calculation. There is no use of a rebus to express phonetic elements in the language. We may *imagine* how these signs might turn into cuneiform, into full writing, but they have not reached that stage yet. Unlike the tablet about barley on p. 63, this tablet is unsigned and was probably some sort of supplementary annotation to the main administrative documents (which we do not have). Nevertheless, it is believed to have been composed by a scribe in the office of Kushim, whose name is on the earlier tablet.

It tabulates in columns the raw materials required to make nine different cereal products and eight different kinds of beer. We do not know what these products were: maybe baked items, such as loaves of bread? Each product is designated and or denoted by a logogram, e.g. . Five different series of numerals are used, sexagesimal and bisexagesimal, pertaining to beer containers, cereal products, and measures of raw materials.

Five major groups of signs on the tablet are singled out for explanation.

Left **Clay tablet used for administrative purposes. Five groups of marks have been analysed** (opposite). **The small incisions made in some of the marks are not always consistent, and since they are not essential to our purpose here, they are ignored. (From Nissen et al)**

 = 10 (noted in the bisexagesimal system)

 = designation of a grain product (baked item?) with the grain content (see numeral system 1, p. 65)

 = amount of barley groats necessary for 10 (see numeral system 3, p. 65)

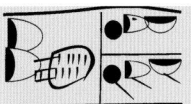

 = 2 x 60 = 120 (noted in the sexagesimal system)

 = jars of a certain type of beer

 = amount of barley groats necessary for beer (see numeral system 3, p. 65)

 = amount of malt necessary (see numeral system 2, p. 65)

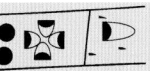

 = 20 (noted in the bisexagesimal system)

 = designation of a grain product (baked item) with the grain content (see numeral system 1, p. 65)

 = amount of barley groats necessary for 20

(see numeral system 3, p. 65) Sign for grain product omitted by scribe

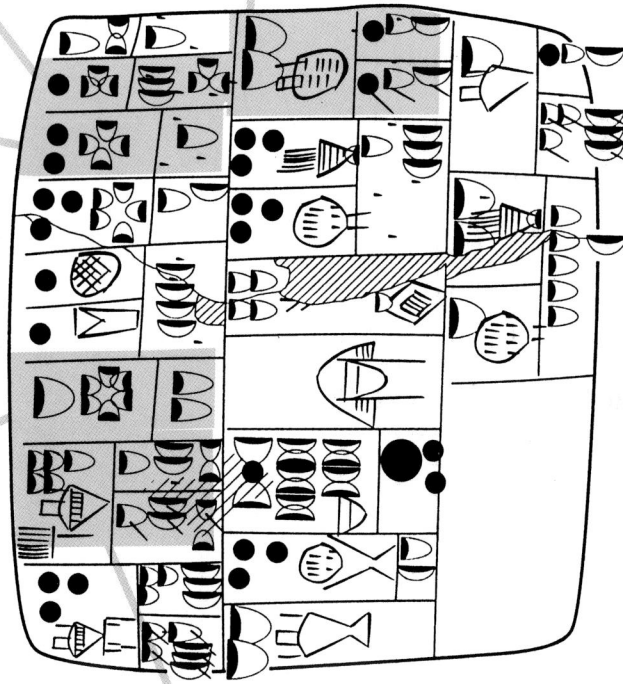

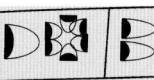

 = 60 (noted in the bisexagesimal system)

 = designation of a grain product (baked item?) with the grain content (see numeral system 1, p. 65)

 = amount of barley groats necessary for 60  (see numeral system 3, p. 65) Sign for grain product omitted by scribe

 = 5

 = large

 = jars of a certain type of beer

 = amount of barley groats necessary for beer (see numeral system 3, p. 65)

 = amount of malt necessary (see numeral system 2, p. 65)

EXTINCT

Top **Boundary stone with cuneiform inscription from Babylonia,** *c.* **1120** BC.
Middle **Text from the Book of the Dead inscribed on a funerary amulet, Egypt, 18th dynasty.**
Bottom **Mesopotamian mace head with 'archaizing' cuneiform, dedicated to the god Meslamta-ea,** *c.* **2250** BC.

II

Today no one speaks Latin, except on certain religious or ceremonial occasions – though millions write in the Roman script. In China, by contrast, both the language and the script used two millennia ago survive today in a modified form. But in Mesopotamia, the ancient languages – Sumerian, Old Akkadian, Babylonian and Assyrian – and the cuneiform script used to write them, have altogether vanished.

WRITING

There have always been far more languages than scripts. And languages have disappeared far more readily than scripts. Often a script has continued in widespread use by virtue of being adapted to a new language, sometimes more than once. This is what happened to cuneiform, to Chinese characters and to the Greek alphabet, but not, significantly, to Egyptian and Mayan hieroglyphs.

The reason why a script survives or perishes is not obvious. Sign simplicity or efficiency in representing the sounds of a language cannot be the sole criteria of survival. If they were, Chinese characters would have disappeared in China and been replaced by an alphabet; and the Japanese would never have borrowed Chinese characters. Political and economic power, religious and cultural prestige and the existence of a major literature all play a part in the historical fate of a script.

Chapter 4 *Cuneiform*

Above **Cylinder seal with modern impression from Babylon. It shows one of the rulers of Ur, Ur-nammu (2112–2095 BC). The cuneiform inscription reads: 'Ur-nammu, strong man, king of Ur: Hash-hamer, governor of Ishkun-Sin, is your servant.' Two goddesses intercede between Hash-hamer, the owner of the seal (*far left*), and the king, who wears the round, high-brimmed head-dress of royalty and sits on a bull-legged throne on a dais beneath a crescent moon.**

Right **Darius hunting lions. Modern impression of his cylinder seal, *c.* 500 BC.**

Ancient Mesopotamia

Today's Iraq does not fit the image conjured by the old name Fertile Crescent. In the second half of the 5th millennium BC, however, climatic change had made Mesopotamia hospitable to human settlement. The result was a fertile alluvial plain and natural conditions, in the words of one scholar, 'like those we might expect to find in the Garden of Eden'.

Agriculture prospered here, then grew cities, regional states, and finally empires, with writing. The first clay tablets were pictographic and date, as we know, from about 3300 BC; they were found at Uruk. By about 2500 BC, these signs had become abstract cuneiform signs in widespread use for writing Sumerian; later they developed into the script of the Babylonian and Assyrian empires; and in the Persian empire of Darius, around 500 BC, a new cuneiform script was invented. The latest inscription in cuneiform is dated AD 75. Thus cuneiform was employed as a writing system for some 3000 years.

Cuneiform gave ancient Mesopotamia a history. Rulers such as Hammurabi of Babylon, Gudea of Lagash and the Assyrian king Sennacherib now speak to us through their inscriptions. But there remain awkward gaps in the record, for which no tablets or inscriptions have been discovered. We tend to assume that economic activity was low in such periods. In fact, the opposite may be true: these may have been periods of peace and prosperity. Unlike in times of strife, perhaps no one's library was being burnt down, no invaluable archive being accidentally baked for posterity.

Writing phase	BC	Historical developments
	3400	Beginning of large-scale settlement of Babylonia
Numerical tablets and clay bullae	3200	First urban centres
Archaic texts from Uruk	3000	Age of early civilization
Archaic texts from Ur		
	2800	
		Formation of large irrigation networks
	2600	
Old Sumerian texts		Rival city states
	2400	
Old Akkadian texts		First regional state
	2200	
		Gudea of Lagash
Old Assyrian texts	2000	Centralized state of the 3rd dynasty of Ur
Old Babylonian texts		
	1800	Hammurabi of Babylon
	1600	
	1400	
	1200	Kassite rule
	1000	
First Aramaic texts	800	Assyrian empire
	600	Babylon occupied by Cyrus in 539
Old Persian texts		Darius I
Revival of cuneiform under the Seleucids	400	

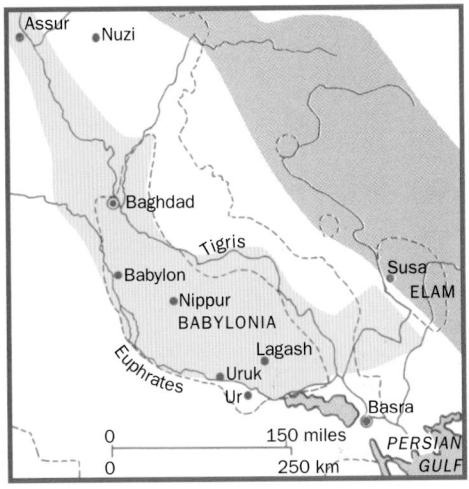

Map of Babylonia and western Iran. The dark shading indicates rain-fed areas; the light shading indicates irrigated agriculture. The hatched lines enclose settlement areas.

The Decipherment of Cuneiform

More than a millennium and a half separate the latest inscriptions in cuneiform from their rediscovery by modern Europe. This occurred at Persepolis, the capital of Darius and the Persian kings of the Achaemenid dynasty, in 1618. The discoverer was the Spanish ambassador to Persia, Garcia Silva Figueroa. He identified the awesome ruins near Shiraz as ancient Persepolis from the descriptions of the site given by ancient Greek and Roman authors. Of the mysterious inscriptions in the ruins, exquisitely carved in black jasper, he concluded that they belonged to no people 'that can be discovered now or to have ever existed'. The letters were not Aramaic, Hebrew, Greek or Arabic but 'triangular, in the shape of a pyramid or miniature obelisk . . . and are all identical except in position and arrangement'.

The first cuneiform inscription was published in 1657. Unlike Egyptian hieroglyphs, it aroused little curiosity: most scholars assumed that the signs, rather than being writing, were ornamental (or even the tracks of birds walking across newly softened clay!). Thomas Hyde, the Regius professor of Hebrew and Laudian professor of Arabic at the University of Oxford, writing in 1700, regarded the signs as an experiment by the architect of Persepolis, who wished to see how many different patterns he could create from a single element. They could not be writing, Hyde said, if only because the same characters were seemingly never repeated.

Hyde did however coin the name cuneiform, 'wedge-like', or rather 'ductuli pyramidales seu Cuneiformes' ('cuneus' being Latin for 'wedge'). In fact, the same characters *were* repeated, often: the copies

Above **Persepolis, capital of the Achaemenid dynasty, destroyed by Alexander the Great in 330 BC. These ruins were identified as Persepolis in 1618.**

Left **Ahura Mazda, floating on a cloud, supreme deity of Zoroastrianism, the religion of the ancient Persians. Avestan, the language of the sacred books of Zoroaster (Zarathustra), written down in the 4th century AD, would provide clues to the decipherment of cuneiform. The drawing is from Thomas Hyde's (misleading) study of the ancient Persians, published in 1700, depicting a scene at Persepolis.**

of the inscriptions available to Hyde were faulty. Better ones were published in 1712 by E. Kaempfer, a physician who visited Persepolis in 1686. It was he who first realized that different scripts might be represented among the inscriptions, because some signs were unique to certain inscriptions.

Other visitors published inscriptions in the first half of the 18th century, but there was no progress in deciphering their meaning until the 1770s. Carsten Niebuhr, a remarkable Danish traveller, noticed that many of the inscriptions were duplicated, enabling him to check one set of readings against another. From the fact that the line-endings in duplicate inscriptions did not always fall in the same place, Niebuhr was able to confirm the left-to-right direction of the writing. By comparing signs in different inscriptions, he distinguished clearly *three* scripts. He also began the process of

Carsten Niebuhr (1733–1815), the first man to draw accurately the cuneiform inscriptions at Persepolis. Niebuhr was an indefatigable traveller and scholar, who returned alone from India to Denmark, via Persepolis. He published his first drawings in 1772. Careful study enabled him to show that there were three different cuneiform scripts at Persepolis.

isolating the simplest signs. The decipherment proper, starting after 1800, was built upon the work of Niebuhr.

One of the Persepolis inscriptions drawn by Niebuhr.

First Successes

The person who took the first serious steps towards decipherment was a German high school teacher in Göttingen, Georg Grotefend. Deciding that the single slanting wedges which occurred at frequent intervals in the inscriptions must be word dividers, Grotefend concluded that the system must be alphabetic: there were too many signs between word dividers – as many as ten – for it to be a syllabic system. This assumption was not wholly correct, but it served well in identifying names, which were indeed spelt alphabetically (as they were in the cartouches of Egyptian hieroglyphs). Two further assumptions were necessary.

First, there was likely to be a royal formula embedded in the inscriptions, reading something like 'X, (great) king, king of kings . . .', since this formula had already been discovered in the much later Persian inscriptions of the Pahlavi kings; further, this formula might be extended to include the royal lineage, i.e. 'X, (great) king, king of kings, son of Y'. Second, the kings in question might be Xerxes, son of Darius, son of Hystaspes (who was not a king).

Grotefend now focused on two different inscriptions. Each was carved above a figure, or rather two different figures, on the doorways at Persepolis. Although the signs

Grotefend's attempted decipherment of Old Persian as an alphabet. In fact, the script is partially syllabic; many of Grotefend's values were therefore incorrect, particularly where he allocated more than one sign to a single sound value, and more than one sound value to a single sign.

liffered, there were many signs in common, and there were even shared groups of signs. For instance:

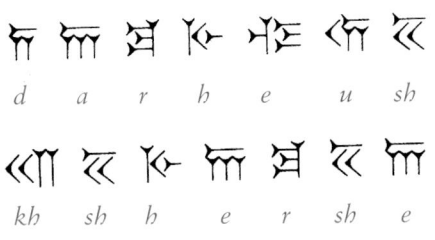

It seemed reasonable that the highlighted group in common (3) might be the name of Darius. Thus the first inscription would celebrate Xerxes, son of Darius, and the second Darius, son of Hystaspes. The first word of each inscription would be the name of the king. The problem then became: how did these two Achaemenid kings spell their names? – certainly not 'Xerxes', 'Darius' and 'Hystaspes', which are from later Greek spellings. Grotefend examined the Greek, Hebrew and Avestan (Zoroastrian) spellings – Avestan being the language likely to be nearest to the inscription – and guessed: Darius = Darheush, Xerxes = Khshhershe. He proceeded to fit these to the cuneiform as follows:

d   a   r   h   e   u   sh

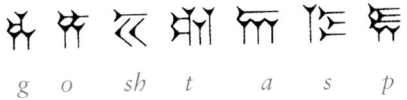

kh   sh   h   e   r   sh   e

Three signs, those for *h*, *r* and *sh*, seemed to be the same in both cases.

Could these tentative sign values be used to 'translate' other words in the inscriptions? Grotefend tackled the word that appeared after the two initial names, which was the same in each inscription (2). It was likely

to mean 'king'. Applying the values, he obtained:

kh   sh   e   h   ?   ?   h

In the *Avesta* – the sacred scriptures of Zoroastrianism – Grotefend located the royal title 'khscheio'. He therefore allocated the sign values *i* and *o* to the blanks above.

What about Hystaspes, the father of Darius? The Avestan spelling appeared to be 'Goshtasp'. This fitted well with the group of signs (1) in the second inscription (these signs did not appear in the first inscription, as was expected, since Hystaspes was *grand*-father to Xerxes):

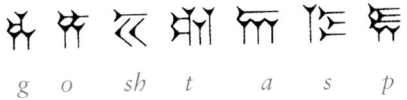

g   o   sh   t   a   s   p

Out of such decipherments, Grotefend compiled an alphabet of Old Persian. Many of his sign values proved to be wrong, particularly when he attempted to extend his system beyond proper names. For the Old Persian script is *not* purely alphabetic, but partially syllabic. This fact, combined with his lack of academic status, deprived Grotefend of some of his due credit at the time of his decipherment. Today, however, he is generally recognized as a pioneer.

The second inscription now reads: 'Darius, the great king, king of kings, king of countries, son of Hystaspes, an Achaemenian, who built this palace.' Its part-syllabic transliteration may be matched with the cuneiform signs (Darius and Hystaspes have been underlined):

da-a-ra-ya-va-u-š /xa-ša-a-ya-θa-i-ya/
va-za-ra-ka/xa-ša-a-ya-θa-i-ya/xa-ša-a-
ya-θa-i-ya-a-na-a-ma/xa-ša-a-ya-θa-i-ya/
da-ha-ya-u-na-a-ma/vi-i-ša-ta-a-sa-pa-ha-ya-
a/pa-u-śa/ha-xa-a-ma-na-i-ša-i-ya/ha-
ya/i-ma-ma/ta-ca-ra-ma/a-ku-u-na-u-ša

Georg Grotefend (1775– 1853), the German high school teacher who began the decipherment of Old Persian cuneiform.

Rawlinson and the Behistun Inscription

If the decipherment was to make progress, longer inscriptions in cuneiform were required. The 'Rosetta Stone' for cuneiform turned out to be the massive inscription of Darius cut into a cliff in the Zagros Mountains of western Iran near the little town of Behistun (today's Bisitun). As at Persepolis, three scripts had been used: Old Persian, Elamite and Babylonian. (Elamite cuneiform is distinct, though we now know it to be a regional variant of Babylonian cuneiform.)

But before this great trilingual could be of use, it had to be copied. This was easier said than done, since there was only a narrow ledge on which to stand (the mountainside seems to have been removed in antiquity, perhaps to make the inscription more prominent and to protect it). The upper portion of the inscription appeared to be completely inaccessible.

The challenge was taken up by an adventurous, polyglot English army officer, Sir Henry Creswicke Rawlinson (1810–95). He had served in India from 1826 to 1833, where he acquired a knowledge of Hindustani, Arabic and modern Persian, and a reputation as an outstanding polo player and athlete. Seconded to Persia to help train the Shah's army, he became an adviser to the governor of Kurdistan. Rawlinson was able to copy the lower lines of the Old Persian inscription by standing on the narrow ledge. Using ladders, he precariously copied higher up, standing on the topmost rung 'with no other support than steadying the body against the rock with the left arm, while the left hand holds the notebook, and the right hand is

employed with the pencil.' But the uppermost inscriptions were beyond his powers. Luckily, 'a wild Kurdish boy' appeared, managed to squeeze himself up a cleft in the cliff, drive a wooden peg into the cleft, cross the face of the inscription, drive in another peg and rig ropes such that he could take papier-mâché casts of the inscription, directed from below by Rawlinson. It was an extraordinary feat of courage and determination. By 1847, after

Above **The rock at Behistun, western Iran, showing the inscriptions that led to the decipherment of cuneiform. They are located more than 300 feet (100 metres) above the road.**

ome ten years' effort, the entire Behistun
scription had been copied.

Reproduced below are the Behistun
scriptions, drawn by Rawlinson (*right*).
uneiform in three languages surrounds
arius who has his foot on his rival and
dges nine others, their hands tied behind
eir backs. Above them floats Ahura
Mazda, the supreme deity of the Persians
nd Zoroastrians). Until Rawlinson read
e Old Persian inscription, some scholars
nagined the scene to show the captive
ibes of Israel.

Rawlinson is generally credited with the
ecipherment of Babylonian cuneiform, but
e never explained how he did it, unlike
ean-François Champollion and Michael
entris (Linear B). Recent study of his
otebooks suggests that he borrowed
rucially without attribution from the work
f the scholar Edward Hincks.

Cuneiform Deciphered

It is not possible to give a complete and coherent account of the decipherment of cuneiform scripts, unlike that of Egyptian hieroglyphs, because Rawlinson and Edward Hincks, the other principal scholar involved, did not spell out all their thinking. Moreover, cuneiform is an extremely complex script when applied to several different languages.

Old Persian cuneiform was the first of the three cuneiform scripts to yield. Grotefend had identified the names of Hystaspes, Darius and Xerxes; Rawlinson was able to identify in the Behistun inscriptions the names of peoples ruled by Darius, mentioned in the Greek histories of the Persian empire. He thereby allotted values to many more signs in Old Persian. Also vital was his knowledge of Avestan and Sanskrit. Both these languages were known to be derived from a common Indo-European ancestor, along with Old Persian – Avestan being the more closely related of the two to Old Persian. Rawlinson therefore knew that he could expect consistent relationships between words of the same meaning in Avestan, Sanskrit and Old Persian. By 1846, he was able to produce a complete translation of the portion of the Behistun inscription in Old Persian.

In doing so, he built on an insight of Christian Lassen, a professor in Bonn, who had noticed that certain cuneiform signs occurred only before particular vowels. Where Grotefend had seen a pure alphabet, Lassen proposed, correctly, a mixed alphabet/syllabary. Rawlinson (and independently Hincks) realized that the proportion of syllabic spelling varied from

Cuneiform inscription on a clay cylinder of Tiglath-Pileser I of Assyria (1120–1074 BC). In 1857 this was translated, thereby confirming the decipherment of Babylonian cuneiform.

ound to sound. For instance *t* was written
the same way if followed by *a* or *i*, but
differently if followed by *u*:

    𒋫 *ta*   𒋾 *ti*   𒌅 *tu*

b, on the other hand, was written
identically, regardless of the following vowel:

    𒉌 *tha*   𒉌 *thi*   𒉌 *thu*

while *d* appeared in three different forms,
depending on the following vowel:

    𒁕 *da*   𒁹 *di*   𒁺 *du*

With the Old Persian texts deciphered,
attention turned to the other two cuneiform
scripts, Babylonian and its regional variant
Elamite. Both were present at Persepolis as
well as at Behistun. Both clearly contained
non-alphabetic elements, given their large
number of different signs. Again, proper
names were the starting point of the
decipherment. But it was not easy to identify
these names, such was the variety of
spellings. Compare the spelling of Hystaspes
in Old Persian, vi-i-ša-ta-a-sa-pa, with that
in Elamite, mi-iš-da-áš-ba, and that in
Babylonian, uš-ta-as-pa. We have seen
Hystaspes written in Old Persian at
Persepolis on p. 75. Here it is, highlighted, in
an Elamite (1) and a Babylonian (2) version
of the same inscription:

1

2

But apart from names, the Elamite
language proved tougher than the Old
Persian. Parallels with Avestan and Sanskrit
were of no avail; today Elamite is thought to
be unrelated to any other known language.
Not so the Babylonian language, which was
related to Hebrew, Aramaic and other
Semitic languages. Unfortunately, this
connection was somewhat misleading for
Rawlinson, Hincks and others, because it
suggested that Babylonian cuneiform would
resemble the scripts of later Semitic
languages, which typically do not mark
vowels. When Rawlinson came across
different Babylonian signs for *ba*, *bi*, *bu*, *ab*,
ib, *ub*, he at first regarded them all as
different ways of writing *b* – that is, they
were homophonous. Conversely, he accepted
that certain signs could stand for more than
one sound – that is, they were polyphonic.
The Babylonian script seemed fiendishly
complex.

A System Established

Careful study proved that the *context* of a
sign narrowed the seemingly intolerable
choice of sign/sound combinations crucially.
(It is always clear from an English sentence
how to pronounce the polyphonic 'o' in
'bow', for instance.) By the mid-1850s,
translations of Babylonian cuneiform could
be made with some confidence. This was
proved by a public examination conducted in
London by the Royal Asiatic Society and
published in 1857. Rawlinson, Hincks and
two other scholars were asked to submit
independent translations of a recently
excavated clay cylinder bearing an
inscription of Tiglath-Pileser I, king of
Assyria: the convergence, especially between
the translations of Rawlinson and Hincks,
was striking. From then on, the decipherment of Babylonian cuneiform was a matter
of refining a generally accepted system.

Cuneiform as an Art

Cuneiform signs were impressed in clay, carved in stone and inscribed on metal, ivory, glass and wax. So far as we know, the script was rarely written in ink, in contrast to Egyptian hieroglyphs, which were inked on papyrus. Though cuneiform signs do not have the mystery and magic of hieroglyphs, at their most finely written they are intriguing works of art.

**Far left Inscription on a statue of Gudea, ruler of Lagash, 2141–2122 BC.
Left Brick inscription of Ur-Nammu, king of Ur, 2112–2095 BC.** It reads: 'For Inanna his lady Ur-Nammu, the mighty man, king of Ur, king of Sumer and Akkad, has built her temple.' Most buildings in Mesopotamia were built of sun-dried mud brick, with baked brick reserved for the façades of temples. From *c.* 2250 BC, kings had their names stamped into bricks; the stamp was made either from clay or from wood. The practice continued down to Nebuchadnezzar II (604–562 BC) of Babylon, and, ironically, was revived by the ruler of Iraq during the 'rebuilding' of ancient Babylon in the 1980s.

Left Part of a gold plaque of Darius, 6th century BC, from the audience hall at Persepolis. Inscribed in Old Persian, Elamite and Babylonian, it asks the supreme deity Ahura Mazda to protect Darius and his throne. Each plaque is matched by a silver duplicate.

Below Cone inscription of Ur-Bau, ruler of Lagash, 2155–2142 BC. In Sumerian times, it was common for the purchaser of a house publicly to hammer a clay cone or nail into its wall as a mark of new ownership. Rulers between c. 2400 BC and 1700 BC were in the habit of placing inscribed nails in the walls of temples or chapels, sometimes by the hundred. The inscriptions range from simple 'name tags' to recitals of historical and cultic events.

Left Two seals (modern impressions). Seals were in use from the earliest period of literate civilization in Mesopotamia. The oval seal (above left), 18th century BC, an Old Babylonian seal made of haematite, is inscribed: 'Ibni-Amurru, son of Ilima-ahi, servant of the god Amurru'. The other seal (left), c. 2600 BC, from the royal cemetery at Ur, in southern Iraq, made of lapis lazuli, is inscribed in cuneiform: 'Pu-abi, queen', and depicts banqueting scenes involving the queen.

Cuneiform as a Craft

Old Babylonian school tablet. The teacher's version is on the left, the pupil's copy is below right. The text is a Sumerian proverb.

By far the majority of cuneiform inscriptions are written on clay. To produce a good clay tablet must have been one of the first tasks of an apprentice scribe. The largest tablets had eleven columns and could be one foot square. One side was generally flat, the obverse side remained convex. The scribe wrote first on the flat side, and when this was full, he turned the tablet over and wrote on the curved side; the first set of signs, being flat, was therefore undamaged by pressure.

When finished, a tablet was usually left to dry out; such tablets could be altered by moistening the clay. Instead, a tablet might be baked, to create a permanent record. If this happened inadvertently in a fire, during the destruction of a library, it might preserve the tablet in perpetuity. Tablets baked in fires are mostly dark grey or black, while those baked today for their better preservation, are dark orange-brown. So-called 'firing holes' were sometimes made in the tablet by pressing a stylus (or similar object) right through (or almost through) the clay. Scholars formerly supposed that these holes were to help the tablet dry out or to stop it from fracturing when baked, but some large tablets were successfully baked without the use of holes. It seems that firing holes, whatever their original purpose was, soon became a matter of tradition: there are copies of literary texts in which the firing holes in the original text have been meticulously reproduced in the copy.

Writing Methods

When inscribing a tablet, a scribe would start at the top left-hand edge of a tablet, work downwards to the bottom edge, return to the top of the next column and repeat the process, thus steadily moving to the right of the tablet in columns. On reaching the bottom right-hand corner, he would turn the tablet over on its bottom edge, begin writing in the top right-hand corner and work leftwards in columns. Thus clay tablets were written and read as we read a modern newspaper, except that the ancient scribes turned over the 'page' along the bottom edge, rather than the side edge.

The stylus was usually made of reed, though occasionally it was of metal or bone. Reed was common in the marshlands of the Near East, and had strength. A scribe could

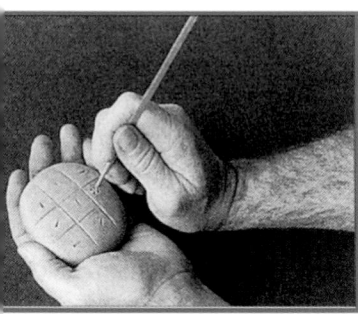
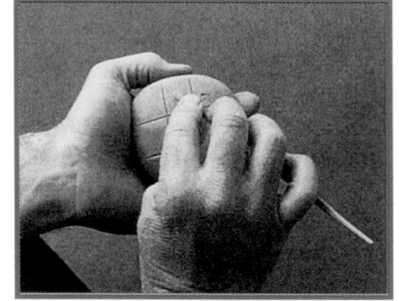

2

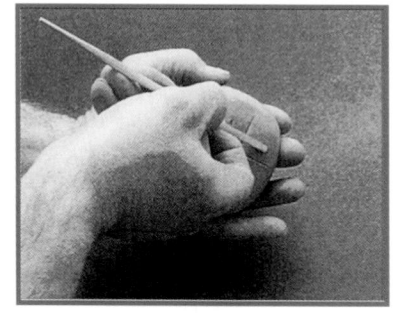

3

sily trim a reed to give a circular end, pointed end, a flat end or a diagonally cut nd. Each shape had its uses, such as npressing the numerals (see 1 *above*), and ome reed shapes generated recognizable yles of scribal hand.

The stylus could obviously be oriented in ny direction the scribe wanted, in relation o the tablet; and if the tablet was small nough, it too could be turned back and orth in the hand. In practice, only a limited nge of sign angles was used. A study of ny cuneiform inscription reveals that idividual wedges seldom point upwards, to ne left, or slant up to the right. (Forgers nd to miss this fact.) We can see why, if we onsider how the tablet was held. Assuming nat most scribes were right-handed, the iblet was held in the left hand and the rylus was held between thumb and fingers iee 2 *above*). In this position a variety of vedges can comfortably be made, but many ossible wedges are awkward (see 3 *above*). Ve find that the first angle of wedge is ommonly found in later cuneiform, while ne second is rare and disappeared from tandard usage in about 2300 BC.

cribal Training

cribes were trained in scribal schools. Boys and a very few girls) practised by copying few lines of cuneiform written by a eacher: the names of gods, a list of technical erms, a brief fragment of literature or

a proverb. Many such school tablets survive, with the teacher's version on one side and the pupil's less competent version on the other.

Once trained, scribes had many roles. The most influential scribes were those at the royal court and the personal secretaries of various city governors in the country. Others were attached to temples, still others to the textile industry, ship-building, pottery workshops and transport services. Most were in agriculture, assisting in the maintenance of irrigation canals, registering the rations of the labour force and the storage of the harvest, and recording the supply and guarding of agricultural tools; they also dealt with the receipt and conveyance of animals. Finally, scribes filled positions in the field of law. Many were probably without real power, but some may have been equivalent to a modern 'secretary' of a major institution. However, scribes in Mesopotamia were definitely less revered than scribes in Egypt.

How cuneiform was written with a reed stylus. The circular end of the stylus was used for making numeral impressions (later on, numerals too were impressed as wedges, not circles). The first wedge (2) is easy to make, the second (3) awkward, hence the common appearance in cuneiform of the first angle of wedge and the rarity of t̶ ̶ ̶ ̶ ̶ngle of wedge.

LOVE!

The Evolution of the Signs

1

2

The origin and evolution of the cuneiform sign meaning 'to eat', in southern Iraq, *c.* 3000–600 BC.

(1) The first tablet (above left), **which concerns temple administration from 3000 BC, shows the pre-cuneiform sign, at the pictographic stage: a profile of a head with a cup of grain at the mouth.**

(2) The second tablet is a temple receipt from *c.* 2100 BC (below left), **in which the pictogram has been turned through 90 degrees so that it rests on the back of the head; the word 'to eat' is now represented part-phonetically by the combined signs for 'head' and 'food'.**

(3) The latest of the three tablets (opposite above), **from *c.* 600 BC, concerns the study of lucky and unlucky days. The sign is now part of a beautiful, intricate hand, which, when magnified, can be read: it is a more abstract pattern of marks, but still has the meaning 'to eat'.**

3

Below **The law code of Hammurabi, king of Babylon (1792–50 BC).**

With the discovery of large numbers of clay tablets from many periods of Mesopotamian history, and the steady decipherment of cuneiform, the evolution of certain signs could be discerned. The early numerical tablets from Uruk, with their recognizably pictographic symbols, were seen to give way to signs made of wedges that still resembled the pictographic symbols; these in turn became further abstracted; and by the time of the Assyrian empire in the 1st millennium, the signs bore almost no resemblance to their pictographic progenitors.

At some point in the later 3rd millennium BC or earlier part of the 2nd millennium BC, the evolving signs underwent a change of orientation. The pictograms on clay tablets became turned through 90 degrees, so that they lay on their backs. And it was the same for the overall direction of the script: instead of being written vertically, it became a horizontally written script (though it was still often partitioned into columns like a modern newspaper); and instead of being written from right to left, it was now written from left to right. But stone monuments continued to be written in the orientation of the archaic script until the middle of the 2nd millennium. So, in order to read the famous law code of Hammurabi (earlier half of the 18th century BC), one must hold one's head down on one's right shoulder (turning the eyes through 90 degrees).

The date of this change is vague, and the reason for it is not clear. Some scholars have proposed that it came about because right-to-left writing tended to obliterate signs through smudging of the clay by the right hand. In fact, with good quality clay, this does not occur. A more likely reason is that the scribes found the new orientation more convenient to the way they held tablet and stylus. Experiments with a tablet and stylus suggest this. In the words of one scholar, 'there must have been from the beginning a strong tendency to *write* the tablet at an angle rather different from that at which it was read.'

Numerals and Arithmetic

From the early clay tablets at Uruk we know that ancient Mesopotamia counted and calculated in a sexagesimal system. We saw the original Sumerian numerals on p. 64. As the cuneiform system developed, these archaic numerals changed into wedge-shaped signs:

60^2 x 10 (36,000)	60^2 (3600)	60 x 10 (600)	60	10	1

By the time of the Old Babylonian period (the first half of the 2nd millennium BC), this system had developed fully. Numbers were now expressed using a place value system, as we use today, where the value of a numeral depends on its position within a number. (Each 5 in the number 555, say, has a different value: 500, 50, 5.) The only serious lack, 4000 years ago, was a symbol for zero; Babylonian scribes apparently trained themselves to keep in mind an empty space within a number while calculating, where we would write a zero.

The symbols in the fully developed place value system were as follows:

5	4	3	2	1

50	40	30	20	10

60^2 x 10 (36,000)	60^2 (3600)	60 x 10 (600)	60

Ambiguity is immediately obvious in the use of the same symbol for 60 and 3,600; ditto for 600 and 36,000. While the numeral with the highest place value is always on the left (as in our decimal system), this still leaves three options for each of the two numbers at the top of the next page:

$60 + 10 + 5 = 75$
or $60^2 + 10 + 5 = 3,615$
or even $1 + (15/60) = 1.25$

$(2 \times 60) + 40 + 5 = 165$
or $(2 \times 60^2) + (40 \times 60) + 5 = 9,605$
or $2 + 45/60 = 2.75$

In Assyrian history, there is a famous case of numerical manipulation of the place value system. After Sennacherib sacked Babylon in 689 BC, he declared that the city must remain deserted for 70 years, by decree of the god Marduk. His son Esarhaddon, coming to the throne in 680, declared that he intended to restore Babylon, on the grounds that Marduk had relented and reversed his original number, making a curse lasting only 11 years:

70   11

Left **Sumerian tablet concerning seed grain (front and back).** It belongs to the same place and period as the tablet concerning bread transcribed below. It records an amount of barley delivered to a 'ploughmaster' called Inimanizi for use on a particular field and as fodder for the oxen that pulled the seed plough. The area of the field is also noted.

Opposite page **Old Babylonian standard combined multiplication table.** The basis is the sexagesimal system, and all numerals are written in cuneiform. Besides multiples of a wide range of numbers, the table lists reciprocal values of numbers from 1 to 10 and their multiples. Such tablets permitted scribes to multiply swiftly using the most important fractions.

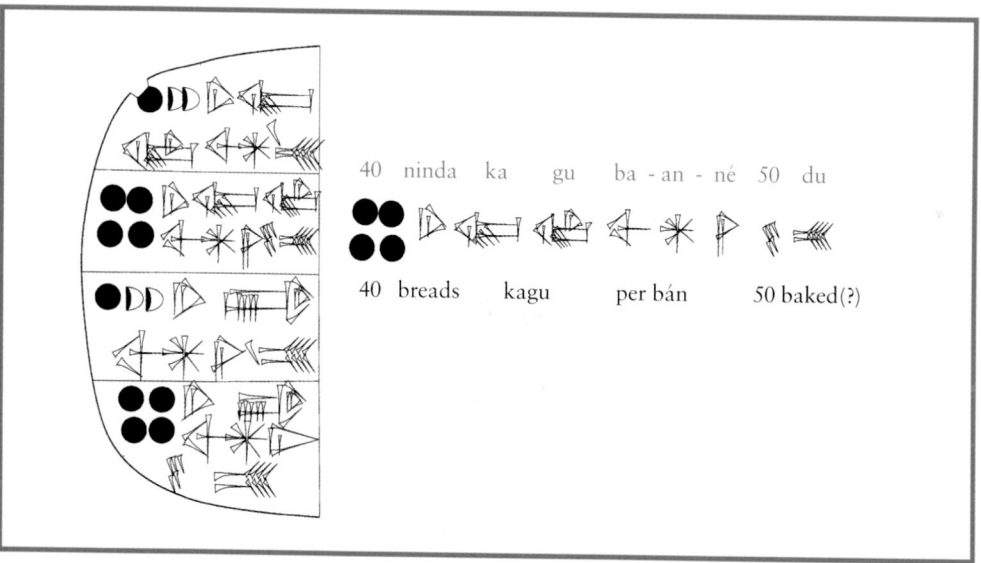

40 ninda ka gu ba - an - né 50 du

40 breads   kagu   per bán   50 baked(?)

The tablet which has been transcribed above comes from Lagash and belongs to the period before 2350 BC. It appears to describe various quantities of two kinds of bread loaf and their ingredients. Two numeral systems are used: the numbers of bread loaves are given in archaic numerals (of the type discussed on pp. 64–5), e.g. 40, while the quantities of the ingredients are given in cuneiform numerals, e.g. 50. Additionally, unlike the older tablets from Uruk, this tablet records *language* (Sumerian), as well as numerals. Even so, it cannot be fully understood, just as accounting ledgers of today cannot be fully grasped, unless one is familiar with their specialized terminology.

Tablet concerning field ownership. The tablet comes
from Shuruppak and belongs to the period around
2600 BC. Its front and back together have 104
entries, each stating the size of a field and the
owner's name or title. These persons include two
tradesmen, several scribes, a fisherman, and many
other 'professions': they were probably in the service
of a temple or palace and were rewarded with a field
to secure their subsistence. The size of the fields
varies between 2.5 and 10 'iku' (2 to 8 acres); the
entire area is 672 'iku' (about 600 acres). Seed
grain (barley) allotments are also recorded,
amounting to about 15 litres per 'iku'.

Computers and Cuneiform

The traditional method of publishing a cuneiform text requires a skilled copyist to draw it. This is still the best way for a complex tablet, such as the one opposite. But for simpler tablets, computer graphics have proved useful. The screen below shows a detail of the photograph of a tablet, a drawing of the detail, and a drawing of the entire tablet. The process works as follows (in outline). A photograph is digitized with a scanner, in which a laser breaks down the image into individual pixels, for processing in the computer. The digitized photograph becomes a drawing template under an empty electronic canvas, so that the tablet's shape, division lines and discernible signs can be traced on the screen. A preliminary copy is then printed out. This is compared with the original tablet, corrected and completed by hand. It is now fed back into the computer and scanned, becoming in its turn a drawing template so as to correct the preliminary copy of the tablet. The final copy can be electronically placed into a manuscript for the purposes of publication.

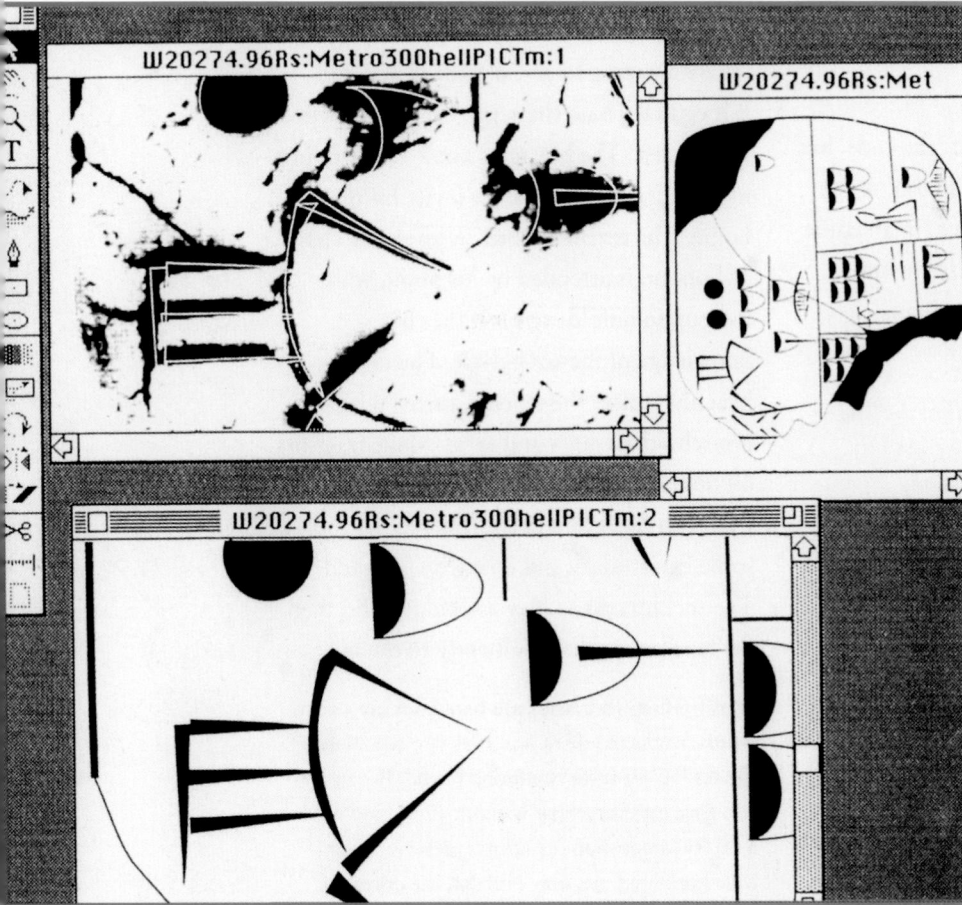

Stages in the computerized drawing of a simple cuneiform tablet.

Cuneiform 'Literature'

We cannot do more than scratch the surface of cuneiform in this book. The clay tablets we have seen may have given the impression that there is no cuneiform literature. Actually there is a considerable body of what may be called literature, notably the Epic of Gilgamesh, and some engaging writing by both kings and commoners. We shall sample just two brief extracts.

The first is from the law code of Hammurabi, king of Babylon:

If a man has harboured in his house a fugitive slave or bondmaid belonging to the state or to a private citizen, and not brought him out at the summons of the public crier, the master of that house shall be slain.

The harshness is typical of the code, but it was surprisingly enlightened too on the subject of women and children, in an effort to protect them from arbitrary treatment, poverty and neglect. In the epilogue, Hammurabi felt able to claim:

In my bosom I carried the people of the land
of Sumer and Akkad;
They prospered under my protection;
I have governed them in peace;
I have sheltered them in my strength.

Some two and a half centuries before this, around 2000 BC, an anonymous school teacher wrote an essay, 'Schooldays', which is one of the most human documents excavated in the Near East. In it, an alumnus of the scribal school, 'Old Grad', looks back nostalgically to his schooldays. 'My headmaster read my tablet, said: "There is something missing," caned me.' Then, one by one, just about everyone in authority

Cuneiform tablets in the library at Ebla, Syria, *c.* 2300 BC. Over 15,000 tablets were discovered here in 1975.

finds an excuse to give a caning. And so 'I [began to] hate the scribal art, neglect the scribal art.' The boy goes home to his father in despair and asks him to invite his teacher home. The teacher comes, is given the chair of honour, is attended by his pupil, who thereupon unfolds to his father his knowledge of the scribal art. The father heartily praises the teacher, turns to his household servants and says: 'Make fragrant oil flow like water on his stomach and back; I want to dress him in a garment, give him some extra salary, put a ring on his hand.' The servants do as they are bidden and then the teacher speaks emolliently to the boy:

Young fellow, [because] you hated not my words, neglected them not, may you complete the scribal art from beginning to end. Because you gave me everything without stint, paid me a salary larger than my efforts [deserve, and] have honoured me, may Nidaba, the queen of guardian angels, be your guardian angel, may your pointed stylus write well for you; may your exercises contain no faults.

Hittite Cuneiform and Hittite Hieroglyphs

The cuneiform script originated by the Sumerians was used to write some 15 languages during the three millennia of its history. These borrowings divide into two clear groups: languages that borrowed the Sumero-Babylonian signs and syllabary (the majority), and languages that borrowed only the principle of the clay wedge, while inventing a new cuneiform script unrelated to the Sumero-Babylonian signs.

The Hittites, an Indo-European-speaking people who appeared in Anatolia around the start of the 2nd millennium BC, belong to the first category. Until the 20th century the Hittites were almost unknown: there were only scattered references to them in the Old Testament and in the Egyptian and Babylonian records. Then, in 1906, excavations of the Hittite capital at Boghazköy (ancient Hattusas) revealed a royal archive of 10,000 cuneiform tablets. Many of these could be read in Babylonian, but the majority were in the unknown Hittite language. However, the Hittite scribes had alternated freely between the given Hittite term and its Sumerian or Babylonian equivalent, when writing historical, legal or ritual texts. This provided a good starting point for the decipherment of Hittite cuneiform, which was essentially completed by 1933.

Hittite Hieroglyphs

The Hittites also wrote in a hieroglyphic script. It was used almost exclusively for display rather than communication, appearing on seals and rock inscriptions. Perhaps it had been invented in response to the beauty of Egyptian hieroglyphs. The Tarkondemos seal has two inscriptions, one in cuneiform, the other in hieroglyphs. The first was transliterated as *n Tar-rik-tim-me sar mat Er-me-e*, 'Tarkondemos, king of the land of Erme' (Tarkondemos was known from Greek sources as a royal name). The second inscription could not be transliterated but it was clear that it was doubled, the same signs appearing on either side of the central figure. Most probably it contained a mixture of phonograms and logograms: the single triangle was thought to stand for 'king' and the double triangle for 'land'. Other probable logograms for 'god' and 'town' were identified. This approach proved productive for scholars: one could take from the Hittite cuneiform records the names of kings, countries, gods and towns, and search for their equivalents among the hieroglyphs adjacent to the appropriate logograms.

No *one* scholar was responsible for the decipherment, which, though lacking glamour, continues today with considerable success.

The Tarkondemos seal, an embossed silver roundel discovered in the late 19th century, bears both cuneiform and hieroglyphic inscriptions. It assisted the decipherment of Hittite hieroglyphs.

Below **Part of a Hittite hieroglyphic inscription and squeeze from Carchemish. The name of the town is located around its logogram 𐊼 , as is the name of the storm god Tarhuns around its logogram ⊕ .**

Left **In the slate palette of King Narmer, from the early dynastic period, hieroglyphs are already used phonetically, employing the rebus principle. Above the head of the king, who is smiting his enemy with a mace, are two hieroglyphs, a catfish ⌐◁ and a chisel ⌙ . These supply, respectively, the phonetic values *nr* and *mr*, making Narmer (properly speaking *n'r*, where ' is a guttural sound found in Semitic languages but not in Indo-European languages).**

Right **Section from a private letter written on papyrus, 11th dynasty. Compare the hieratic signs with their hieroglyphic equivalents on the left.**

The Development of Egyptian Writing

Probably the most controversial question about Egyptian hieroglyphs is where did they spring from? Unlike cuneiform, they do not appear to have evolved over centuries: suddenly, in about 3100 BC, just prior to the beginning of dynastic Egypt, the hieroglyphs come into existence, virtually fully developed. Many designs/signs have been found belonging to the centuries preceding this period, the pre-dynastic period. The designs are painted on pottery and worked into weapons, amulets, ornaments, tools, etc. Some of these picto-grams resemble closely or are identical with the hieroglyphic pictograms of dynastic Egypt. They show such things as topograph-ical features (e.g. land, village, mountains), geographical features (e.g. stars, moon, earth), 'standards' that totemically represent tribes and deities, and signs representing concepts, (e.g. hoes, the symbol for the 'ka', soul, spirit). Can these designs be regarded as the precursors of the hieroglyphs? Some scholars think so, but most prefer to regard the pre-dynastic signs as a slowly evolved artistic repertoire, from which the first hieroglyphs were chosen.

Sumerian Influence?

The stimulus for the creation of the hieroglyphic script may have been the system of writing that had started in Mesopotamia around 3300 BC. The idea of writing could easily have diffused into Egypt from such a comparatively nearby area. (By 3500 BC, lapis lazuli had reached Egypt, presumably from Afghanistan, its nearest and most important source, much farther away than Sumer.) But we do not know for

sure: the Egyptians may have stumbled on the phonetic principle independently. There are certainly profound differences between early Egyptian hieroglyphs and Sumerian pictograms: in the shapes of the signs, in the consonantal rather than syllabic nature of the script (the hieroglyphic script does not mark vowels), and in the greater degree of phonography in Egyptian compared to Sum-erian. Still, it is tempting to believe that the basic idea of phonography was borrowed by the Egyptians from the Sumerians.

From hieroglyphs, two cursive scripts developed, hieratic and from it demotic, the first dating almost from the invention of hieroglyphs, the second from after about 650 BC. (Demotic was the standard docu-mentary script by the time of the Rosetta Stone, in the period of Greek domination.) These two names are somewhat confusing. Hieratic became a priestly script, as suggested by its name, only *after* it was ousted by demotic; originally hieratic was ... everyday administrative and business ... And demotic had nothing to do with ... reading of literacy 'to the people': its ... derived from 'demotikos', meaning 'in ... mon use'.

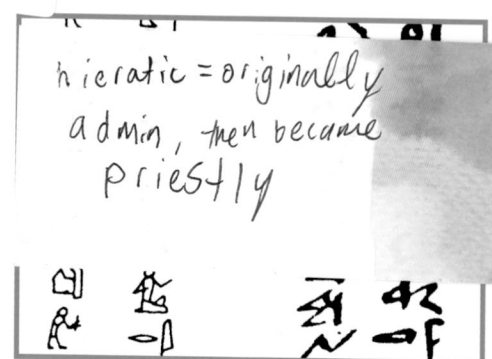

handwritten note: hieratic = originally admin, then became priestly

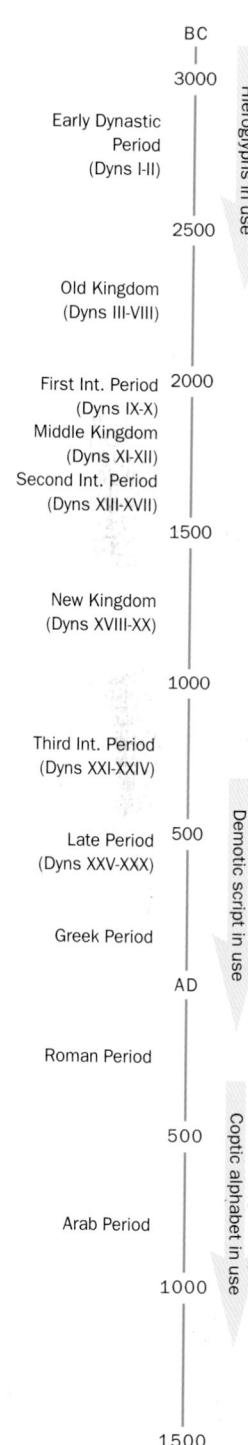

	BC	
	3000	Hieroglyphs in use
Early Dynastic Period (Dyns I-II)		
	2500	
Old Kingdom (Dyns III-VIII)		
First Int. Period (Dyns IX-X)	2000	
Middle Kingdom (Dyns XI-XII)		
Second Int. Period (Dyns XIII-XVII)		
	1500	
New Kingdom (Dyns XVIII-XX)		
	1000	
Third Int. Period (Dyns XXI-XXIV)		Demotic script in use
Late Period (Dyns XXV-XXX)	500	
Greek Period		
	AD	
Roman Period		
	500	Coptic alphabet in use
Arab Period		
	1000	
	1500	

The Direction of Egyptian Writing

In the history of writing, there is no general rule about the direction in which scripts have been written, left to right, right to left, or boustrophedon ('as the ox turns' in ploughing), i.e. alternating left to right, right to left and so on. Experiments with children learning to write suggest that there is a fundamental conflict between the natural starting position of a novice and the natural stroke production of an experienced writer, and that this conflict has destabilized writing systems. A right-handed child starts naturally at a five o'clock position, where the hand comes in contact with the paper; but with learning, the child's hand migrates towards an eleven o'clock position, where adults begin a piece of writing.

Egyptian hieroglyphs were written and read both from right to left and from left to right. Always, whichever direction was chosen, the individual signs faced in such a way that the reader's eye passed over them from front to back. Thus, if one looks at a line of hieroglyphs and sees the signs (birds, humans, animals etc.) facing to the right, then the direction of writing is from right to left – and vice versa.

That said, the Egyptians usually chose to write from right to left when there was no reason to choose one direction over another. Reasons for differing included aesthetic appeal and symmetry, the showing of respect towards images of gods, kings and others, and ease of reading. A nice example is the so-called false door of Khut-en-Ptah, shown opposite. Such doors marked the boundary in an Egyptian tomb between the closed and forbidden domain of the dead and a relatively accessible area where friends and relatives of the deceased could make prayers and offerings. Khut-en-Ptah is shown twice at the bottom to the left of the door, and twice to the right, in each case facing inwards. The columns of hieroglyphs directly above her images all face inwards too; those on the right are therefore mirror images of those on the left (though they are not in exactly the same order). The sculptor did, however, make one apparent mistake, carving a sign the wrong way round. See if you can spot it in the portion shown below. (The answer is given on p. 226.)

The symmetry is pleasing, and it is also the natural way for a 'person' passing through the false door to view and read the hieroglyphs on either side: from right to left, to the left of the door, and from left to right, to the right of the door. The lines of hieroglyphs *above* the door are, by contrast, read naturally in only one direction, and so they are written from right to left.

(The answer is given on p. 226.)

The false door of Khut-en-Ptah, *c.* 2000 BC. It demonstrates the way in which the direction of Egyptian hieroglyphs varied, depending on their context.

Khut-en-Ptah was a noblewoman; this 'false door' to her tomb bears the same inscription on each side. One set of hieroglyphs faces left to right, another right to left, to allow whoever passes 'through' the door to read each side naturally. The inscription on each long column (shown below in part) reads: 'One venerated before Ptah and Sokar, the king's noblewoman, Khut-en-Ptah'. (After Zauzich)

writing direction is not innately one direction
— hieroglyphs → direction is based around which signs are facing

The Sound of Ancient Egyptian

No one knows how the ancient Egyptians sounded in conversation. The spellings of Egyptian words and names adopted by Egyptologists, such as Tutankhamun, Ptah, Ramesses and so on, are conventions. Nefertiti is the queen's conventional spelling in the English-speaking world; the Germans call her Nofretete. Imenhetep occurs as Amenhotep, Amunhotpe, Amenhetep. One particular name is spelt in 34 different ways!

The problem is partly the obvious one, that the ancient Egyptian language is long extinct. But it is also the result of the ancient Egyptians' not marking the vowels in the hieroglyphic script. Recognizing this fact, Egyptologists usually insert a short 'e' between the consonants. Thus *mn* is pronounced (for Egyptological purposes) *men*, *wbn* as *weben*, *nfrt* as *nefret*.

But it would be wrong to imply that we have no idea at all of the original pronunciation of the hieroglyphs. There are two important clues to it. The first comes from Coptic, the last stage of Egyptian and the only stage in which the vowels were written. Coptic, which is still used in the Coptic church, is written mainly in Greek letters (as we have seen) which we can more or less pronounce. No doubt Coptic's pronunciation, even in the early centuries AD, was considerably different from Greek and even more different from that of Egyptian spoken in the Old Kingdom, but it is still a useful pointer. Although the vocabulary of Coptic contains Greek and other foreign words, the bulk of it is of pharaonic ancestry. Some examples (*above*) show Coptic on the right, hieroglyphs on the left.

	mn (remain)	ⲘⲞⲨⲚ	*moun*
	mdw (speak)	ⲘⲞⲨⲦⲈ	*moute*
	pdt (bow)	ⲠⲒⲦⲈ	*pite*
	nfr (good)	ⲚⲞⲨϤⲈ	*noufe*
	r(m)t (man)	ⲢⲰⲘⲈ	*rōme*

The second clue to pronunciation comes from other ancient languages – Assyrian and Babylonian – in which the vowels *were* marked. Their inscriptions contain fully vocalized transcriptions of Egyptian words, in the same way that English borrows French words, e.g. 'fiancé', and, vice versa, 'le weekend'. We have already come across this in the decipherment of the Rosetta Stone, where the 'foreign names clue' was of pivotal importance. The earliest and most significant of these transcriptions are in cuneiform documents contemporary with the New Kingdom in Egypt. *R'-mss* (Ramesses), for instance, is transliterated in cuneiform as *Riamesesa*, *'Imn-ḥtp* (Imenhetep) as *Amanhatpi*.

By combining the evidence from the Coptic language and from foreign texts contemporary with the Egyptian scripts, scholars can make informed guesses about the pronunciation of both consonants and vowels in ancient Egyptian. But they cannot, alas, ever know for certain if their guesses are correct.

The Hieroglyphic 'Alphabet'

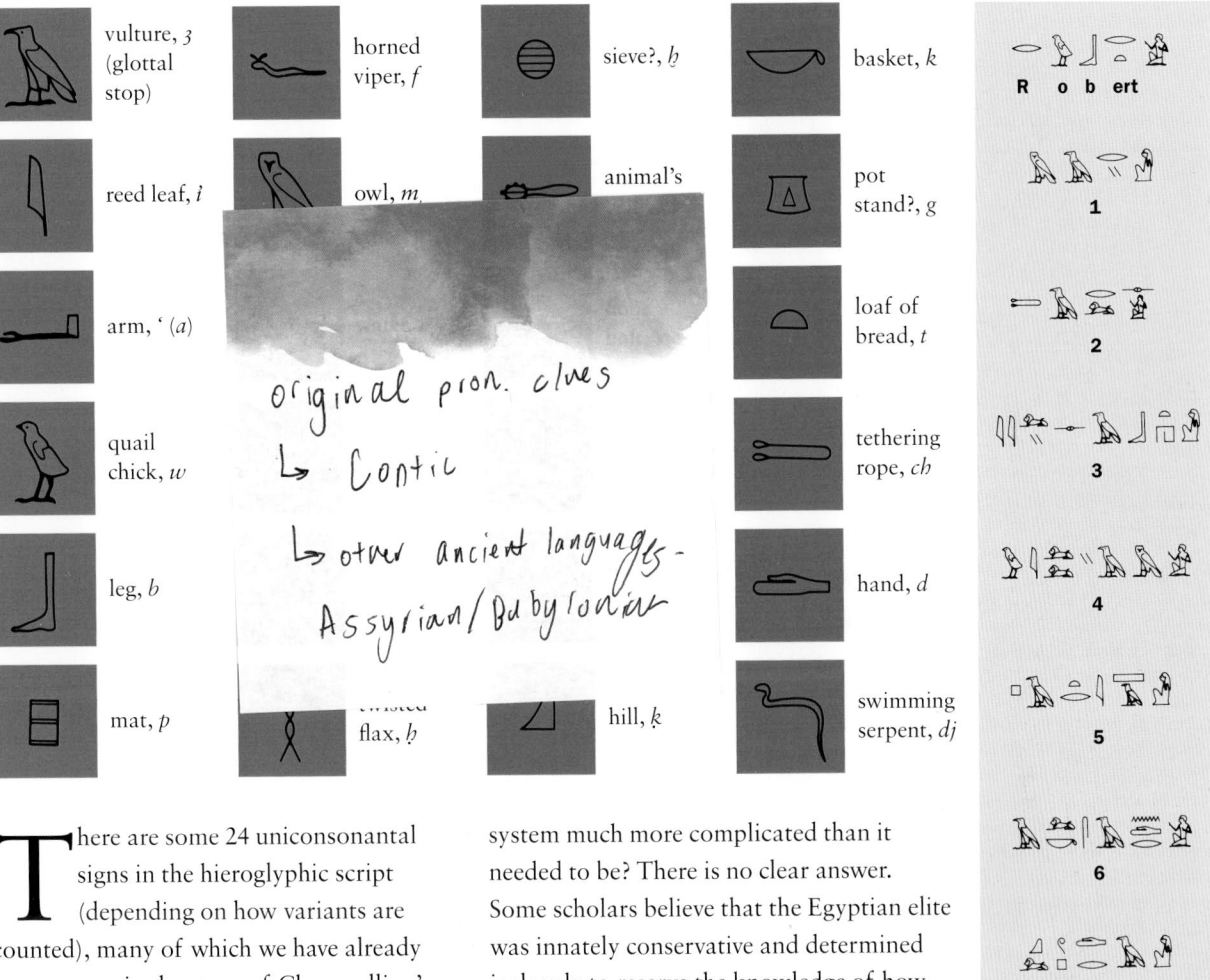

vulture, *3* (glottal stop)	horned viper, *f*	sieve?, *ḫ*	basket, *k*		R o b ert
reed leaf, *i*	owl, *m*	animal's	pot stand?, *g*		1
arm, *'* (*a*)			loaf of bread, *t*		2
quail chick, *w*			tethering rope, *ch*		3
leg, *b*			hand, *d*		4
mat, *p*	flax, *ḥ*	hill, *k*	swimming serpent, *dj*		5

original pron. clues
↳ Coptic
↳ other ancient languages –
Assyrian / Babylonian

There are some 24 uniconsonantal signs in the hieroglyphic script (depending on how variants are counted), many of which we have already come across in the story of Champollion's decipherment. In addition, the script used biconsonantal and triconsonantal signs, and various non-phonetic signs. The few uniconsonantal signs are often referred to as an 'alphabet', despite their not including true vowels and despite the fact that their usage is not distinct from that of other kinds of hieroglyphic phonetic sign. But if the Egyptians had an alphabet nearly 5000 years ago, why did they need all the other signs in the hieroglyphic script? Why did they apparently choose to make their writing system much more complicated than it needed to be? There is no clear answer. Some scholars believe that the Egyptian elite was innately conservative and determined jealously to reserve the knowledge of how to write and read hieroglyphs to an exclusive few; other scholars maintain that the hieroglyphic system seems complex to us but would not have seemed so to the ancient Egyptians. According to the latter group, a mixed system of several hundred phonograms and logograms, with a high proportion of the latter, was actually a *more* efficient way to represent the Egyptian language accurately than by writing it with only a few alphabetic signs. Evidence can be adduced to support both views.

Some familiar modern first names have been written in hieroglyphs. The first one is transcribed; try to read the rest – answers on p. 226. (After Zauzich)

The Hidden Power of Hieroglyphs

Left **Wooden mirror case of Tutankhamun, shaped as an 'ankh'.**

Right **'Boasting made permanent'. Hieroglyphs at the temple of Amun-Re, Karnak, glorify King Senusret I (1965–1920 BC The god Atum conducts th king to his divine father Amun-Re. Egyptian gods, unlike the gods of classica Greece and Rome, did not generally embody abstract ideas.**

Hieroglyphic inscriptions have been described as 'boasting made permanent'. But at their finest, they also exert a mysterious charm exceeding all other ancient scripts. The two inscriptions shown here are magnificent examples, in which writing fuses with art. The skilful integration of hieroglyphs with the objects they adorn is a quintessential feature of Egyptian writing. The 'ankh' is both a hieroglyph and a symbol of life.

Here it is a wooden case for a hand mirror found in Tutankhamun's tomb. The familiar cartouche of the pharaoh appears at the bottom of the handle. The cartouche above it is another of Tutankhamun's names, Nebkheperure; it is also inlaid in glass paste at the centre of the case. The 'basket' (light blue) has the value *neb*; the scarab beetle has the value *kheper*; the three strokes below the scarab have the value *u*; and the 'sun' (red) has the value *re*.

Types of Hieroglyph

With that caveat, hieroglyphs may be classified as follows:

    i. uniconsonantal signs (the 'alphabet');

    ii. biconsonantal signs;

    iii. triconsonantal signs;

    iv. phonetic complements;

    v. determinatives/logograms.

The uniconsonantal signs are listed on p. 97. Here are some of the biconsonantal and triconsonantal signs:

Biconsonantal signs

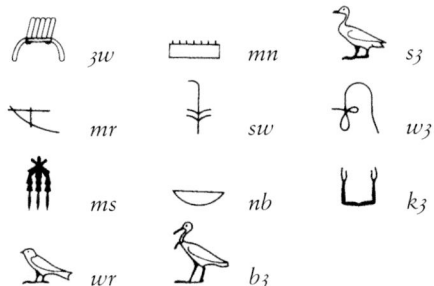

Triconsonantal signs

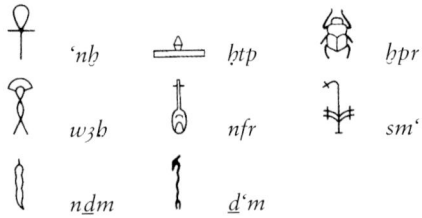

Left **Thoth, the divine patron of scribes, offers 'all life and dominion' to Osiris. From the funerary papyrus of the royal scribe and steward of King Sety I, Memphis, XIX dynasty, c. 1310 BC.**

We have already come across the basic elements of hieroglyphic spelling in the cartouche of Tutankhamun (pp. 34–5), and in some other words deciphered by Champollion. We know that the script is a mixture of phonograms and logograms, and that many symbols may be either phonographic or [lo]graphic, depending on context. The [bo]undaries are not hard and fast: hiero-[glyp]hs do not maintain caste distinctions.

'Phonetic complementing' means the addition of a uniconsonantal sign (or signs) to a word in order to emphasize or confirm the pronunciation of the word. It is somewhat as if we were to add the letter 'b' to a picture of an insect and the letter 'w' to another similar picture, in order to differentiate 'bee' from 'wasp'.

With hieroglyphs, the usual phonetic complement is a single sign reiterating the final consonant of the main sign.

Some phonetic complements are highlighted:

But it is common to add two or even three signs:

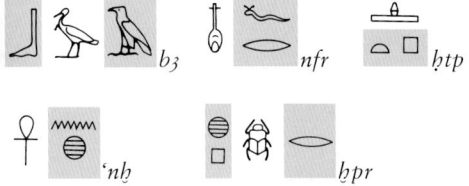

Determinatives are logograms added to the end of phonograms to indicate a word's meaning, and to discriminate where two or more meanings are possible. (The cartouche is a sort of determinative, as is the capital letter used in English to mark a proper name.) Many determinatives (highlighted below) are clearly pictographic:

The 'striking man' determinative shown in the last word is also used in the words for 'education' and 'taxes'! It determines words which involve forceful activity or action of some kind.

An exquisite example of determinatives is provided by the word *wn* (*wen*) which consists of a biconsonantal sign and a phonetic complement ᗡᗡᗡ , that may be combined with the following six determinatives (shown highlighted below):

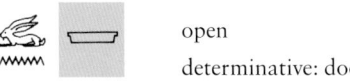 open
determinative: door

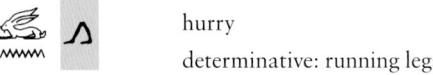 hurry
determinative: running legs

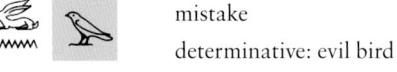 mistake
determinative: evil bird

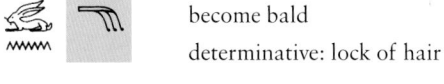 become bald
determinative: lock of hair

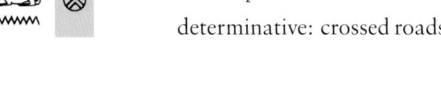 Hermopolis
determinative: crossed roads

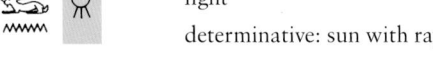 light
determinative: sun with rays

Sometimes more than one determinative is used:

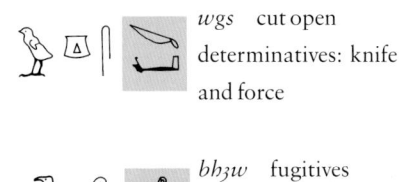 *wgs* cut open
determinatives: knife and force

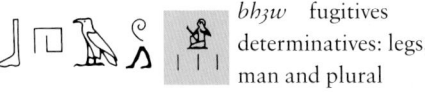 *bḥ3w* fugitives
determinatives: legs, man and plural

The Book of the Dead

There were many copies of The Book of the Dead in ancient Egypt, not just one. They consisted of religious spells written and illustrated on rolls of papyrus; stored in the tomb of the deceased, they were thought to ensure happiness in the other world. Their quality varied enormously, depending on the wealth of the individual named in the book: some were specially commissioned with an individual choice of texts and beautiful illustrations, others were standard copies, without much artistry, in which a space had been left to add the buyer's name and titles.

This example (*right*), one of the finest, belonged to a man named *Pꜣ-wiꜣ-n-ꜥdꜣ* (Pawiaenadja). The text on the left is written in hieratic, that on the right in hieroglyphs. The picture is surrounded by a frame that is itself made of hieroglyphs: at the bottom is the earth sign *tꜣ*, at the top the sign for heaven *p.t*, and at the left and right are two *wꜣs* sceptres. The dead man, at right, is pouring cool water on some offerings piled upon an altar before the god Osiris.

The hieroglyphic text begins, not on the far left or right of the inscription, but second from the left, as marked with an arrow. It is read vertically downwards, but printed here horizontally, to be read from left to right as follows (the transliteration of each sign is shown next to the sign in question):

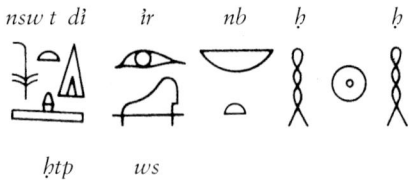

nsw t di *ir* *nb* *ḥ* *ḥ*

ḥtp *ws*

Ḥtp-di-nsw.t Wsir nb (n)ḥḥ

This may be translated as follows: 'An offering which the king gives to Osiris, lord of eternity'. (The small ⌒ under the *neb* sign was apparently a scribal mistake; *nḥḥ* is written here without the initial *n*, as is often the case.)

The hieroglyphic inscription continues, in translation: 'the great god, foremost of the West, that he may give a good burial to the god's father of Amun-Re, king of gods, Pawiaenadja, true of voice.'

The last line of the hieroglyphic inscription, on the far right, includes the sign of a child holding its hand to its mouth: the equivalent derived *hieratic* sign can be spotted at the beginning – i.e. at the far right-hand end – of the second line of hieratic.

Some Hieroglyphic Words

As we saw, a given hieroglyph can play various roles, depending on the word in which it appears. It may be a logogram in one word and a phonogram in another (the rebus principle), and in both cases also a pictogram. A good example is ⸓ , the 'sedge plant', the heraldic plant of Upper Egypt:

 *sw.t* sedge plant

Here, ⸓ is a logogram, with a phonetic complement ⌒ and a determinative ⎮ , which indicates that ⸓ is functioning as a logogram.

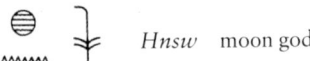 *Hnsw* moon god

Here, ⸓ is a biconsonantal phonogram, and the first two signs are uniconsonantal.

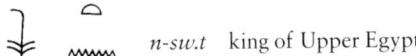 *n-sw.t* king of Upper Egypt

Here, ⸓ is both a logogram and a phonogram. It has been moved to the beginning of the word, as a sign of respect for the royal emblem: relying only on sign order, we would expect to read the word *sw-t-n*, rather than *n-sw.t*.

The *t* at the end of these two words is a feminine ending, separated from the rest of the transliteration with a dot for that reason. Thus:

 *nb* lord

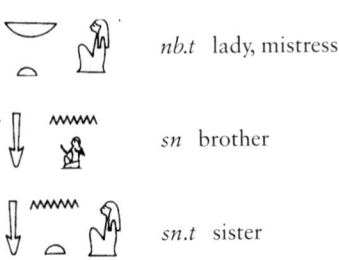 *nb.t* lady, mistress

sn brother

sn.t sister

(But not every *t* ending a word is a feminine ending.) Plurals are indicated logographically in at least two basic ways. Three strokes may be added:

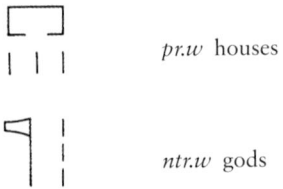 *pr.w* houses

ntr.w gods

Or the logogram itself may be tripled:

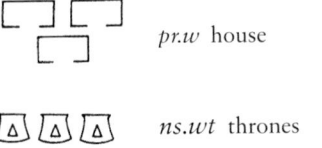 *pr.w* house

ns.wt thrones

They are transliterated with a *w* ending if the noun is masculine, a *wt* ending if it is feminine; and a separating dot indicates that the ending is a plural termination.

To form a genitive, two expressions can often simply be joined together.

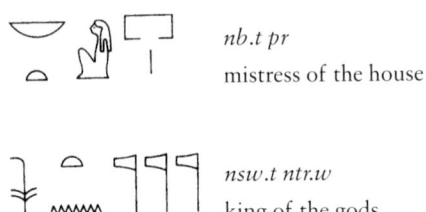 *nb.t pr*
mistress of the house

nsw.t ntr.w
king of the gods

A Glazed Tile of Ramesses II

This is the 'praenomen' (throne name) of Ramesses II in blue faience inlaid with white faience. The hieroglyphs may be transliterated as follows:

 (sun) logogram: the god Re

 (jackal head) triconsonantal *wsr*: 'be strong'

 (goddess with a feather) logogram: the goddess of justice, Maat (*Mȝ'̣t*), who carries an 'ankh' (life)

 (adze on a block of wood) triconsonantal *stp*: 'chosen'

 (water) 'alphabetic' sign *n*.

The name of the sun god Re occurs twice. In both cases it has been moved forward to show respect to the god. The signs are therefore to be read:

Wsr- mȝ'̣.t-R'-stp-n-R'
(User-maatre-setepenre)

The first part of the praenomen is the original form of Ozymandias, the title of Shelley's poem about one of the ruined statues of Ramesses II at Luxor, with its famous lines:

My name is Ozymandias, king of kings:
Look on my works, ye Mighty, and despair!

The rest of the translation of the praenomen is very uncertain, like many other royal statements in ancient Egypt. The most favoured translation is: 'the Maat of Re is strong, one chosen for Re'. Another possibility is: 'Strong with regard to the Maat of Re, whom Re chose'.

The Profession of Scribe

'A princely profession'. This limestone statue, excavated at Saqqara, is 4500 years old. A scribe named Kay sits in the customary cross-legged posture, on his lap a partially opened roll of papyrus. The eyes are inlaid with white quartz, crystal and ebony.

It is not easy to estimate what proportion of the population of ancient Egypt was literate. The population itself is imprecisely known; it appears to have risen from one million during the Old Kingdom to four and a half million in the Graeco-Roman period (today Egypt's population is nearly 80 million people). Of these, perhaps one per cent was literate, with Greeks forming the majority of the literate later on. Thus, during the Old Kingdom, there were probably fewer than

10,000 people who could read and write hieratic, still fewer who knew hieroglyphs; during the Greek period, this number may well have declined further, since the priests in the temples consciously made the hieroglyphic script more complicated in order to exclude secular people.

As in Mesopotamia, the life of an ancient Egyptian scribe was a comparatively attractive one. But we know less about it, because the evidence was written on

Below Hieroglyphic, hieratic and demotic forms of the sign for scribe.

1. hieroglyphic, *c.* 1500 BC
2. hieroglyphic, 500–100 BC
3. hieroglyphic book script, *c.* 1500 BC
4. hieratic, *c.* 1900 BC
5. hieratic, *c.* 1300 BC
6. hieratic, *c.* 200 BC
7. demotic, 400–100 BC.

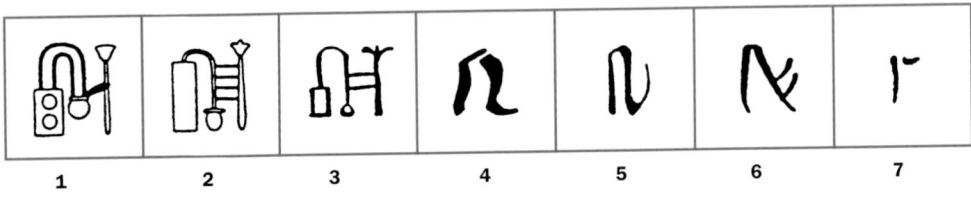

| 1 | 2 | 3 | 4 | 5 | 6 | 7 |

papyrus (the lives of scribes rarely intruded into the hieroglyphic inscriptions); and papyri have not endured like clay tablets. Fragments of papyri have survived that contain moral advice to apprentice scribes reminiscent of that in cuneiform tablets. A teacher writes to his pupil: 'I know that you frequently abandon your studies and whirl around in pleasure, that you wander from street to street and every house stinks of beer when you leave it . . . You, boy! You do not listen when I speak! You are thicker than a tall obelisk 100 cubits high and 10 cubits wide.' Another work portrays a father taking his son to school and advising him to be diligent if he is to avoid a life of back-breaking manual labour. 'I have seen the smith at his work beside his furnace,' the father declares. 'His fingers are like crocodile skin, and he stinks worse than fish roe.' Then the father disparages each manual trade in turn. Yet another papyrus concludes: 'The profession of scribe is a princely profession. His writing materials and his rolls of books bring pleasantness and riches.'

Papyrus

The name papyrus seems to derive from the Egyptian 'pa-en-per-aa', meaning 'that which belonged to the king': most likely papyrus was manufactured and issued under royal monopoly. The process began with the pith of the tall papyrus reed, which was cut lengthways into thin slivers. Placed side by side vertically just touching, then covered horizontally with a similar layer of slivers, this 'mat' would be beaten with a mallet, and left under a heavy weight for several days. When dry, the natural sap would bond the pith into a firm sheet. Sheets could then be stuck together to make long rolls; the side with horizontally laid fibres had to be on top to ensure that the sheet, when rolled, did not crack on the written side.

Left **The chief of the royal scribes, Hesire, from Saqqara, *c.* 2700–2650 BC. In this wood carving, Hesire holds in his left hand his writing implements; the hieroglyphs above his head contain the sign for scribe. Hesire was also chief dentist!**

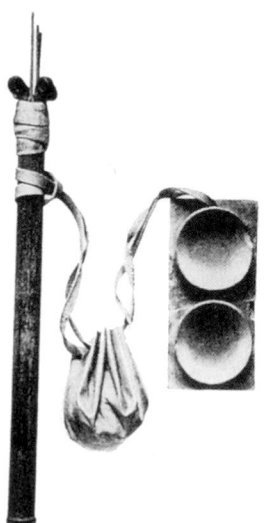

Above **Writing implements. The slate palette has two depressions for holding ink cakes, a wooden case for a brush made from a softened maritime reed, and a jug for water needed to moisten the brush.**

Left **Tutankhamun's writing implements:** (left to right) **ivory palette, gilded wood palette, ivory and gold papyrus burnisher, elaborate pen case of gilded and inlaid wood.**

Chapter 6 *Linear B*

Portrait of Sir Arthur Evans (1851–1941) at Knossos by Sir W. B. Richmond. Evans holds a Linear B clay tablet, a clear signal of his early obsession with the script. The portrait was painted in 1907; when Evans died in 1941, he had made little progress in deciphering Linear B.

'Room of the Throne' in the palace of Knossos, restored according to the ideas of Evans. Evans was convinced that one of the common signs in Linear B was a pictogram for the throne, another sign was a pictogram for 'double-axe', a motif found at various points in the palace (a double-axe is visible through the door) – beliefs that were in fact wholly incorrect, linguistically speaking.

Below **The first Linear B tablet to be published. Evans published it in 1900.**

In *The Odyssey* (book 19), Homer sings: 'Out in the middle of the wine-dark sea there is a land called Crete, a rich and lovely land, washed by the sea on every side; and in it are many peoples and ninety cities. There, one language mingles with another . . Among the cities is Knossos, a great city; and there Minos was nine years king, the boon companion of mighty Zeus.'

More than 2500 years after Homer, in 1900, the archaeologist Arthur Evans began to dig up and reconstruct the 'great city' of Knossos. He discovered what he believed was the palace of King Minos, with its notorious labyrinth, home of the Minotaur. He also discovered caches of clay tablets, written in a script that bore no resemblance to Egyptian hieroglyphs, Sumerian cuneiform or the later Greek alphabet. Evans was quite convinced that the language written by the script could not be Greek: he therefore coined the term Minoan for it, named the unknown writing 'Linear Script of Class B', and spent the last 40 years of his long life hoping to decipher it. He failed. The eventual decipherment of Linear B, in 1952, by a British architect, Michael Ventris, ranks second only to that of Jean-François Champollion's decipherment of Egyptian hieroglyphs in 1823. Both decipherments were chiefly the work of a single gifted individual. Linear B is the earliest European script we can understand. Although it is a millennium and a half younger than the earliest writing of Sumer and Egypt, it predates the Greek alphabetic inscriptions by as much as half a millennium.

Arthur Evans as Decipherer

lthough Evans failed to decipher Linear B, he did take some significant steps in the right direction. For a start, he recognized the existence of at least three distinct scripts in ancient Crete: a 'hieroglyphic' script, Linear A and Linear B. The hieroglyphic script had been found on sealstones and was so named for its superficial resemblance to Egyptian hieroglyphs; it need not detain us here (see p. 149). Linear A had been found inscribed on clay tablets, mainly at a Minoan palace in the south of Crete; very little Linear A was found in Knossos. Linear B had been found exclusively at Knossos, though it would later turn up – to everyone's great surprise and somewhat to the discomfort of Evans – in *mainland* Greece (discovered in 1939 in a large cache of tablets found at ancient Pylos). Although Linear A and B are clearly related, there are many signs which do not match. Today Linear A remains largely undeciphered.

Concentrating on Linear B, Evans identified the short upright lines that frequently recurred near the line as word dividers:

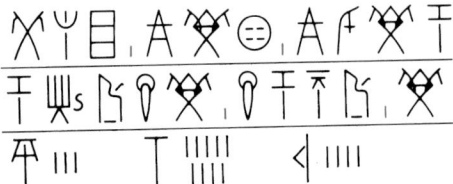

He worked out the system of counting as follows:

| = 1 unit   — = 1 ten

○ = 1 hundred   ⬦ = 1 thousand

Here are two examples of numbers in Linear B tablets, 362 and 1350:

Evans also understood that many tablets were inventories, with a total at the bottom, often involving a pictogram. For example:

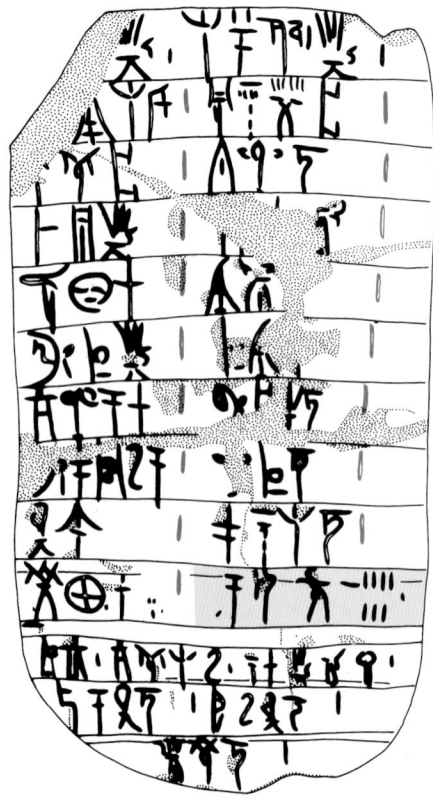

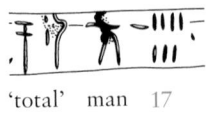

'total'   man   17

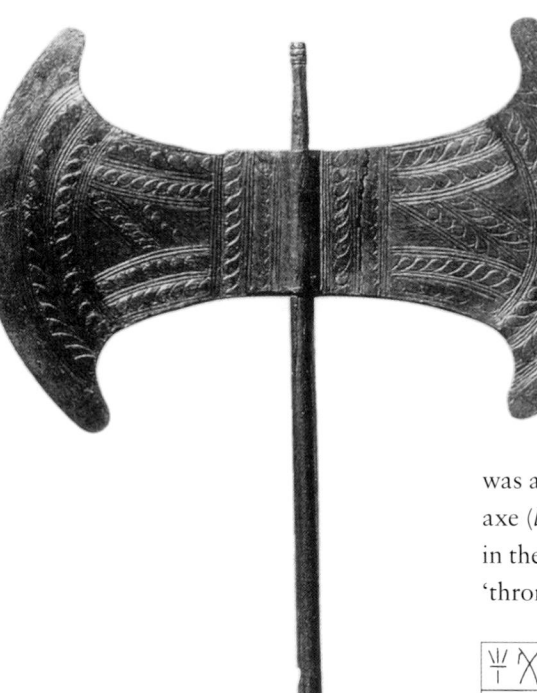

astray in respect of the Linear B signary. He looked for pictography: naturally he found it, and then – under the influence of the determinatives found in Egyptian hieroglyphs – he proceeded to treat the supposed Linear B pictograms as logograms. Thus ⊤, a frequent sign at the beginning of a word, Evans decided was a representation of the Minoan double-axe (*left*); and ⬡, which appears five times in the tablet below, Evans decided was a 'throne-and-sceptre'.

Left **Minoan gold double-axe from Arkalochori, Crete, *c.* 1500 BC. The double-axe is a motif found in various parts of the palace at Knossos and in various forms.**

There were other pictograms that were obviously logographic, representing words, such as:

woman   horse   wheel

jar   cup

and there were a number of pictograms that came in two forms:

Evans recognized that these stood for male and female animals, presumably counted for the palace of Minos. But he could not determine which pictogram was male and which female. The pictograms led Evans

Given the shape and apparent significance of the real throne Evans had already excavated, his second analogy was not an unreasonable one.

Where Linear B tablets were discovered, and when. According to Evans, Linear B should have been found *only* on Crete.

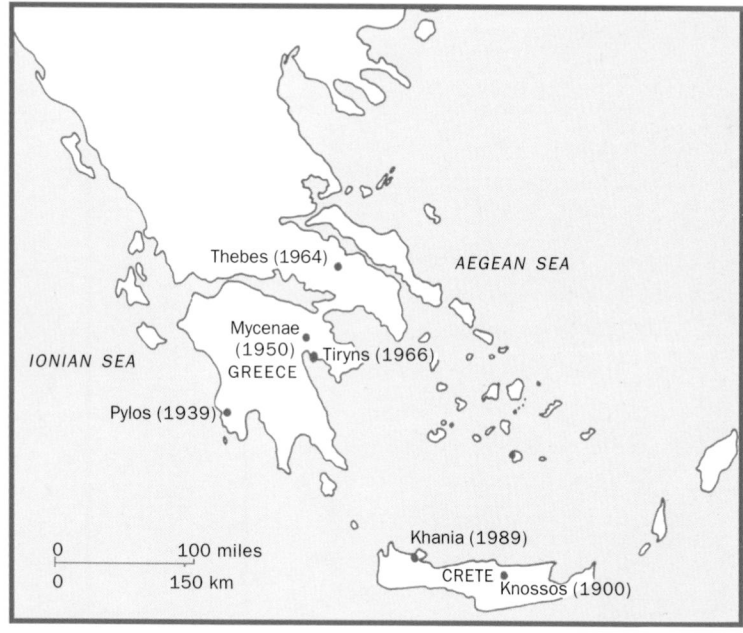

The Cypriot Clue

In search of further clues to Linear B's decipherment, Evans turned east, to Cyprus. Here was another island on which an ancient script had been found. But unlike Linear B, the Cypriot script had been deciphered. It appeared in bilingual inscriptions such as this one (*above*), which is almost contemporary with the Parthenon at Athens and therefore a thousand years or so younger than Linear B. The top two lines are in classical Greek script, the bottom line (shown separately) in Cypriot script.

With both scripts, the *language* is Greek (a dialect of Greek in the case of the Cypriot script). The reason for this was that Greek-speakers were thought to have brought Greek to Cyprus, fleeing the Trojan War. Since the sounds of the Greek alphabetic signs were known, the sounds of the Cypriot script could be deciphered: a task first performed in the 1870s. The script turned out to be a syllabic one. Evans now hoped that the *known* sounds of the Cypriot script could help him to decipher the *unknown* sounds of the Linear B script. His theory was that the Cypriot script was somehow derived from Linear B. Minoan-speaking people, possibly traders to begin with, must have settled in Cyprus, bringing their script with them. That was why, according to Evans, some of the Cypriot signs looked so similar to the Linear B signs.

Here are the eight most similar signs and their sound values in Cypriot:

Linear B	Cypriot	Cypriot sound values
		*po*
		*ta*
		*lo*
		*to*
		*se*
		*pa*
		*na*
		*ti*

Evans decided to test these values on a promising-looking tablet from Knossos. He noticed on the tablet six horse-heads, two of which were incomplete. (The join in the tablet was made after Evans' death by John Chadwick, so Evans' drawing does not include the left-hand portion.) Of the four horse-heads in the middle and on the right of the tablet, two had manes and two did not. The ones without manes, foals presumably, were preceded by the same pair of signs:

According to the Cypriot sound values, the two signs should read *po-lo*. What might 'polo' mean in the Minoan language? Evans noted that it resembled the classical Greek word 'pōlos', young horse or foal, (and its dual form 'pōlō', two foals); in fact the English word 'foal' is from the same source as Greek 'pōlos'. If the Minoan language and the Greek language were related after all, Minoan 'polo' could easily be the equivalent of classical Greek 'pōlos'. The tablet would then mean:

horses 2	*polo* foals
polo foals 2	horses 4

If the guess was right, the word  ('polo') had been added by the Minoan scribe to make absolutely clear that the maneless pictogram was a *foal* and not an adult animal.

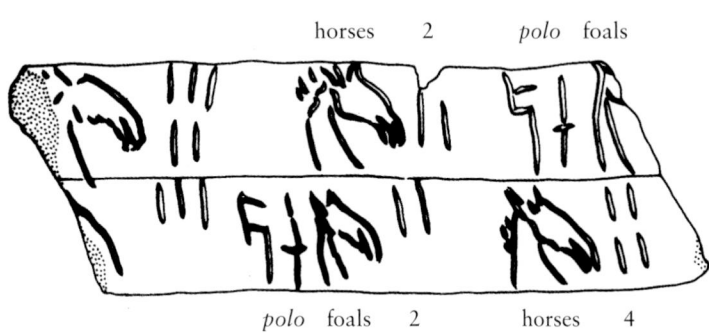

horses	2	*polo* foals
polo foals	2	horses 4

Evans, however, rejected this plausible beginning, almost out of hand. He refused to accept that the Minoans spoke and wrote an archaic form of Greek, which they took with them to Cyprus. In Evans' view, it was Minos and the Minoans, *not* the mainland Greeks, who ruled the roost: the Minoan language could not possibly be Greek. Only a few archaeologists dared to differ from him. Evans dismissed the similarity of the Linear B and Cypriot signs in the case of 'polo' as a mere coincidence without significance.

Sanctuary of Aphrodite, Paphos, Cyprus. Evans correctly proposed that signs found on inscriptions in Cyprus were similar to those found in Crete.

Deciphering Linear B

When Evans died in 1941, he left a disorganized legacy with regard to Linear B. Of the well over 3000 tablets excavated by him and others, less than 200 had been published. Those who tackled the decipherment in the 1940s did not have much to go on. Nevertheless, Alice Kober, an American classical scholar with a logical turn of mind, made important progress. Though it was Michael Ventris who finally made sense of Linear B, Kober provided a vital insight, subsequently applied by Ventris.

Kober acted upon a suggestion made by Evans: that there was evidence of declension in Linear B. She was familiar with declension from Latin and Greek, where noun endings decline with the case of a noun, and verb endings conjugate. There is relatively little declension/conjugation in English, more in French, e.g. j'aime/ tu aimes/ il aime/ nous aim**ons**/ vous aim**ez**/ ils aim**ent**. In Linear B, in the Knossos tablets, Kober identified five groups of words, with three words in each group – later dubbed 'Kober's triplets' by Ventris – which suggested to her the presence of declension. She could not know what the words meant, but their context in the tablets made it likely that they were nouns, maybe personal names or place names.

Here are two of the triplets:

We can see the inflection more clearly if we highlight the word endings:

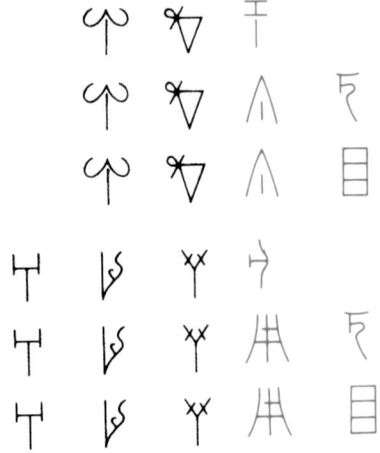

An English parallel might be:

Ca-na-da	Ar-ge(n)-ti-na
Ca-na-di-a(n)	Ar-ge(n)-ti-ni-a(n)
Ca-na-di-a-(ns)	Ar-ge(n)-ti-ni-a(ns)

If such parallels were right (assuming Linear B was syllabic, like the Cypriot script), $\math=$ and $\rightarrow$ would have different consonants (C) but the same vowel (V), like *da* and *na* above, i.e.:

So would $\wedge$ and ⊞ like *di* and *ni* above:

the same token, using the other three plets, Kober arrived at what she called 'the ginning of a tentative phonetic pattern':

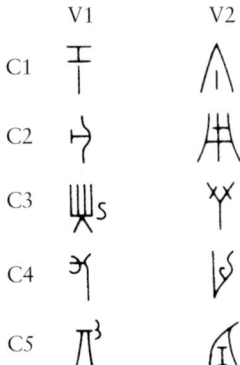

	V1	V2
C1		
C2		
C3		
C4		
C5		

he sounds of these syllables were as yet nknown, but their interrelationships, like e blanks in a crossword, were (tentatively) stablished. This analytical principle, called 'grid' by Ventris, was seminal in rganizing the Linear B material for ecipherment.

Michael Ventris

entris was a schoolboy when he first ecame interested in Linear B. His classics aster, Patrick Hunter, took a party ncluding Ventris to see an exhibition on the Minoan world arranged by Evans in 1936. vans himself, then 85 years old, was resent, and showed the boys some Linear B ablets. At that moment Hunter heard entris ask Evans, very politely: 'Did you say hat they haven't been deciphered, sir?' From 936 until June 1952, when he made his reakthrough, Ventris worked at under-tanding Linear B, as and when he could btain access to more drawings of tablets. rom January 1951, he began circulating his deas to other scholars in the form of 'Work Notes', sometimes including 'grids'. Shown ere is part of Work Note 15, compiled in Athens on 28 September 1951.

Michael Ventris (1922–56) in 1937, at the age of 15.

From 1951, Ventris started to use 'Work Notes' which he circulated to other scholars. Long before this, in 1942, he had remarked: 'one can remain sure that no Champollion is working quietly in a corner and preparing a full and startling revelation, as no one has access to sufficient reproductions.'

Breakthrough

Ventris used many analytical techniques, besides comparison of the 'triplets', to extract the inter-relationships of Linear B signs. The frequency of certain signs and the regularity with which they appeared in a particular context in the tablets, was a useful clue. By February 1952, he was able to compile a promising grid (*opposite*).

But how was he to guess the actual sound values of these signs? He began by allotting the pure vowel *a* to the 'double-axe' ⟨†⟩, pure vowel 5 on the grid. This sign appeared frequently at the beginning of a word. In all syllabic scripts, vowels display high initial frequencies. Other evidence suggested that if the 'double-axe' was a vowel, it was probably *a*.

For his second guess Ventris turned to the Cypriot clue once tried by Evans: comparison of the shapes of Linear B signs with those of the Cypriot script. Ventris had studiously avoided using this comparison before because he distrusted it; but he had continued to believe in some kind of historic link between the languages of Crete, Cyprus and the Aegean. He now hazarded that Linear B ⟨†⟩ was equivalent to ⟨T⟩ – *na* in Cypriot, and that Linear B ⟨/\⟩ was equivalent to ⟨↑⟩ – *ti* in Cypriot. If these guesses were correct, then consonant 8 must be *n* and vowel 1 must be *i*, which meant that ⟨Υ⟩ was *ni*, according to the grid.

Ventris' next step was inspired. He had for some time suspected that the Knossos tablets studied by Kober contained place names; and he had noticed that the 'triplets' occurred only in the tablets from Knossos, never in the tablets from mainland Greece.

Could each triplet refer to a different town in Crete? What about Amnisos, the port of Knossos? Amnisos spelt syllabically would be *A-mi-ni-so*, with no final *s* – this *s* being a classical Greek inflexion. (Remember that Evans had made the same speculation about 'polo' and 'pōlos'.)

From the grid with its new values added, *A-mi-ni-so* would be spelt:

$$ \text{†} - ? - \text{Υ} - ? $$

The first word in one triplet was ⟨† ⏐⟩ Υ ⟩⟩ . If it meant Amnisos, then

$$ \text{⏐⟩} = mi \qquad \text{⟩⟩} = so. $$

Then, according to the grid, consonant 9 must be *m*, and vowel 2 must be *o*. This would mean, in turn, that ⟨Щs⟩ = *no*.

The first word in another triplet was ⟨？ Щs ⟩⟩⟩. Using the grid, this translated as ? - *no* - *so*. If ⟨？⟩ = *ko*, the name could be Knossos itself! In due course Ventris was to extract from the five triplets the names of three more Cretan towns:

⟨♡ 关 ⟩⟩⟩	*Tu-li-so*	(Tulissos)
⟨‡ Щ ∓⟩	*Pa-i-to*	(Phaistos)
⟨ᗣ ∇ ∓⟩	*Lu-ki-to*	(Luktos).

An entire triplet now transliterated as:

⟨† ⏐⟩ Υ ⟩⟩⟩	*A-mi-ni-so* (Amnisos)
⟨† ⏐⟩ Υ 舟 ℉⟩	*A-mi-ni-si-jo* (Amnisian men)
⟨† ⏐⟩ Υ 舟 目⟩	*A-mi-ni-si-ja* (Amnisian women).

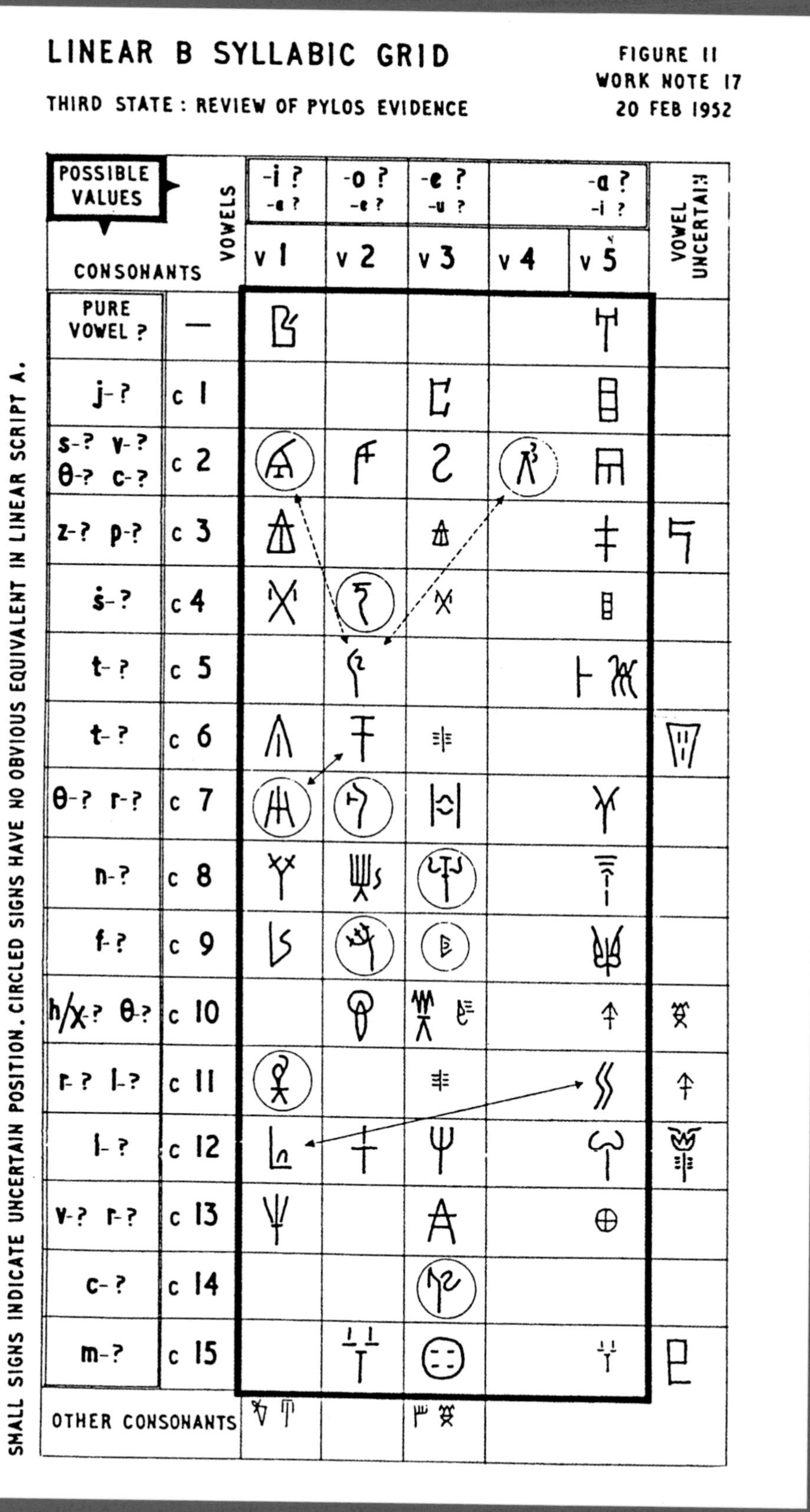

LINEAR B SYLLABIC GRID

THIRD STATE: REVIEW OF PYLOS EVIDENCE

FIGURE II
WORK NOTE 17
20 FEB 1952

SMALL SIGNS INDICATE UNCERTAIN POSITION. CIRCLED SIGNS HAVE NO OBVIOUS EQUIVALENT IN LINEAR SCRIPT A.

Work Note 17 by Michael Ventris, 20 February 1952. By now the inter-relationships of many Linear B signs were known, but the actual sound values of the signs were still unknown. It is clear from the grid, however, that Ventris had made guesses at the sound values of both vowels and consonants. Later in 1952, he used this grid – and some inspired guesswork – to determine many of the sound values. For instance, vowel 1 turned out to have the value *i*, consonant 8 the value *n*, and the sign to have the value *ni*. (Ventris' other workings need not concern us.)

'The tablets are in GREEK'

Many of the deciphered words were easily recognizable as an archaic form of Greek. At first Ventris was highly sceptical of this result: like Evans, he was convinced that the Minoan language was unrelated to Greek – related rather to the unknown language of the Etruscans. But over the coming months of 1952–53, Ventris, with the help of John Chadwick, a specialist in early Greek, showed that more and more of the tablets yielded to the 'Greek solution'. It began to seem that the Minoans and the Mycenaeans of mainland Greece had been speaking and writing Greek centuries before Homer.

In mid-1953 – at the same moment that the structure of DNA was decoded and Everest was climbed, by strange coincidence – Linear B was finally cracked beyond reasonable doubt. Confirmation came from a new tablet find, made at ancient Pylos on the Greek mainland by the American archaeologist Carl Blegen. As soon as the tablet had been cleaned, Blegen applied the values worked out by Ventris and Chadwick. Suddenly the mute signs, writing pre-dating the Trojan War, were made to speak after more than three millennia of silence.

a	e	i	o	u
da	de	di	do	du
ja	je		jo	ju
ka	ke	ki	ko	ku
ma	me	mi	mo	mu
na	ne	ni	no	nu
pa	pe	pi	po	pu
qa	qe	qi	qo	
ra	re	ri	ro	ru
sa	se	si	so	su
ta	te	ti	to	tu
wa	we	wi	wo	
za	ze		zo	

Above **The basic Linear B syllabary.**

Left **The Pylos tablet that confirmed the decipherment of Linear B, with its transliteration into Greek and translation into English on the opposite page.**

tiripode   aikeu   keresijo   weke   2

(tripod cauldrons of Cretan workmanship of the
aikeu type 2)

tiripo   eme   pode   owowe   1

(tripod cauldron with a single handle
on one foot 1)

tiripo   keresijo   weke

(tripod cauldron of Cretan workmanship)

apu   kekaumeno   kerea

(burnt at the legs)

qeto   3

(wine jars 3)

dipa   mezoe   qetorowe   1

(larger-sized goblet with four handles 1)

dipae   mezoe   tiriowee   2

(larger-sized goblet with three handles 2)

dipa   mewijo   qetorowe   1

(smaller-sized goblet with four handles 1)

dipa   mewijo   tirijowe   1

(smaller-sized goblet with three handles 1)

dipa   mewijo   anowe   1

(smaller-sized goblet without a handle)

This is not the Greek of Homer, still less the
classical Greek of Euripides – as modern
English is not the English of Chaucer or
Shakespeare. There proved to be nothing of
literary value in Linear B: the tablets merely
recorded prosaic details of palace
administration, such as lists of names and
their trades – shepherd, potter, bronzesmith,
etc. – and lists of goods. Linear B tells us not
one word about the names of kings and the
deeds of heroes. But Greek it certainly was.
As Ventris remarked at the time, with
characteristic modesty, to his former classics
master Patrick Hunter:

*Not quite the Greek you taught
me, I'm afraid!
Best wishes ——— Michael*

In great excitement,
Ventris began to apply the
sound values in the Linear
B grid to unknown words
in the tablets. In mid-June
1952 he wrote a letter to
the retired professor of
ancient history at Oxford
University, Sir John Myres,
friend of Evans and editor
of the Knossos tablets.
Ventris admitted: 'though
it runs completely counter
to everything I've said in
the past, I'm now almost
completely convinced that
the [Linear B] tablets are
in GREEK.'

This photograph shows
Ventris at the time of the
conclusive decipherment of
Linear B, mid-1953. He was
a superb draughtsman; all
the signs on this page and
the tablet drawing opposite
are his. He was only 34
when he died in a car crash
three years later.

Chapter 7   *Mayan Glyphs*

A page from the Dresden Codex, key to the decipherment of Mayan glyphs. It was probably painted by Maya scribes just before the Spanish conquest of Mexico and then taken to Europe by Cortés. In 1739, it was apparently purchased by the royal library of the court of Saxony in Dresden. At the height of Maya power, between AD 250 and 800, codices had jaguar-skin covers, and were painted by scribes using brush or feather pens dipped in black or red paint held in cut conch-shell inkpots.

The Myth of the Ancient Maya

The page opposite is taken from one of only four surviving 'books' of the ancient Maya of Central America. Actually, it is one of 39 leaves from the Dresden Codex, a folding screen the size of a Michelin travel guide, which opens out to a length of nearly 12 ft (3.5m). On each leaf, which has been sized with a fine coat of lime, the artist has painted with extreme care a series of gods and animals, often in many colours, accompanied by hieroglyphic symbols.

It is difficult to believe that the hieroglyphs in the codex are part of a full writing system. They bear no resemblance to Sumerian cuneiform, the Linear B script or even Egyptian hieroglyphs; they seem, rather, like cabalistic symbols, designed for the rituals of some esoteric cult. And that is exactly how they were viewed by most scholars until as recently as the 1950s and 1960s. Sir Eric Thompson, the leading

Mayanist, asserted in 1972: 'Maya writing is not syllabic or alphabetic in part or in whole.' The ancient Maya themselves were thought of as a theocracy, time worshippers with an immensely sophisticated calendar and a deeply spiritual outlook. Their ideal was said to be 'moderation in all things', their motto 'live and let live', and their character to have 'an emphasis on discipline, cooperation, patience, and consideration for others'. Theirs was a civilization unlike any other, maintained Thompson, who looked to the Maya as a source of spiritual values in a modern world that placed far more importance on material prosperity.

As Evans worshipped the noble Minoans, and sought to distance them from the vulgar Greeks, so Thompson revered the ancient Maya and abstracted them from the brutal, human-sacrificing Aztecs who followed them. Only after Evans' death in 1941 was the myth fully exposed, and the mundane subject matter of the Linear B tablets revealed. Something similar happened in the years following Thompson's death in 1975.

Today we know, thanks to the recent phonetic decipherment of the glyphs, that the Maya were obsessed with war, and that both the rulers and the gods liked to take hallucinogenic or inebriating enemas using special syringes. 'The highest goal of these lineage-proud dynasts was to capture the ruler of a rival city-state in battle, to torture and humiliate him (sometimes for years), and then to subject him to decapitation following a ball game which the prisoner was always destined to lose,' says Michael Coe, a contemporary Mayanist who assisted the decipherment.

The page of the Dresden Codex opposite shows a dog and, above it, the glyph for 'dog':

According to Sir Eric Thompson (left, 1898–1975), the two signs were strictly pictographic/logographic: the first depicted the ribs of an animal, while the second was the symbol of death. The combined meaning of 'dog' was implied by the fact that the dog was known in Maya belief to accompany the shades of the dead to the world beyond the grave. In actual fact each sign is phonetic, representing a syllable: the first has the value *tzu*, the second the value *l(u)*; the word 'tzul' means 'dog' in one of the Mayan languages spoken today.

Who are the Maya?

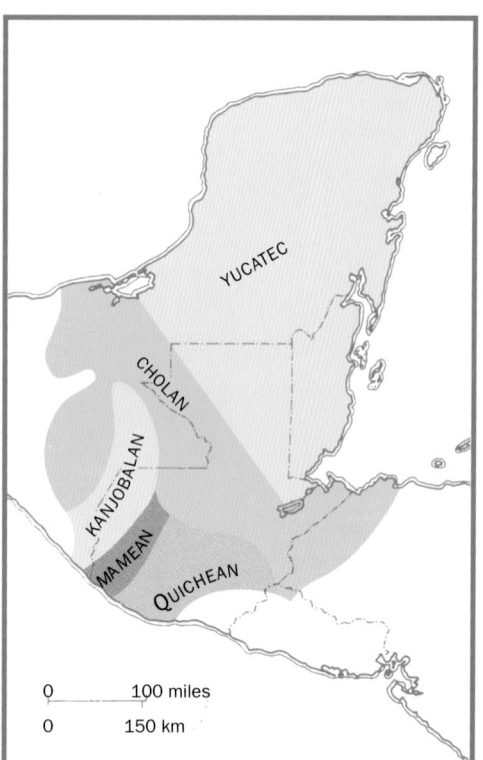

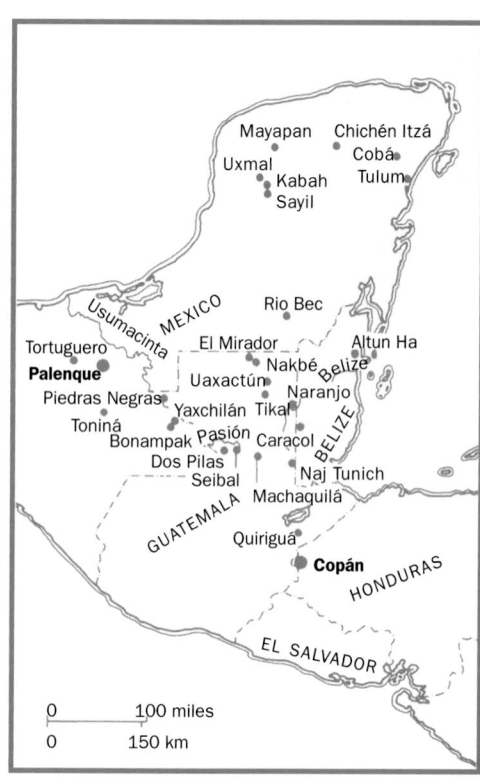

The Maya area, with major sites.

The Mayan language groups. There are some 3 Mayan languages in all.

The first Europeans to encounter Maya civilization were the Spanish, who conquered Mexico in the 16th century; they left accounts of astonishing monuments buried in the jungle, and they recorded invaluable clues as to the meaning of the glyphs. But it was not until the 1840s that the Maya entered modern consciousness: an intrepid American traveller, John Lloyd Stephens, and his companion, the Englishman Frederick Catherwood, a brilliant illustrator, published what became one of the bestsellers of the 19th century, *Incidents of Travel in Central America, Chiapas, and Yucatan*. The authors felt that they had stumbled upon wonders comparable to that of ancient Egypt,

explored by Napoleon's scholars 40 years before. Speaking of the buildings of Copán, Stephens wrote that, 'If a like discovery had been made in Italy, Greece, Egypt, or Asia, within reach of European travel, it would have created an interest not inferior to the discovery of Pompeii.' He was firmly convinced that the elaborate glyphs on the monuments, drawn by Catherwood, were writing: 'No Champollion has yet brought to them the energies of his inquiring mind. Who shall read them?'

As Champollion had been aided by Coptic, the descendant of the language of the ancient Egyptians, so the decipherers of Mayan writing have been helped by the languages of the living Maya. About seven illion Maya live today in the same area as heir ancestors. Although they are mostly atholics – in consequence of the Spanish onquest – they speak various Mayan anguages and preserve a distinctive culture; heir relationship with the governments of Mexico, Guatemala and the other countries n which they live has been fraught with ppression and bloodshed. (Rigoberta Menchú, the Maya woman who won the Nobel peace prize in 1992, lost most of her amily to the death squads.) While they annot read the glyphs of their ancestors, he modern Maya use vocabulary that lies ehind the glyphs in many cases.

The linguistic situation is complex, owever. Besides being difficult to learn (for peakers of European languages), Mayan anguages number 30 or so. Some of these are as closely related as, say, Dutch is to English, others differ as much as English does from French. A major division is that between Cholan and Yucatec. The monumental texts at Copán and Palenque, two of the greatest cities of the ancient Maya, are in Cholan languages; while three of the four surviving codices are in Yucatec (though Cholan influence can be detected in the codex at Dresden).

Nevertheless, dictionaries of these languages as spoken in recent centuries have yielded words that fit the ancient inscriptions. And native speakers of Mayan languages, with the help of American and European epigraphers, have been able to suggest insights into the glyphs based on their unique knowledge of their own language and culture.

This painting by Tatiana Proskouriakoff, a pioneer decipherer of the Mayan glyphs, reconstructs the principal group of buildings at Copán as they would have looked at their zenith in the late 8th century AD. In the centre is the Hieroglyphic Stairway, which consists of multiple glyphs, one of which is the so-called emblem glyph of Copán (below), signifying that the carrier of the glyph was the 'blood lord' of Copán (the beads on the left represent blood, the two signs at the top mean 'lord').

Maya Numbers and Time

The numbers were the first part of the Mayan writing system to be deciphered by scholars during the 19th century. The system turned out to be remarkably sophisticated. Like us (and like the Babylonians), the Maya used the idea of place value. But where we have a place value that increases from right to left in multiples of 10, the Maya system has a place value that increases in multiples of 20 (i.e. 1, 20, 400, 8000 etc.). A shell symbolized zero, an advance that the Maya (and the Hindus) made over the Romans and Babylonians, and which reached Europe only much later. A dot stood for 1, a bar for five. Here are some examples:

| 0 | 1 | 4 | 6 | 19 |

Instead of the place value increasing horizontally from right to left, as with our own system, among the Maya it increased vertically, moving up the page:

$$= 1 \times 20 = 20$$

$$= 0 \times 1 = 0$$

Total: 20

$$= 2 \times 20 = 40$$

$$= 15 \times 1 = 15$$

Total: 55

$$= 12 \times 20 = 240$$

$$= 9 \times 1 = 9$$

Total: 249

$$= 2 \times 400 = 800$$

$$= 0 \times 20 = 0$$

$$= 19 \times 1 = 19$$

Total: 819

$$= 9 \times 8000 = 72,000$$

$$= 0 \times 400 = 0$$

$$= 3 \times 20 = 60$$

$$= 3 \times 1 = 3$$

Total: 72, 063

This is not the end of the numeral system, however. Maya scribes loved decoration and complexity for its own sake. Each number from 1 to 20 could therefore also be expressed by the face of a god, sometimes by several alternative faces: a hint of the daunting diversity of the writing system as a whole. Here are some examples:

In measuring time, the Maya began by combining the numerals 1 to 13 with 20 named days. We can visualize this with two interlocking wheels; the days are on the upper wheel, with their glyphs and their names in Yucatec Mayan. The date shown is:

1   Imix

(earth being, world, crocodile)

In 4 days' time the date will be (revolve the wheels in your mind):

5   Chicchan

(snake)

In 13 days' time the lower wheel will have completely revolved and the date will be:

1   Ix

(jaguar)

In 20 days' time, the upper wheel will have completely revolved and the date will be:

8   Imix

The Dresden Codex is full of dates like these, as we shall see shortly.

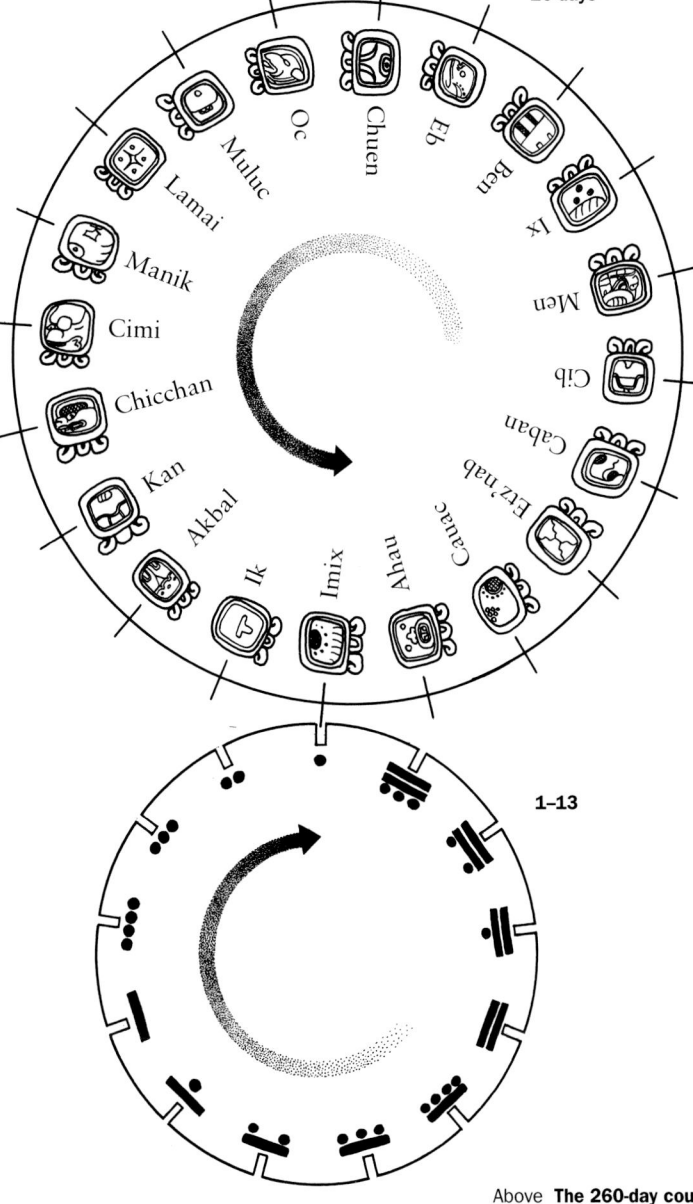

20 days

1–13

Above **The 260-day count of the Maya. (From Coe, 2005)**

Rabbit god writing in a folding-screen codex with jaguar-skin covers. This painting is not from a codex but from a cylindrical vase in codex style, 8th century AD.

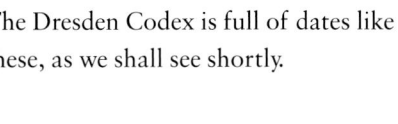

Maya Dates

The Maya expanded the 260-day count by meshing the named days with a third wheel representing the approximate year of 365 days. It consisted of 18 named months (compared to our 12), each of 20 days' duration, and one month of 5 days called Uayeb, making altogether a 'vague year' of $(18 \times 20) + (1 \times 5) = 365$ days: 'vague' because the extra one quarter of a day in a solar year, which we solve by adding a leap year, the Maya chose to ignore.

The three wheels opposite intermesh to show how the date changes (the month wheel is Cumku). The date shown is 4 Ahau 8 Cumku. In 4 days' time the wheels show that the date will be: 8 Kan 12 Cumku.

If the wheels keep turning, 52 'vague' years will pass before the same date, 4 Ahau 8 Cumku, recurs. This is long enough to be sufficient for everyday life, but not for historical purposes. It would be as if we were to date both the beginning of the French Revolution and the building of the Eiffel Tower as '89, or the American Declaration of Independence and its bicentenary as '76. So the Maya needed to invent an equivalent for our 'Long Count' of years, an endless march of time extending into the past and into the future, independent of the 260-day count until the two counts were correlated by the Maya. Their 'zero on the Long Counter' correlates with 4 Ahau 8 Cumku and corresponds with 13 August 3114 BC in our Gregorian calendar. For the Maya, it is 0.0.0.0.0. – the beginning of the latest Great Cycle of time. This was due to end on 23 December AD 2012. Each Great Cycle the Maya divided into smaller cycles, just as we have millennia, centuries and decades.

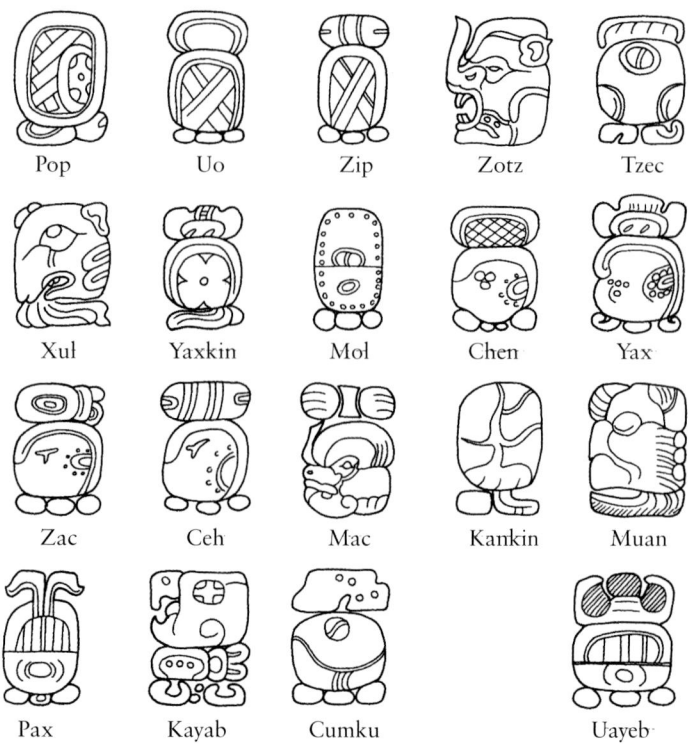

Pop   Uo   Zip   Zotz   Tzec

Xul   Yaxkin   Mol   Chen   Yax

Zac   Ceh   Mac   Kankin   Muan

Pax   Kayab   Cumku   Uayeb

The month glyphs with the names in Yucatec Mayan. Each month consists of 20 days, except for Uayeb which lasts only 5 days. (From Coe, 2005)

Right **The 52-year count of the Maya.**

A Maya date therefore consists of a series of numerals, beginning with the number of the largest cycles of time elapsed since the 'zero' point, working through the numbers of successively shorter cycles, and finally correlating with the 52-'vague year' count, e.g. the date 9.15.4.6.4. 8 Kan 17 Muan, the first five numerals of which mean:

9 cycles of 144,000 days = 1,296,000 days
15 cycles of 7,200 days = 108,000 days
4 cycles of 360 days = 1,440 days
6 cycles of 20 days = 120 days
4 cycles of 1 day = 4 days
TOTAL   **1,405,564 days**

That is 1,405,564 days from the beginning of the last Great Cycle (13 August 3114 BC) – which is 29 November AD 735.

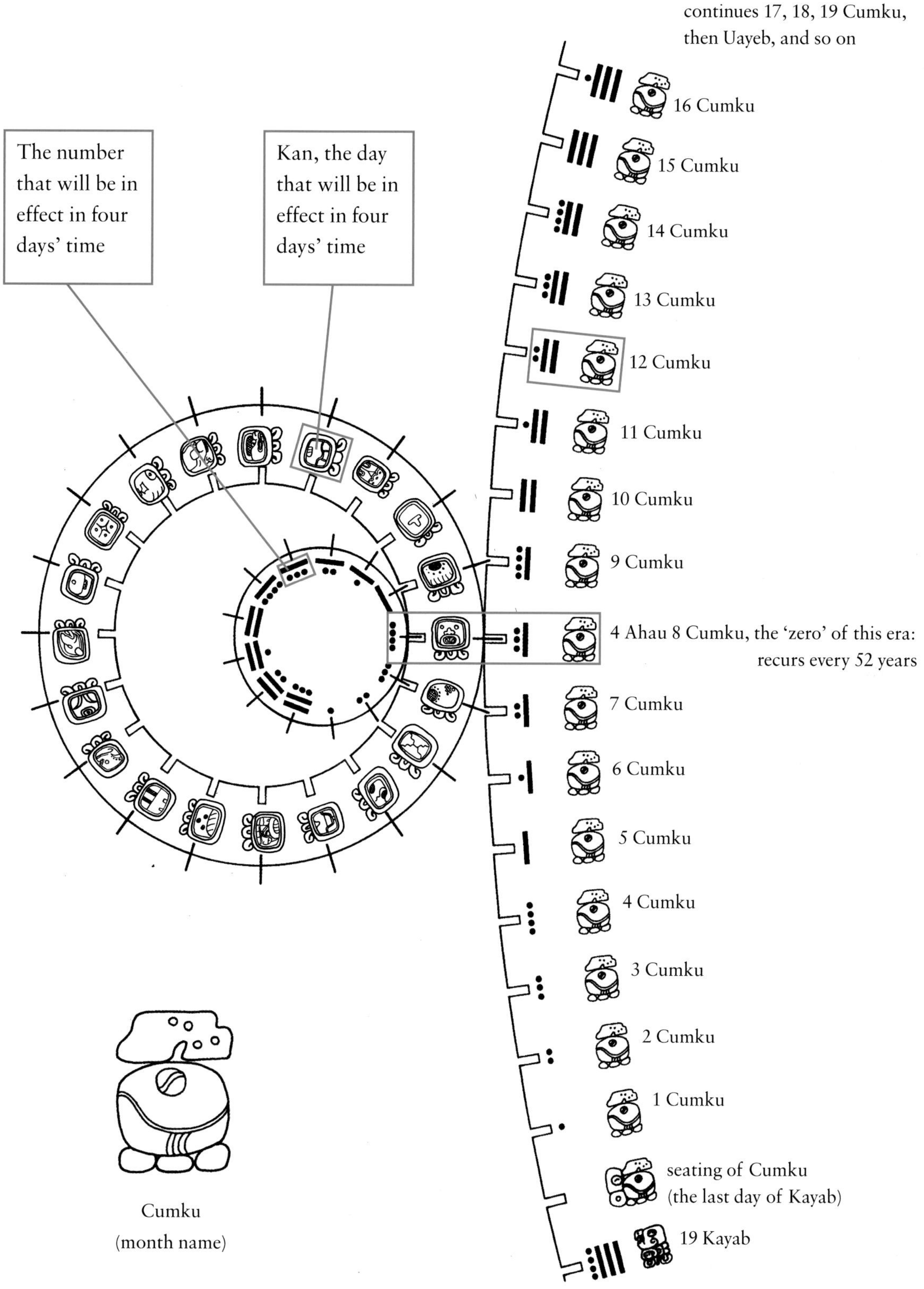

continues 17, 18, 19 Cumku,
then Uayeb, and so on

16 Cumku

15 Cumku

14 Cumku

13 Cumku

12 Cumku

11 Cumku

10 Cumku

9 Cumku

4 Ahau 8 Cumku, the 'zero' of this era:
recurs every 52 years

7 Cumku

6 Cumku

5 Cumku

4 Cumku

3 Cumku

2 Cumku

1 Cumku

seating of Cumku
(the last day of Kayab)

19 Kayab

The number
that will be in
effect in four
days' time

Kan, the day
that will be in
effect in four
days' time

Cumku
(month name)

The Dresden Codex

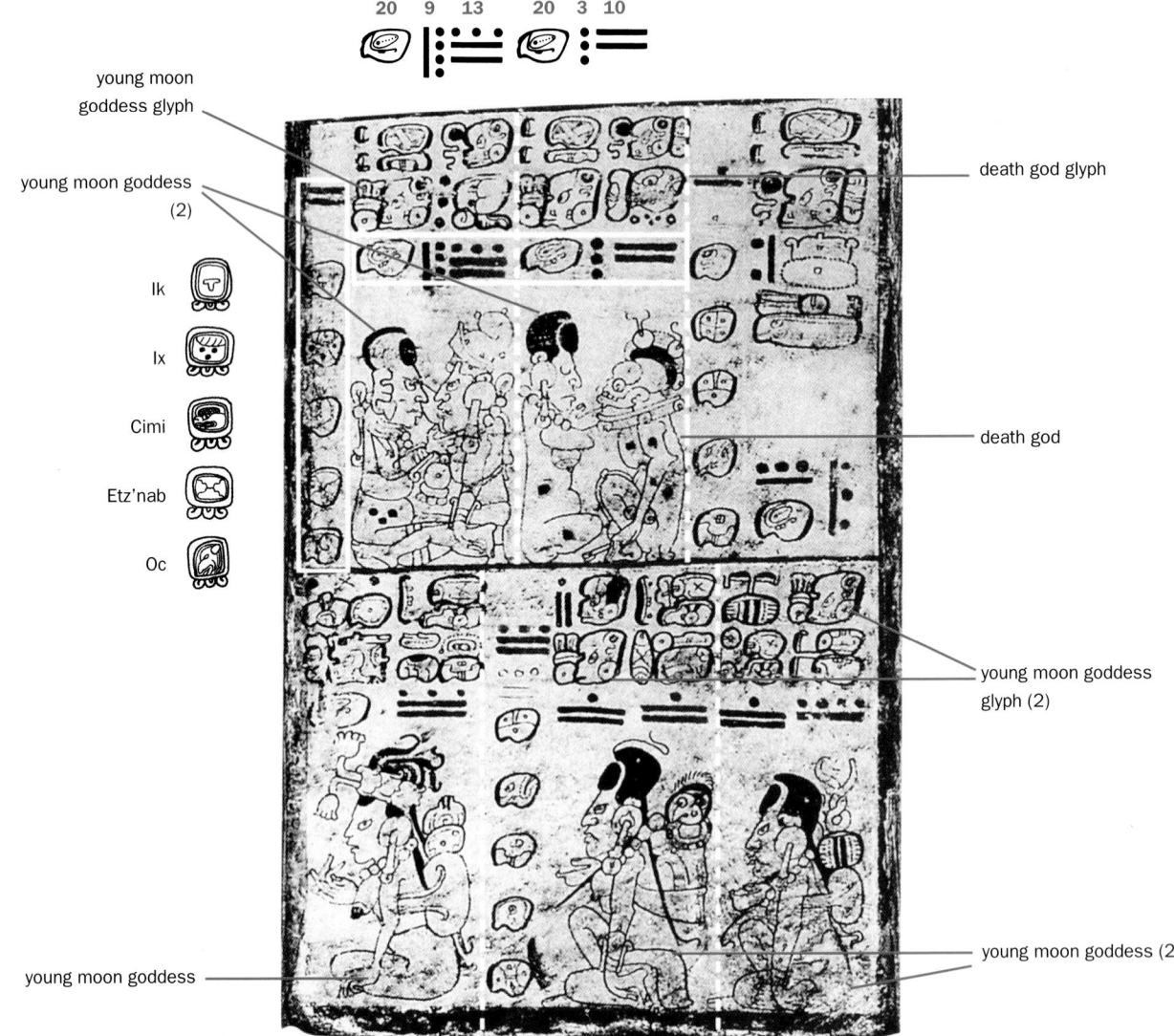

The Dresden Codex is full of dates. It is an almanac for divination, in which each day is linked to other days by complex astronomical calculations (using eclipses and the movements of Venus) and is thereby given an astrological significance – auspicious or otherwise – expressed in the deeds and moods of a bewildering variety of gods, goddesses and half-recognizable deified animals. Each god and goddess is named with a glyph written above his or her portrait. We can think of the codex as being a bit like a strip-cartoon about Maya gods and goddesses. Rather than the captions being written close to the character in a bubble, in the codex they are

generally written above the character. There are also not many dividing lines to tell the reader of the codex that he or she has moved from one picture caption to the next (dotted white lines have been added as a guide, opposite). Five dates have been extracted from the section of the codex opposite, enclosed within the first red box (vertical). The month glyphs have been drawn to show them more clearly. We can make a calculation using the numerals in the second red box (horizontal) to link these dates together.

These numerals connect up 10 Ik, 10 Ix, 10 Cimi, 10 Etz'nab and 10 Oc. We can see this by revolving the two wheels of the 260-day count (see *below*).

We start at 10 Ik. Revolving the wheels in our mind through 20 + 9 = 29 positions (day names), we reach 13 Chuen. Now revolve the wheels again in your mind through 20 + 3 = 23 (day names). You should find that the new date is 10 Ix. 10 Ix is 29 + 23 days after 10 Ik. If we repeat this calculation four more times, we move from 10 Ix to 10 Cimi to 10 Etz'nab to 10 Oc and back to 10 Ik. The almanac therefore covers 5 × 52 = 260 days, a vital number to the Maya.

Stone head and torso of the young maize god, from Copán.

260-day count used for calculating dates in Dresden Codex.

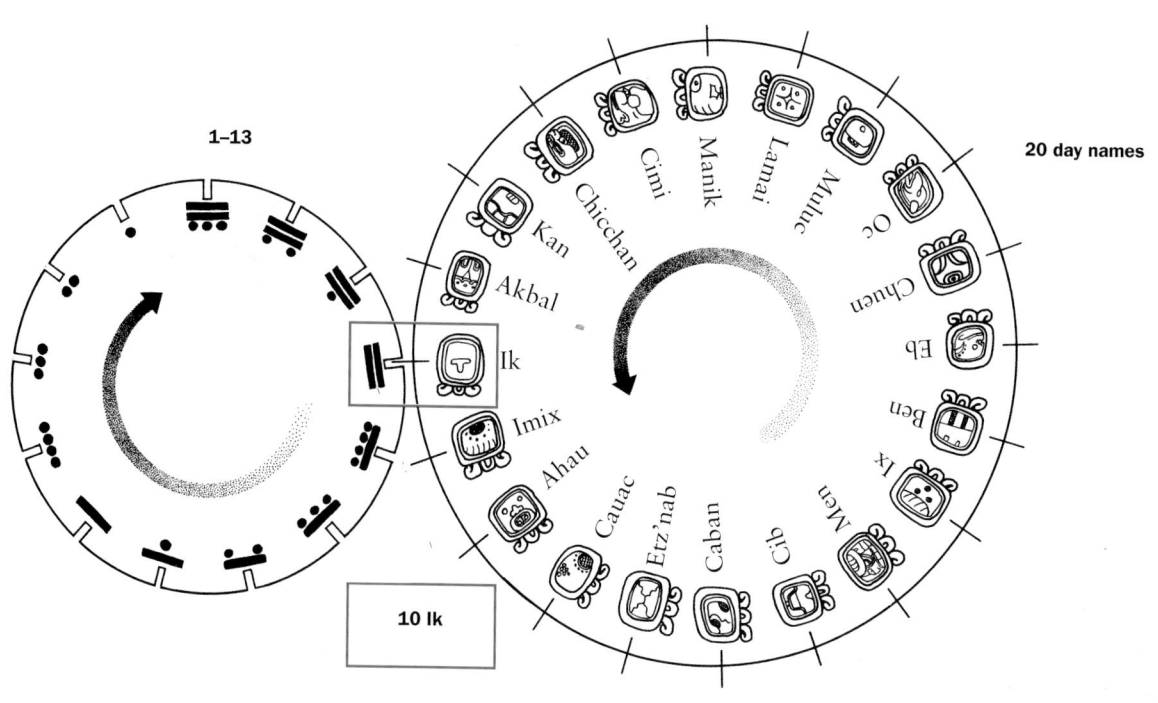

1–13

20 day names

10 Ik

The Mayan 'Alphabet'

The next major step in the decipherment of Mayan glyphs – the realization that they were partially phonetic – dates back to the time of the Spanish Inquisition. One of the ironies of history is that we owe almost all our direct knowledge of the ancient Maya to Spanish inquisitors, who were also responsible for eradicating almost all Mayan writing and many of their customs. The most important inquisitor was Fray Diego de Landa, in Yucatán from 1561 and later bishop of Yucatán. It is Landa's *Relación de las Cosas de Yucatán* (An Account of the Things of Yucatán) – written by Landa in exculpation of charges of excessive zeal brought against him by the Spanish authorities – that contains the Mayan 'alphabet', which proved to be the key to deciphering Mayan glyphs in the 20th century.

Plainly it is no ordinary alphabet, since it contains more than one sign for some letters, as well as syllabic signs. We now know that the 'alphabet' was a mixture of right and wrong interpretations, based on a fundamental misunderstanding. Landa, speaking in Spanish, had interrogated a senior Maya man with whom he was friendly, and neither man had properly understood the other. (The very name Yucatán is derived from 'uic athan' – the phrase spoken to the Spanish 'conquistadores' by the Maya when asked what their land was called: it means 'what do you say, we do not understand you'.) Landa tended to assume that the Maya wrote like 16th-century Spaniards, using an alphabet. For instance, seeing a picture in a codex of a noose around the leg of a deer, and knowing from his knowledge of Yucatec

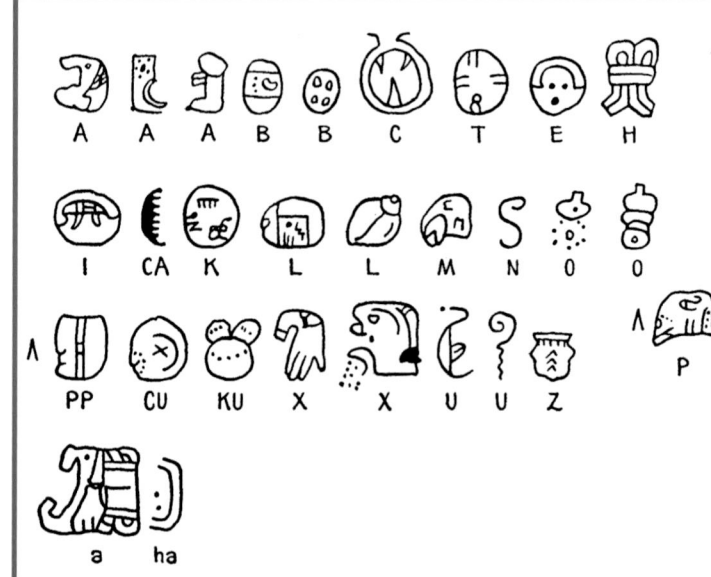

Mayan that 'noose' is pronounced *le* in that language, Landa must have pointed to the drawing and said: 'Kindly show me how you write *le*. It has two letters.' He must then have given the two letters their Spanish names and pronounced the complete word again: '*ele, e: le*'. This must have puzzled his informant, who nevertheless wrote:

 *le*

This in turn must have surprised Landa. How could *four* glyphs be required to spell *two* letters? And why was it necessary to repeat each glyph? The truth was that the writing was basically *syllabic* with an admixture of pure vowels: ☺ had the value *e*, 🖼 had the value *le*. Landa, never having encountered a syllabic writing system, was confused by his evidence, though he obviously understood that some of the glyphs were syllables. He also knew

The Mayan 'alphabet', reproduced from the surviving copy of Diego de Landa's original manuscript.

Fray Diego de Landa (1524–79), bishop of Yucatán from 1572 until his death. Landa is one of the more fascinating figures in the story of Mayan hieroglyphs. He burnt most of the surviving codices, but gave posterity the key to understanding those that remained; he tortured the Maya, but he also loved them, regarding them as moral beings, worthy of salvation – unlike his Catholic superiors, who disallowed torture but regarded the Maya as beyond the pale of civilization. In the late 1560s, Landa had to return to Spain and face charges; he was exonerated, and eventually returned to his beloved Maya as bishop. This portrait of Landa hangs in the cathedral of Izamal in northern Yucatán, where Landa served and where today crowds of Maya, descendants of those tortured by Landa, come to take Holy Communion.

Above left **The building known as 'the Church', Chichén Itzá, Yucatán, one of many remarkable Maya buildings admired by Landa. The central mask of the facade depicts the curled, projecting nose of the rain god Chac.**

hat Mayan consonants could change their meaning depending on whether they were nglottalized or glottalized (that is, whether the throat was unconstricted or not). The ollowing examples are from Yucatec Mayan Coe, 1999):

Unglottalized	Glottalized
'pop' (mat)	'p'op' (to shell squash seeds)
'cutz' (turkey)	'kutz' (tobacco)
'tzul' (to put in order)	'dzul' (foreigner)
'muc' (to bury)	'muk' (to permit)

Landa expressed the contrast by writing ⟨⟩ for *cu*, and ⟨⟩ for *ku*. However, his communication with his informant clearly broke down, as we can see from the following phrase:

ma i n ka ti

which means 'I don't want to' – presumably the informant's response to Landa on being requested to write further sound values of the mysterious glyphs.

Decipherment Begins

Could the Landa 'alphabet' be applied to the glyphs in the Maya codices? During the later 19th century, many attempts to do so were made, some sensible, others nonsensical. The glyphs for certain animals, such as dog, turkey, parrot and jaguar, had been identified by comparing their positions with pictures of these creatures (the same technique had been used to identify the glyphs for gods and goddesses). In 1876, Léon de Rosny applied the Landa alphabet to the first sign in the glyph for 'turkey' in the Madrid Codex:

He read the first sign as *cu*, by comparing it with Landa's:

 cu

He then hazarded a guess that the entire glyph might read *cutz(u)*, since the Yucatec Mayan word for turkey is 'cutz'. Rosny went on to propose that Mayan writing was a phonetic system, based on syllables.

Other scholars produced nonsensical readings, however, and discredited the phonetic approach. Thompson, whom we met earlier (p. 121) and who dominated Maya studies during the middle of the 20th century, rejected Landa's 'alphabet' and phoneticism in Mayan glyphs almost entirely; he favoured a logographic explanation of the glyph for 'dog', for instance, in which one sign represented 'ribs' and the other represented 'death'.

In 1952, this was challenged from an unexpected quarter, Leningrad. Yuri Knorosov, a Russian scholar who had never been near Central America, proposed phonetic readings of many glyphs, including the one for dog. Knorosov noticed that the first sign in the dog glyph was the same as the second sign in the turkey glyph:

Yuri Valentinovich Knorosov (1922–99), the chief initiator of the decipherment of Mayan glyphs. Knorosov was a young artilleryman in the attack on Berlin in 1945; it was a book on the Maya from Berlin's National Library taken to Moscow – the one-volume edition (published in Guatemala in 1933) of the Dresden, Madrid and Paris codices – that sparked Knorosov's interest in Mayan writing. From the 1950s he published important papers on the subject in Russia; but he was unable personally to visit the Maya ruins in Guatemala until 1990. It would take well over a quarter of a century after Knorosov's first Mayan publication in Russian in 1952, before his insights would be generally accepted.

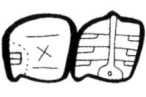

turkey glyph

turkey

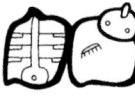

dog glyph

turkey glyph

If the first sign in the dog glyph had the [s]ound value *tzu* (as proposed by Rosny), the [se]cond sign could be assigned the value *l(u)*, [o]n the basis of its resemblance to Landa's [s]ymbol:

 *l*

[H]ence the dog glyph might stand for *tzul*:

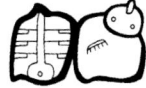

tzu   l(u)

[W]as there a Yucatec word 'tzul'? There was. [I]t meant 'dog'.

Knorosov was able to take this line of [d]ecipherment further. On a certain page of [t]he Dresden Codex, instead of the expected [b]ar and dot numeral for 11, or its equivalent [g]od-face, there appears a glyph consisting of [t]hree signs:

(1 is damaged in the codex)

['E]leven' in Yucatec Mayan is 'buluc'. Could [t]he glyph be made up of *bu*, *lu* and *cu*, as [f]ollows? (*bu* is damaged)

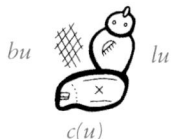

[A] damaged glyph on another page of the [D]resden Codex (*above right*) consisted of [t]wo signs that appeared, from Knorosov's [l]ine of argument, to mean *lub(u)*.

lu *bu*

The word 'lub' in Yucatec Mayan means 'to [f]all' or 'to rain'. The drawing in the codex [s]uggested that the idea might be correct: rain [i]s shown falling on the central character.

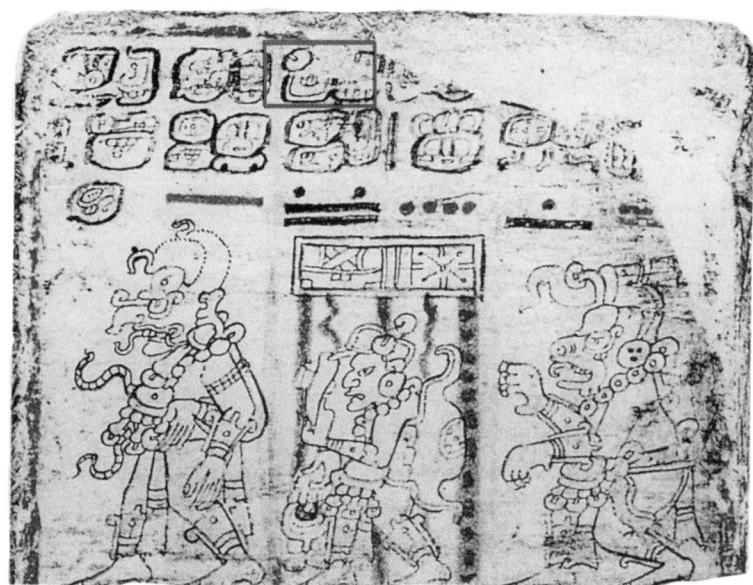

Above **Part of the Dresden Codex. The highlighted glyph means 'to rain'.**

Left **Proposed decipherments of Mayan glyphs by Yuri Knorosov, 1950s. Not all proved correct, but Knorosov's basic approach was sound.**

1.		*c(u).*	11		*cutz*
2.		*tz(u).*	12.		*tzul.*
3.		*l(u)*	13		*buluc*
4.		*b(u)*	14		*can tzuc*
5		*x(a)*	15		*lub*
6		*m(a)*	16		*xati*
7		*t(i)*	17		*xam*
8.		*u*	18.		*uxah*
9.		*h(a)*	19		*pax*
10		*p(a)*	20.		*Mam*

Knorosov produced a series of such decipherments. They were bitterly ridiculed by Thompson, who began a kind of private war against him, taking his tone from the Cold War of the 1950s. But some of the younger Mayanists in the United States decided that Knorosov was onto something important.

A Mixed Writing System

There were two basic kinds of obstacle facing the Mayanists who wanted to follow Knorosov's lead. First, the Mayan languages in the 1950s were not, and still are not, well known to scholars. If a scholar could not locate in the Mayan dictionaries an obviously appropriate word, such as 'cutz' (turkey) or 'tzul' (dog) in Yucatec, there was no way to confirm or reject a proposed decipherment.

Second, there was the mixed character of the writing system, combining phonography and logography. Although Egyptian hieroglyphs were similarly mixed, Mayan hieroglyphs were far more unpredictable; the same word could be written in several ways, not just two or three. Furthermore, the individual glyphs were often 'soldered' together (a feature also found in Chinese writing, though not in Egyptian) – so intimately that the constituent glyphs could only be discerned by a highly trained eye. The problems encountered by Ventris in discriminating between Linear B signs were as nothing compared to the problems faced by would-be decipherers of Mayan glyphs.

Here, for instance, two glyphs spelling 'chum tun' have been conflated in three different ways; all four spellings of the word are acceptable (lower case letters indicate a phonogram, upper case a logogram):

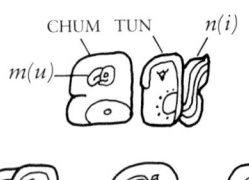

Here are five acceptable spellings of 'balam' (jaguar) showing differing proportions of phonography and logography:

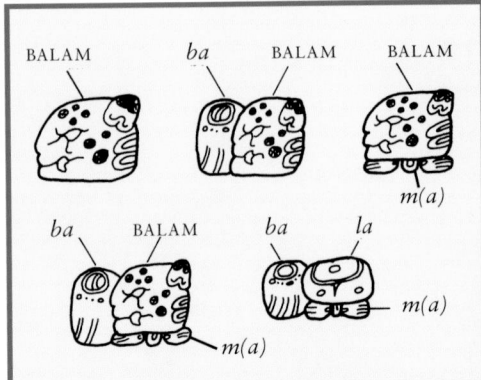

The first is wholly logographic (and pictographic), the last wholly phonographic (and sans pictography).

Below **Stone lintel from Yaxchilán, *c.* 770 AD. The scene shows Bird-Jaguar, wearing a skull and skeletal serpent headdress, and one of his wives, Lady Balam Ix, performing acts of ritual bloodletting. The glyphs describe the scene, as shown in the lintel on the opposite page.**

We can see the mixture of phonographic and logographic elements in a striking relief celebrating a victory of 'Bird-Jaguar' of Yaxchilán (*right*). Bird-Jaguar is on the right, wearing a splendid headdress, and grasping his captive 'Jewelled-Skull' by the arm, while on the left Bird-Jaguar's lieutenant K'an Tok seizes a second captive by the hair. The various glyphs – which are not fully understood – have been labelled.

The date is 7 Imix 14 Tzec (try checking the numerals and the day/month glyphs using the information on pp. 124–7) – which corresponds to 9 May AD 755. Bird-Jaguar is so called, because his glyph combines a bird and a jaguar:

His Mayan name may have been Yaxun Balam. The glyph immediately below his name is the 'emblem' glyph of Yaxchilán. Each Maya city state, generally speaking, had its emblem glyph, discovered in the late 1950s by Heinrich Berlin. Here are eight such glyphs, each of which contains a pair of phonetic signs now known to stand for 'ahaw' (lord):

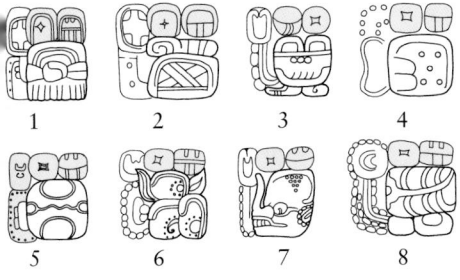

A second pair of signs (marked in 5) stands for Yucatec 'k'ul' (divine).
The sites are:
1. Tikal, 2. Naranjo, 3. Yaxchilán,
4. Piedras Negras, 5. Palenque, 6. Seibal,
7. Copán, 8. Quiriguá (see map on p. 122).

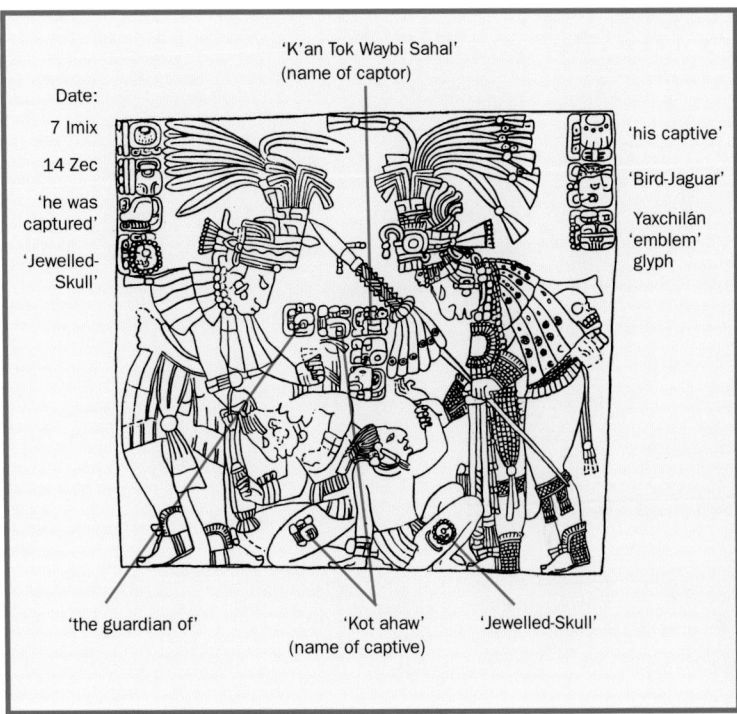

Date:
7 Imix
14 Zec
'he was captured'
'Jewelled-Skull'

'K'an Tok Waybi Sahal' (name of captor)

'his captive'
'Bird-Jaguar'
Yaxchilán 'emblem' glyph

'the guardian of'

'Kot ahaw' (name of captive)

'Jewelled-Skull'

Then there are two words in the Yaxchilán relief spelt purely phonetically:

chu — *h(a)*
ca

chucah(a) (he was captured)

Here, two of the three syllabic signs are found in Landa's 'alphabet':

ca ha

And, second, there is the glyph:

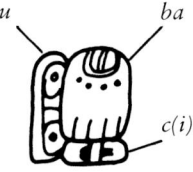

u ba
c(i)

u bac(i) (his captive)

A Mayan Syllabary

Today, more than 50 years after Knorosov's first published decipherment, the work of dozens of scholars, mostly Americans, has yielded the adjacent syllabic chart. Not every glyphic position is universally agreed, but a large proportion is. It is now true that the great majority of the Mayan glyphs can be 'read', in the sense that their meaning can be understood with some precision, if not always the way they were pronounced in Mayan.

The complexity of the Mayan script is evident, even without the hundreds of non-syllabic glyphs. The most obvious feature of the chart is the large number of variant signs for a single sound, for instance thirteen glyphs for the pure vowel *u* and six glyphs for the syllable *na*. There is nothing comparable in the Linear B syllabary (p. 118); without Landa's 'alphabet' to help the decipherment, no one would have had a chance to create this Mayan equivalent of the Linear B 'grid'. Moreover, besides their homophony, some syllabic signs can also act as logograms.

The degree of homophony built into the system is indicated by three different glyphs, all pronounced *can* in Yucatec Mayan (the phonetic elements in the first and third of these are noted):

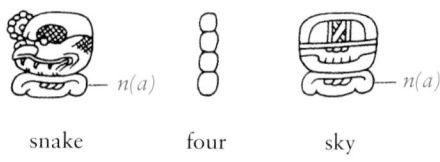

snake   four   sky

The degree of polyphony, by contrast, i.e. one sign with several different pronunciations, is shown by the following three glyphs:

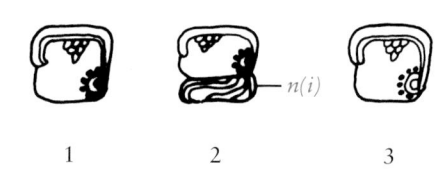

1   2   3

1 is Cauac, a day name, 2 has the phonetic complement *n(i)* and is pronounced *tun*, 3 is the syllable *cu*.

Right This syllabic chart, representing the combined work of many scholars since the 1950s, is still in the process of change. Blanks indicate syllables for which no glyph has yet been discovered. (Based on Coe and Van Stone, 2001)

Below Painted design on a ceramic cylinder vase, Guatemala, *c.* 672–830, showing artists with their tools (stylus and shell paint pot). One paints a codex, the other holds a mask. Glyphic texts in front of each figure indicate the names and/or titles of the artists.

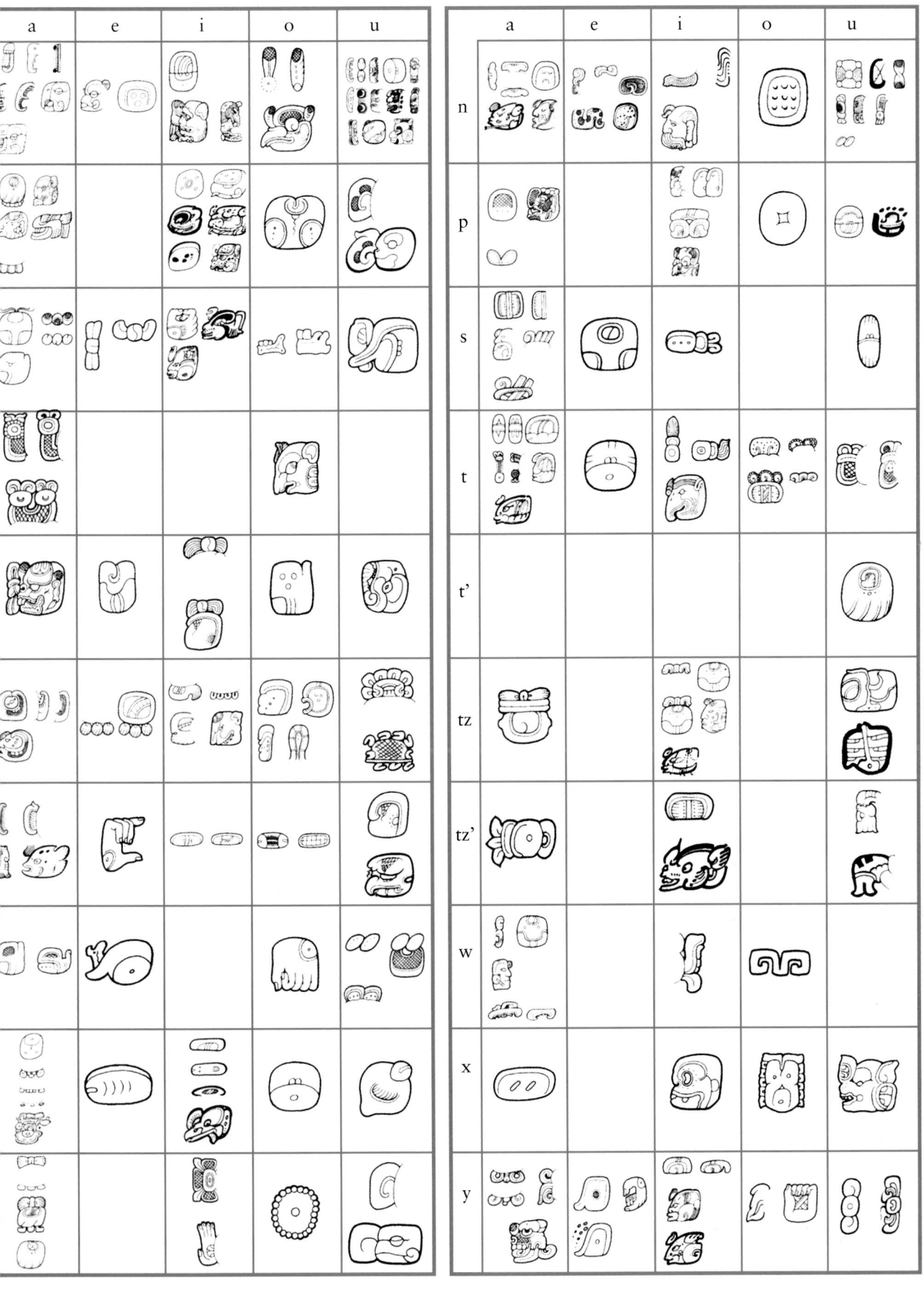

A Maya 'Tutankhamun'

An archaeological discovery that in due course provided one of the breakthroughs in the decipherment of the Mayan script took place in 1952. It can almost stand comparison with the discovery of the tomb of Tutankhamun. The Mexican archaeologist Alberto Ruz was investigating the Temple of the Inscriptions at Palenque, when he came across a large stone slab in the floor with a double row of holes provided with removable stone stoppers; removing it, he saw a vaulted stairway leading down into the interior of the pyramid, but deliberately choked with rubble. It took him four field seasons to clear the stairway and reach a chamber on about the same level as the base of the pyramid, which was also filled with rubble; on its floor he found the skeletons of five or six young adults, probably all sacrifices. At its far end, the way was blocked by a huge triangular slab. When this too was finally removed, Ruz gazed into the great funerary crypt, about 80 ft (24 m) below the floor of the upper temple. He was the first person to see it for some 13 centuries.

A giant rectangular sarcophagus cover concealed the remains of an ancient Maya ruler. Inside was a treasure-trove of jade with the corpse: a life-sized mosaic mask of jade lay over the ruler's face, jade and mother-of-pearl discs served as ear spools, several necklaces of tubular jade beads festooned the chest, and the fingers were adorned with jade rings. In each hand and in the mouth was a large jade – a custom documented for the late Yucatec Maya, the Aztecs and the Chinese. Two jade figures, one representing the sun god, lay beside the ruler.

The carving on the sarcophagus shows the ruler (who is clearly club-footed) falling down the great trunk of the World Tree from the celestial bird (symbolizing heaven) into the open jaws of the Otherworld. As he falls, he is accompanied by the image of a half-skeletal monster carrying a bowl of sacrifice marked with the glyph of the sun. The glyph represents the sun in transition between life and death. Like the sun, the king will rise again in the east after his journey through the Otherworld.

Right **Pacal's sarcophagus cover, funerary crypt, Temple of the Inscriptions, Palenque, discovered in 1952.**

Below **Lifesize jade mosaic mask from the funerary crypt, Temple of the Inscriptions, Palenque, AD 683. The eyes are made from shell and obsidian. The wooden backing has rotted away.**

The Birth and Death of Pacal

1 2 3 4 5 6 7 8

pa

ca

la

Who was this great Maya ruler of Palenque? Eight glyphs carved along one edge of the sarcophagus give a partial explanation. They include various numerals, day names and month names: try working them out.

1 is the date 8 Ahau.

2 is the date 13 Pop.

3 is the glyph signifying birth (nicknamed the 'up-ended frog'). So the ruler was born on 8 Ahau 13 Pop, which, when correlated with the 'Long Count', is 26 March AD 603.

4 is the date 6 Etz'nab.

5 is the date 11 Yax.

6 refers to 4 cycles of 7200 days in the 'Long Count', i.e. about 80 years.

7 is a glyph signifying death. So the ruler died on 8 Ahau 13 Pop, that is 31 August AD 683.

8 is the name of the ruler, known as 'Hand Shield', derived pictographically from the sign at bottom right in the ruler's glyph.

But what did the Maya ruler call himself? A clue came from a glyph in the temple up above the funerary crypt. From its context, the glyph was clearly the name of the ruler buried beneath, yet it was quite different from the glyph on the sarcophagus. In 1973, scholars meeting at Palenque suddenly realized that the name glyph on the sarcophagus was *logographic*, while that in the temple was *phonographic*. The glyph in the temple could be translated as shown on the right (refer to the syllabary on p. 137). So the Maya 'Tutankhamun' was called Pacal (which means 'shield').

Here are three variant spellings of Pacal's name, with the phonetic elements indicated by lower-case letters:

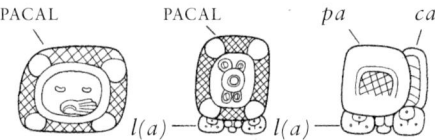

PACAL   PACAL   pa   ca

l(a) —   l(a) —

If the inscription tells the truth – which obviously cannot be taken for granted – Pacal was 80 years old when he died. From other glyphs we can tell that he was only 12 years old when he came to the throne; Pacal therefore ruled for some 68 years – longer than Queen Victoria. We can also identify the names of Pacal's father Kan-Bahlum-Mo' and his mother Lady Zac-Kuk, and other relatives. Intriguingly, his father never ruled (dying on 1 January AD 643), while his mother did briefly rule, from 612 until her son's accession in 615 (she died on 12 September 640). Here at Palenque, and at other Maya sites, the decipherment has given the Maya a detailed dynastic history, of which the world was totally unaware just a few decades ago.

**Edge of the
sarcophagus of Pacal
(AD 603–83):**
his life and death in
glyphs (transcribed
opposite).

1

2

3

4

5

6

7

8

The Murals of Bonampak

The second great post-war Maya archaeological discovery was that of the murals of Bonampak, not far from Yaxchilán. Two American adventurers who had been living with Lacandón Indians were taken to the ruins of Bonampak in 1946; a few months later the Indians showed the murals to the photographer Giles Healey, who published photographs that caused a sensation. For scholars, the interest of the murals lies less in what they tell us about Mayan writing than in what they show of life among the Classic Maya in the late 8th century AD, just before the Maya civilization collapsed. Some glyphs in the murals are yet to be deciphered.

The murals show a single narrative, a story of a successful battle, its aftermath, and the victory celebrations. In the scene below, the miserable prisoners have been stripped, and are being tortured by having their fingernails pulled; nearby lies a severed head. A naked figure seated on the summit of the platform pleads with the central figure, the great lord Chaan-muan, ruler of Bonampak, who is clad in a jaguar-skin battle jacket and surrounded by subordinates arrayed in gorgeous costume. One of the spectators is a lady in a white robe, carrying a folding screen fan in her hand; she is Chaan-muan's principal wife, identified as coming from Yaxchilán by the glyphic text.

The Bonampak murals, 8th century AD, were never completed, because Bonampak was abandoned. They seem to have been painted in connection with the consecration of a little male heir to the throne of Yaxchilán, with ritual battles, torture and decapitation, mummery, dancing, music and the shedding of blood by noble lords and ladies. Presumably all the ceremony was in vain.

A Maya Chocolate Cup

Of all the weird and wonderful art produced by the Maya, their ceramic paintings are perhaps the most appealing. In the last few decades, many specimens have been looted from Maya sites and passed to art dealers in America, Europe and elsewhere. A good effect of this trade, however, has been to help the decipherment of Mayan glyphs.

In 1971, the Mayanist Michael Coe was organizing an exhibition of Maya ceramics in New York when he noticed that the sequence of glyphs around the rim of many pots was similar. Coe termed it the Primary Standard Sequence and hazarded that it referred to Maya mythical adventures in the Otherworld, like those in the Egyptian Book of the Dead, since these appeared to be the subject matter of much of the art on the ceramics and since, in addition, the purpose of the ceramics was thought to be funerary.

In fact the sequence turned out to have a rather different meaning. One of the Primary Standard Sequence's commonest glyphs occurs in this order:

Phonetic decipherment suggests that the glyph means *uch'ibi*:

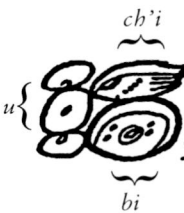

In Cholan Mayan, *uchi'i* means 'to drink'. The glyph therefore probably means, 'the drinking cup of'. It begins to look as if Maya nobles, like some people today, wanted their drinking mugs name-tagged.

Further decipherment was even more revealing. The Primary Standard Sequence includes the following glyph, in which phonetic values can be substituted with a little imagination:

Cacao! And when scrapings from Maya pots bearing this glyph were submitted to the Hershey Foods Corporation, the answer came back that the residues were indeed the chemical remains of cacao.

Maya ceramic vessel from Rio Azul, Guatemala. The glyph in the centre stands for cacao. Chemical tests have confirmed the presence of cacao residues at the bottom of the pot. In the words of Diego de Landa, the first European to study the Maya: 'They make of ground maize and cacao a kind of foaming drink which is very savoury, and with which they celebrate their feasts. And they get from cacao a grease which resembles butter, and from this and maize they make another beverage which is very savoury and highly thought of.' It is fitting that Landa's 'alphabet', written down in the 1560s, should in the late 20th century help to confirm the accuracy of Landa's account of Maya civilization.

Chapter 8   *Undeciphered Scripts*

This stone seal is from the Indus Valley civilization that flourished in northwest India and what is now Pakistan some four millennia ago. It is one of many such seals, bearing signs that are probably full writing. No one can say for certain, because no one has been able to decipher the meaning of the signs. The Indus script is perhaps the most intriguing of the many scripts from all parts of the world and almost all periods that remain undeciphered.

Difficulties of Decipherment

The major undeciphered scripts are listed in the table below. They are distinguished from other undeciphered scripts by the fact that they are associated with a culture that is of clear significance. Thus the Etruscan script was used by a people who produced works of art and funerary monuments of beauty, and who strongly influenced the Romans; the Linear A script of Crete was used by the Minoans, prior to and contemporaneous with the Linear B script deciphered by Michael Ventris; and the 'Rongorongo' script of Easter Island (Rapanui) may have been used by the sculptors of the celebrated giant stone statues scattered over the island. By contrast, the few undeciphered signs found in an excavation in Romania in 1961, known as the Tartaria tablets, have not attracted comparable attention – at least partly because the other products of the excavation have not been very striking.

The Definition of 'Deciphered'

Of course many scripts are neither undeciphered nor deciphered, rather they are partially deciphered. This is true of Hittite hieroglyphs and the Mayan script, as we have seen, of the Linear B script, and even of Egyptian hieroglyphs – in increasing degree of decipherment.

Undeciphered scripts may be resolved into three basic categories: an unknown script writing a known language, a known script writing an unknown language, and an unknown script writing an unknown language. Mayan writing was until recently an example of the first category; Etruscan writing is an example of the second; and the Indus Valley and Rongorongo scripts are examples of the last category.

Ventris gave the following masterly summary of decipherment techniques in general. 'Each operation needs to be planned in three phases: an exhaustive *analysis* of the signs, words and contexts in all the available inscriptions, designed to extract every possible clue as to the spelling system, meaning and language structure; an experimental *substitution* of phonetic values to give possible words and inflections in a known or postulated language; and a decisive *check*, preferably with the aid of virgin material, to ensure that the apparent results are not due to fantasy, coincidence or circular reasoning . . . Prerequisites are that the material should be large enough for the analysis to yield usable results, and (in the case of an unreadable script without bilinguals or identifiable proper names) that the concealed language should be related to one which we already know.'

Major undeciphered scripts. An asterisk * indicates cases in which there is no scholarly consensus on the nature of the script and/or its underlying language.

Name of script	Where found	Earliest known	Script known?	Language known?
Proto-Elamite	Iran/Iraq	c. 3000 BC	Partially	No
Indus	Pakistan/N.W. India	c. 2500 BC	No	*
'Pseudo-hieroglyphic'	Byblos (Lebanon)	2nd mill. BC	No	No
Linear A	Crete	18th cent. BC	Partially	No
Phaistos Disc	Phaistos (Crete)	18th cent. BC	No	No
Etruscan	N. Italy	8th cent. BC	Yes	Partially
Zapotec	Mesoamerica	c. 600 BC	Partially	Partially
Meroïtic	Meroë (Sudan)	c. 200 BC	Yes	Partially
Isthmian	Mesoamerica	c. AD 150	*	*
Rongorongo	Easter Island	pre-19th cent. AD	No	No

Seal Secrets of the Indus

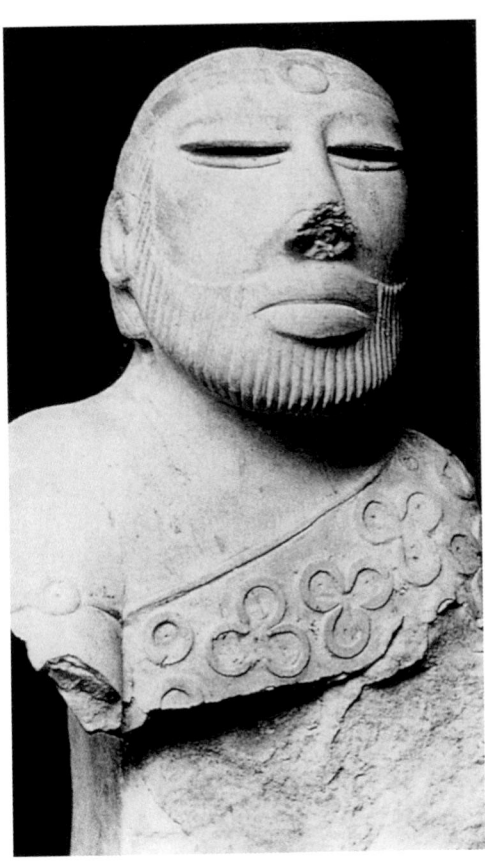

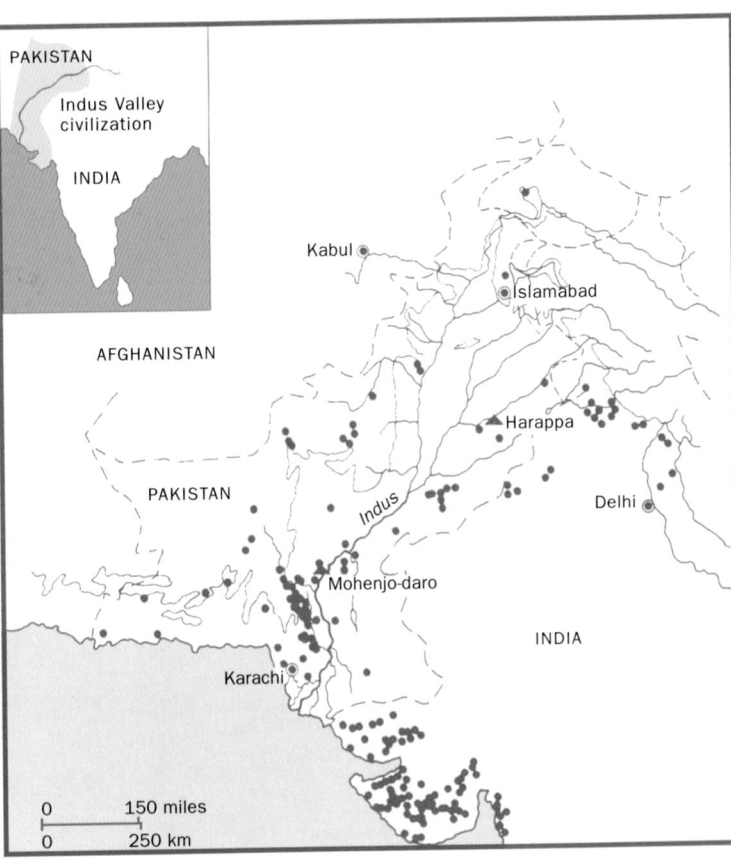

The six-inch (15-cm) steatite sculpture shown here, known as the 'priest-king', was discovered in the early 1920s on the banks of the river Indus, at a ruin mound called Mohenjo-daro, in what is now Pakistan. Nothing is known about his identity and significance, though the trefoil designs on his garment are assumed to have an astral meaning. The object is perhaps 4000 years old – predating the invasion of India by Alexander by nearly two millennia – and is the most famous surviving object from the Indus Valley civilization.

The remains of this civilization cover an area of Pakistan and northwest India approximately a quarter the size of Europe. At its peak, between 2500 and 1900 BC, its major cities could be compared with those of contemporary Mesopotamia and Egypt. They cannot boast great pyramids, statues and hordes of gold, but their well-planned streets and advanced drainage put to shame all but the town planning of the 20th century. Yet prior to 1921, no one had even suspected the existence of such a civilization in India.

As far back as the 1870s, though, archaeologists had been aware of an undeciphered script from the Indus area. Since the 1920s scholars of many nationalities have attempted a decipherment.

The extent of the Indus civilization. The map is based on archaeological finds showing a clear commonality of culture. Mohenjo-daro and Harappa, the two chief cities, are highlighted.

Above left **The 'priest-king' of the Indus civilization, discovered at Mohenjo-daro in the 1920s.**

The Indus Script

The Indus script appears not on walls, tombs, statues, clay tablets and papyri, but on seal stones, terracotta sealings, pottery, copper tablets, bronze implements and ivory and bone rods, found scattered in the houses and streets of Mohenjo-daro and other urban settlements. About 3500 inscriptions are known, most of them on seal stones.

The inscriptions are tantalizingly brief: the average has less than four signs in a line and five signs in a text, the longest inscription is only 20 signs in three lines on the sides of two terracotta prisms. In addition to the signs, many seal stones are incised with an outline of animals, which are often recognizable – rhinoceroses, elephants, tigers, buffaloes, for instance – and also include a one-horned animal, a 'unicorn', and some unidentified anthropomorphic figures that may be gods and goddesses. Some scholars have suggested that these figures are precursors of the Hindu deities.

Deciphering the Indus Script

Any attempt to decipher the Indus script has to begin with two considerations. Do the signs themselves yield to analysis, in the way that Kober, Ventris and others established patterns in Linear B? And can we guess the language underlying the signs (Greek in the case of Linear B)?

To begin with the signs themselves, we might look for resemblances with the scripts of other cultures, as Ventris compared Linear B with the Cypriot script. Caution is necessary, because such resemblances can occur accidentally. In fact there is no resemblance at all between the Indus signs and the signs of ancient Iran, Sumer and Egypt. There is, however, a striking resemblance between 40–50 Indus signs and signs from – of all unexpected places – Easter Island.

Sir John Marshall, who excavated Mohenjo-daro, speculated that the cross-legged figure surrounded by animals (*below*) was 'proto-Shiva' – Shiva being one of the most important gods in the (later) Hindu pantheon. The presence of stars and a fig branch in the headdress of the second figure, and the adjacent fish signs, may also be connected – but any 'decipherment' can at best be tentative.

These signs from Easter Island (above right) are of unknown age, possibly a mere two centuries old. Is it conceivable that the Indus signs (above left) were transmitted over 3500 years and across 13,000 miles of ocean from the Indus to an isolated island in the Pacific? A few scholars in the 1930s seriously thought so, but today the idea seems incredible. Most of the Indus script appears on seals (below). Some of their images are easy to grasp; others, such as these two figures sitting in a yogic posture, are puzzling.

Sign Number and Direction of Writing

Can we establish how many Indus signs there are? To attempt this means to decide whether the following three signs are variants of the same sign or different signs:

Scholars disagree on such details, but nevertheless agree that there are about 400 signs in all (plus or minus 25 signs). This is too many signs for an alphabet or syllabary (such as Linear B), and so the Indus script is likely to be a 'mixed' script like the scripts of Mesopotamia and Egypt.

Which way was it written, from left to right or right to left? We can be nearly sure that it was usually written from right to left, because we come across 'overflow' of signs on the next line, always on the left, cramping of signs for lack of space towards the left, and signs written on the top, left and bottom edges of a seal, leaving the right edge blank.

The Language of the Indus Script

What did the Indus Valley dwellers sound like? There are three possibilities. First, their language might have died out altogether. Second, it may be related to Sanskrit, the classical language of India. Third, it may be related to Dravidian, the family of languages that preceded Sanskrit and which are now spoken in south India and, intriguingly, in the mountain valleys and plateaux of Baluchistan and Afghanistan not far from the Indus Valley (the language is known as Brahui). The Dravidian hypothesis seems the most likely of the last two, because Sanskrit descends from the language of the Aryans who invaded India, probably in two waves between 1900 and 1700 BC, and conquered the pre-existent Indus Valley civilization.

The Aryans never penetrated to south India, thus allowing the region to preserve its own languages, which (it is postulated) are related to that of the Indus dwellers.

If the Dravidian hypothesis is correct, it might be possible to match words from the old form of Tamil, a Dravidian language spoken in today's Madras, with suitable Indus signs. A very common Indus sign is the fish. The old Tamil word for fish is 'mīn'. But 'mīn' has another meaning too – 'star' or 'planet'. Could the fish sign be a rebus signifying an astral name? The occurrence of fish signs with stars and anthropomorphic images (see seal on previous page) supports this interpretation, as does Indus Valley pottery in which fishes and stars are adjacent:

The fish also sometimes appears with six strokes before it in the script, indicating '(constellation) of six stars', i.e. the Pleiades, known as 'aru-mīn' in the most ancient Dravidian texts.

We are still a very long way from a decipherment of the Indus script. Asko Parpola, the leading scholar and would-be Ventris of the Indus script, wrote in 1994: 'Many of the signs of the Indus script are so simplified and schematic that it is very difficult to understand their pictorial meaning unambiguously and objectively. Another drawback is the scantiness of the material . . . It looks most unlikely that the Indus script will ever be deciphered fully, unless radically different source material becomes available.'

Cretan Linear A

Along with the Linear B tablets at Knossos, Sir Arthur Evans discovered two other scripts in Crete (as mentioned earlier): a 'hieroglyphic' script, and the Linear A script. The 'hieroglyphic' signs are almost all found on seal stones and sealings, rarely are they incised in clay; Linear A, by contrast, is found mainly on clay tablets – many fewer of them than of Linear B tablets. The hieroglyphic script is undoubtedly the older of the two, occurring as early as 1900 BC; Linear A probably evolved from it and lasted until the collapse of the Minoan civilization in the 15th century BC. Linear A was the script of that civilization, including the Minoan overseas possessions in the southern Aegean, while Linear B was the script used by the Greeks and Minoans after the Greek conquest of Knossos and other parts of Crete. Linear A was used to write Minoan; Linear B, of course, wrote Greek.

There is undoubtedly a close relationship between Linear A and Linear B, but it is not a clear one. The Linear A signs strongly resemble those of the later Linear B. Can the sound values of Linear B be applied to Linear A signs? Only with caution. It is reasonable to expect that Linear B is a script borrowed from Linear A, with some changes, in order to write Greek rather than Minoan. We can substitute the sound values of Linear B in a Linear A inscription, and obtain words – but since we do not know the Minoan language, we cannot be sure if the words are correct or not.

We can, however, be definite that the language behind Linear A is not Greek. This emerges from a tablet such as the one above.

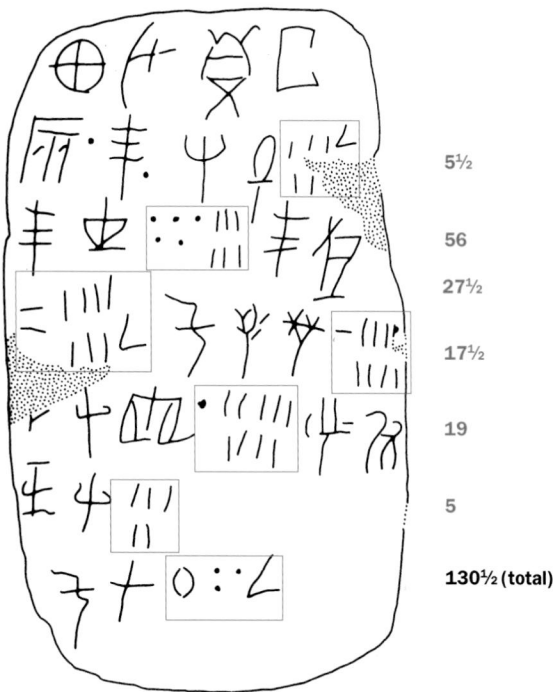

	5½
	56
	27½
	17½
	19
	5
	130½ (total)

The first line is probably a place name. The second line begins (on the left) with a sign identical to the Linear B logogram for 'wine', followed by an unknown sign that may mean 'paid out' or 'issued'. Then come six words, each followed by a numeral: these are probably personal names, each associated with a quantity of wine. The numerals, which follow the same system as in Linear B, add up to 130½ (the numeral in the last line), preceded by two signs which regularly appear in this position and may mean 'total'. On the Linear B tablets, the 'totalling' signs are different and translate as 'to-so', a recognizably Greek word. But if we substitute the Linear B values for the two signs in Linear A, the word that emerges is 'ku-ro', which *cannot* be related to any Greek word of suitable meaning.

'Hieroglyphs' from Crete published by Arthur Evans. This is the earliest known script on Crete, from which Linear A appears to have developed; neither script has been deciphered.

The Phaistos Disc

The Phaistos disc. It is about 6¼ in (16 cm) in diameter and about ½ in (1.2 cm) thick. There is a total of 242 signs either stamped or punched on the two faces, arranged into 61 groups demarcated into boxes by lines. It appears that the signs were written from the outer edge, and spiral inwards in a clockwise direction.

The greatest puzzle among the scripts of ancient Crete is the unique Phaistos disc. It was discovered in 1908 by an Italian excavator in the ruins of a palace at Phaistos in southern Crete, in an archaeological context suggesting that the date of the disc was not later than about 1700 BC – in other words contemporary with Linear A. It is made of baked clay and on either side is an inscription, which consists of signs impressed on the wet clay with a punch or stamp. The Phaistos disc is there-fore 'the world's first typewritten document', in the words of John Chadwick, the collaborator of Michael Ventris.

But why should anyone have bothered to produce a punch/stamp, rather than inscribing each sign afresh as in Linear A and B? If it was to 'print' many copies of documents, then why have no other documents in this script been found in some 100 years of excavation? And why do the signs on the Phaistos disc fail to resemble any of the signs of the 'hieroglyphic' script, Linear A or Linear B? Could the disc have been imported into Crete? Could it be a fake? There are very few clues as to the meaning of the script, and no reliable answers. The signs themselves are of little help since they resemble no other Minoan signs, are few in number and enigmatic in appearance; and the language behind the signs is a total unknown. The context of discovery is of no help either, since only one sample of the script exists. The only hope of a decipherment is for a cache of similar inscriptions to be found. Until then, the frequent attempts at decipherment (many of them cranky) are pointless, said Chadwick. 'We must curb our impatience, and admit that if King Minos himself were to reveal to someone in a dream the true interpretation, it would be quite impossible for him to convince anyone else that his was the one and only possible solution.'

Proto-Elamite

lamite, the language of ancient Elam, an area that corresponds very roughly with today's Iranian oil fields, is one of the three languages written in cuneiform in the Behistun inscription of Darius (see p. 76–9). Some two and a half millennia before this, a quasi-pictographic script was used to write the language of Elam; it is known as proto-Elamite and is as yet undeciphered. Clay tablets written in proto-Elamite have been found in Susa, the ancient capital of Elam, but they also occur as far east as the Iranian border with Afghanistan. They are roughly contemporaneous with the earliest Sumerian tablets from Uruk.

It may be that the proto-Elamite script was invented on the Iranian plateau, or it could have been borrowed from the city-dwellers of Mesopotamia. We do not know.

A substantial body of proto-Elamite writing is available, but despite intense study there has been little progress apart from the deciphering of the complex numerical system. The Elamite language of the Behistun inscription has proved absolutely resistant to comparison with other languages – and the same is true, *a fortiori*, of the attempts to reconstruct the language of the proto-Elamite inscriptions.

Left **Biscript dedication in Akkadian cuneiform and linear Elamite, from Susa, *c.* 2200 BC.**
The cuneiform identifies the dedicator as Puzur-Insusinak. Linear Elamite is more than half a millennium younger than proto-Elamite. Some linear Elamite signs can be read with certainty, but the connection between the two scripts is unresolved.

Below left **A proto-Elamite clay tablet from Susa, *c.* 3000 BC. The significance of the signs is largely unknown.**

Below **Proto-Elamite settlements on the Iranian plateau, with tablet finds marked. (After Lamberg-Karlowsky)**

Greek but not Greek: Etruscan

The Etruscans were the principal intermediaries between the Greeks and non-Greeks, or 'barbarians', of the west. The Greeks first settled in Italy in about 775 BC, at Pithekoussai (modern Ischia). The Phoenicians were already established in western Sicily and Sardinia, and were commercially and politically allied with the Etruscans. Phoenician influence on the Etruscans was important, but Greek culture was paramount. Later the Etruscans transmitted it, including the alphabet, to the neighbouring Latins. By the 1st century BC, the Etruscans had been absorbed into the Roman empire and ceased to exist as a separate people, though Etruscan families and traditions survived in Rome. In AD 408, when Alaric, king of the Goths, threatened to destroy Rome, some Etruscan priests recited prayers and incantations; but Rome was still sacked. This was the last time that the Etruscan language was spoken.

Close study of Latin vocabulary shows that many words were originally Etruscan. Most were connected with luxurious living and higher culture, including writing. Four examples to do with writing are 'elementum' (letter of the alphabet), 'litterae', writing (derived from Greek 'diphthera', skin, a material on which people wrote), 'stilus', writing implement, and 'cera', wax (for wax tablets on which to take notes).

The Etruscan Language and Script

Unfortunately, most of the Etruscan language is completely unknown. Efforts have been made to link it with every European language, and languages such as Hebrew and Turkish, but it remains stubbornly isolated. This is particularly ironic, because the language was faithfully written in the Greek alphabet. We can easily read the 13,000 or so Etruscan inscriptions scattered over central Italy, but we cannot understand much of what they say – which is, in any case, often limited to the names of people and places, and dates. Deciphering Etruscan in this way is like trying to learn English by reading only gravestones.

A good example is the bilingual discovered in 1964 at Pyrgi, a major Etruscan seaport 25 miles (40 km) west of Rome. The date of these gold plaques is about 500 BC. The plaque on the left is in the Phoenician script, the one on the right in the Etruscan/Greek script. They are thank offerings from an Etruscan ruler to a goddess, marking his third year on the throne; each bears the same message, but the translation is not word-for-word. In fact the discovery of the bilingual added only one word to the known Etruscan vocabulary: 'ci', the number three.

Right Gold plaques from Pyrgi, *c.* 500 BC. The plaque on the left is written in Phoenician, the one on the right is in the Etruscan/Greek script. The Greeks borrowed the alphabetic principle from the Phoenicians and then gave it to the Etruscans, including the signs of the alphabet.

Ancient Italy and its peoples, 8th–6th centuries BC.

Etruscan Inscriptions

The Etruscans took over the alphabet of the Greeks, but they did not in practice use four of the letters; similarly, Italian children learn the signs 'k', 'j', 'w' and 'y', which never appear in Italian words. We can use the Etruscan alphabet to read engraved gems, such as:

Hercle = Hercules   *Achle* = Achilles

We can also use the alphabet to read the inscriptions on the backs of mirrors. There are about 3000 mirrors in all, many of them carrying inscriptions in bronze; one example is drawn above. Moving from right to left,

the figures are: Menle (Menelaos), Uthste (Odysseus), Clutmsta (Clytemnestra), Palmithe written Talmithe (Palamedes). By placing these characters together, was the Etruscan artist illustrating some unknown version of the myths of the Trojan War – or were these characters simply stock figures labelled with names favoured by the craftsmen of the time? Judging from the large number of mirrors that survive, 'mass production' of certain models is quite likely.

This is not true of the impressive sarcophagi of wealthy Etruscans. The one shown here, belonging to a late period, when the Etruscans had become part of the Roman empire, carries the inscription:

seianti hanunia tlesnasa

The first letter of Hanunia looks like a θ (theta), but is in fact a ⊟ . This is the family name, judging from the existence of six other inscriptions mentioning Hanunia, all from the same vicinity. Regrettably, as usual with an Etruscan inscription, that is all we learn about the Etruscan language: three names.

Left **This Etruscan mirror from the 3rd century BC shows four figures from the story of the Trojan War.**

Below **Terracotta sarcophagus, from Chiusi, *c.* 150 BC. When the skeleton inside was analysed in 1989, the woman was found to have been at least 80 years old.**

Rongorongo

Rongorongo means 'chants or recitations' in the language of Easter Island. It has also been applied to the script of Easter Island, inscribed on wooden boards and tablets, which was, it seems, chanted while being read. There are 29 examples of the script on pieces of wood scattered around the world's museums, and these contain over 14,000 'glyphs', engraved with a shark's tooth, a flake of obsidian, or a sharpened bird bone. The signs are mostly stylized outlines of objects or creatures, with (according to one scholar) some 120 basic elements, combined to form between 1500 and 2000 compound signs.

There are two basic questions to be asked about the Rongorongo script, which remain unanswered. Is it really writing? And more importantly, did the islanders invent it unprompted, or did they bring it from another country such as Peru or China (even the Indus Valley civilization has been put forward as a possible source, remember), or invent it after the visit of Europeans to Easter Island in 1770, having seen European writing? If the writing did exist before the Europeans came, then Easter Island would be unique among the islands of Polynesia. Were independent invention to be proved, it would enormously strengthen the position of those who believe in *origins* – as opposed to *an* origin – of writing.

The evidence is inconclusive. The last Easter Islanders who knew how to read the script properly were apparently taken away in Peruvian slave raids in 1862. When, in the 1860s and 1870s, Bishop Jaussen of Tahiti persuaded an islander to chant some Rongorongo texts for him and translate

Rongorongo board from Easter Island, date unknown. The square board was obtained by Bishop Jaussen of Tahiti in 1868 and is now in the Congregation of the Sacred Heart, in Rome. The signs cannot be read, but we do know the direction of writing: boustrophedon, in which the reader had to turn the board through 180 degrees at the end of each line. This rare feature of the script is also found on the Tiahuanaco 'Gateway of the Sun' in Peru – which has prompted speculation about a Peruvian origin of the Easter Island script. Other suggestions include China, Sumatra, New Zealand, and even the Indus Valley civilization (see p. 147). The archaeological evidence, however, overwhelmingly supports human colonization of Easter Island from the west, from Polynesia.

them, the results were full of inaccuracies (the bishop's Rongorongo dictionary lists five different signs for 'porcelain', a material unknown on Easter Island!). There are echoes here of Diego de Landa, bishop of Yucatán, interrogating his Maya informant three centuries before, in order to write down his Mayan 'alphabet'.

Most probably, Rongorongo is a developed form of proto-writing, involving both phonetic and logographic elements, in which the signs were as much cues to the memory of the chanter, as conventional symbols for 'full' writing. In the judgment of a group of Russian scholars, among them Yuri Knorosov who led the decipherment of the Mayan glyphs, Rongorongo 'may be compared with the ancient Egyptian hieroglyphs at an early stage of their development.'

LIVING

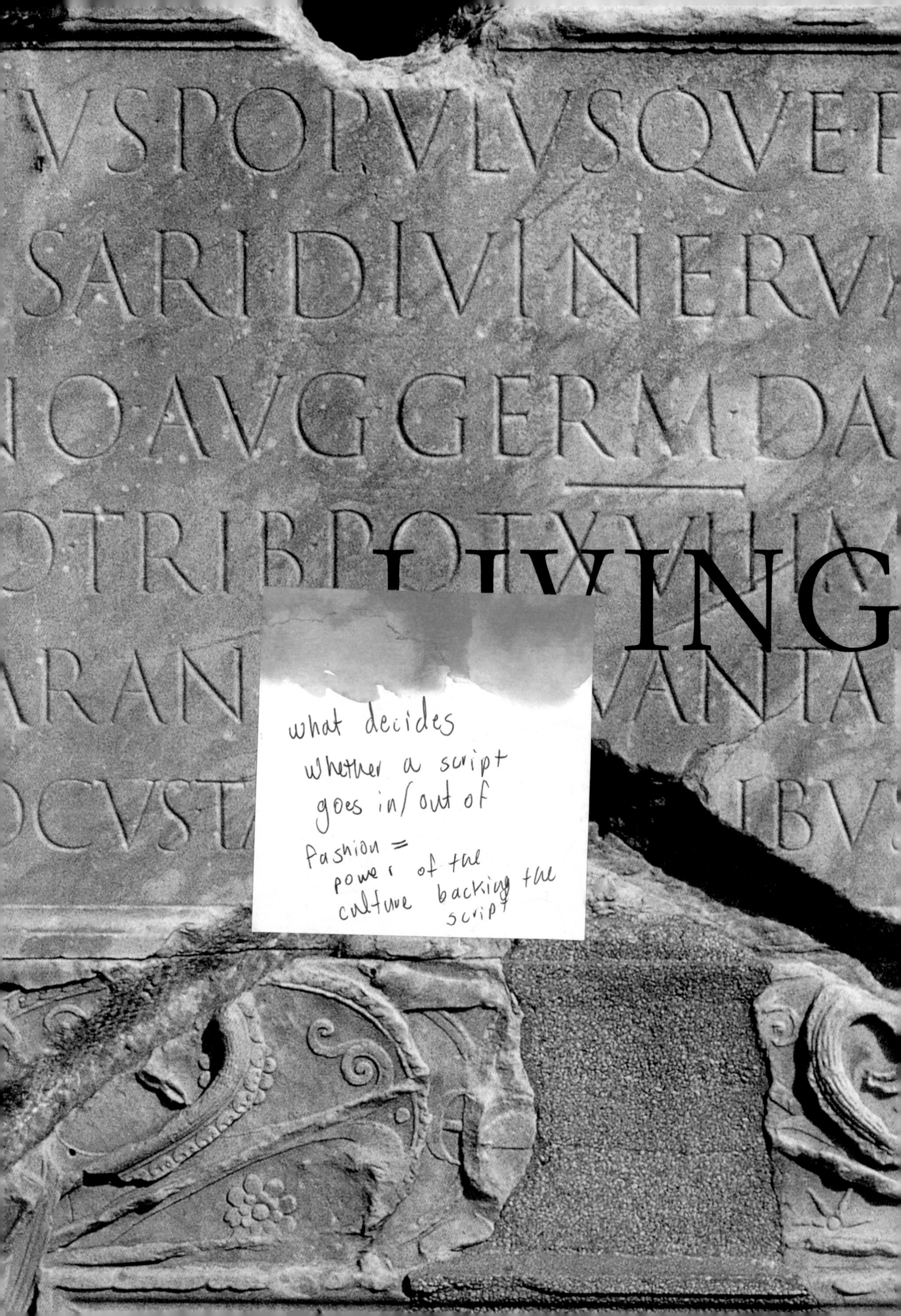
VSPOPVLVSQVE
SARIDIVINERV
IOAVGGERMDA
OTRIBPOTXVIIIM
ARAN
VANIA
OCVSTA
IBVS
what decides
whether a script
goes in/out of
fashion =
power of the
culture backing the
script

III

Mesopotamian cuneiform, Egyptian hieroglyphs, Linear B and the other scripts of the preceding section are now the preserve of scholars. Today most of us write in scripts that derive either from the earliest alphabet or from Chinese characters, though the actual signs differ unrecognizably. The Chinese characters have the longest history of continuous use of any script, living or extinct, and Roman letters are

WRITING

still employed after more than two millennia. One day, however, all these scripts will probably go the way of earlier scripts, and become extinct. What extinguishes or preserves the use of a script is not its efficiency in representing a language – at least not primarily that; it is rather the power, prestige and vitality of the cultures which use the script. Thus the Iraqis and Egyptians now use the Arabic script, the Maya use the Roman script, and the Japanese use the Chinese script. So dominant is the culture of the West (and the English language) worldwide that there have been calls in all countries to 'romanize' their scripts. It is just conceivable to imagine this happening in, say, Egypt or Japan. But try to imagine the converse – that the USA should turn over to the Arabic script, for instance – and the importance of which culture backs a particular script becomes evident.

Trajan's Column, Rome, erected AD **113**

Chapter 9   *The First Alphabet*

The birthplace of the alphabet? The convenience of an alphabet would surely have assisted the process of interstate trade, polyglot haggling and record-keeping in the bazaars of ancient Palestine, Lebanon and Syria, where several cultures met. Left Modern souk, Aleppo, Syria.

The Riddle of the Alphabet

The origin of writing is, as we have seen, full of riddles. Perhaps the most perplexing one of all is that of the alphabet. That it reached the modern world via the ancient Greeks is well known, but we have no clear idea of how and when it appeared in Greece, and how, even more fundamentally, the idea of an alphabet first occurred to the pre-Greek societies at the eastern end of the Mediterranean during the 2nd millennium BC. Scholars have devoted their lives to these questions, but the evidence is too scanty for firm conclusions. Did the alphabet evolve from the scripts of Mesopotamia, Egypt and Crete – or did it strike a single unknown individual in a flash? And why was an alphabet thought necessary? Was it the result of commercial imperatives, as seems most likely? In other words, did business require a simpler and quicker means of recording transactions than, say, Babylonian cuneiform or Egyptian hieroglyphs, and also a convenient way to write the babel of languages of the various empires and groups trading with each other around the Mediterranean? If so, then it is surprising that there is zero evidence of trade and commerce in the early inscriptions of Greece. This, and other considerations, have led some scholars to postulate that the Greek alphabet was invented in order to record the epics of Homer.

In the absence of proof, anecdote and myth have filled the vacuum. Children are often evoked as inventors of the alphabet, because they do not have the preconceptions and investment in existing scripts that adults have. One possibility is that a bright Canaanite child in northern Syria, fed up

with having to learn cuneiform, took the uniconsonantal idea from Egyptian hieroglyphs and invented some new signs for the basic consonantal sounds of his own Semitic language. Perhaps he doodled them first in the dust of some ancient street: a simple outline of a house, 'beth' (the 'bet' in 'alphabet'), became the sign for 'b'. In our own time, Rudyard Kipling's child protagonist in *How The Alphabet Was Made*, Taffimai, designs what she calls 'noise-pictures'. The letter A is a picture of a carp with its mouth wide open; this, Taffy tells her father, looks like his open mouth when he utters the sound *ah*. The letter O matches the egg-or-stone shape and resembles her father's mouth saying *oh*. The letter S represents a snake, and stands for the hissing sound of the snake. In this somewhat far-fetched way, a whole alphabet is created by Taffimai.

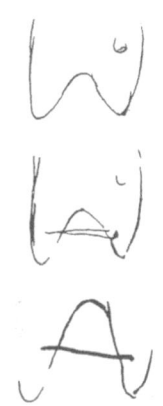

According to Rudyard Kipling, the letters of the alphabet were invented by the child Taffimai. Here Kipling drew the birth of 'A'.

The Middle East when the alphabet was born, *c.* 1500 BC. Was the alphabet the result of the need for more efficient commerce?

The Earliest 'Alphabetic' Inscriptions

In *Jerusalem*, the poet William Blake wrote of 'God . . . in mysterious Sinai's awful cave/ To Man the wond'rous art of writing gave.' A small sphinx in the British Museum once seemed to show that Blake was right, at least about the origin of the alphabet. The sphinx was found in 1905 at Serabit el-Khadim in Sinai, a desolate place remote from civilization, by the archaeologist Sir Flinders Petrie. He was excavating some old turquoise mines that were active in ancient Egyptian times. Petrie dated the sphinx to the middle of the 18th dynasty; nowadays its date is thought to be about 1500 BC. On one side of it is a strange inscription. On the other, and between the paws, there are further inscriptions of the same kind, plus some Egyptian hieroglyphs which read: 'beloved of Hathor, mistress of turquoise'.

There were other inscriptions written on the rocks of this remote area, such as these:

etrie guessed that the script was probably n alphabet, because it consisted of less than 0 signs; and he thought that its language as probably Semitic, since he knew that emites from Canaan – modern Israel and ebanon – had worked these mines for the haraohs, in many cases as slaves. Ten years ter, the Egyptologist Sir Alan Gardiner udied the 'Proto-Sinaitic' signs and noted esemblances between some of them and ertain pictographic Egyptian hieroglyphs. ardiner now named each sign with the emitic word equivalent to the sign's meaning in Egyptian (the Semitic words ere known from biblical scholarship):

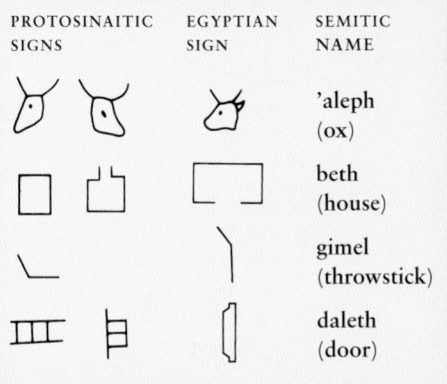

PROTOSINAITIC SIGNS	EGYPTIAN SIGN	SEMITIC NAME
		'aleph (ox)
		beth (house)
		gimel (throwstick)
		daleth (door)

hese Semitic names are the same as the ames of the letters of the Hebrew alphabet a fact that did not surprise Gardiner, since e knew that the Hebrews

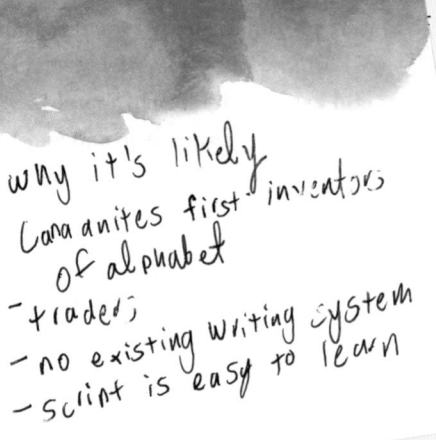

why it's likely Canaanites first invented of alphabet
- traders;
- no existing writing system
- script is easy to learn

In English transcription, this would be 'Baalat', with the vowels spelt out. Hebrew and other Semitic scripts do not indicate vowels; the reader guesses the vowels from his or her knowledge of the language. Gardiner's reading made sense: Baalat means 'the Lady' and is a recognized Semitic name for the goddess Hathor in the Sinai region. So the inscription on the sphinx seemed to be a bilingual. Unfortunately no further decipherment proved tenable, mainly because of lack of material and the fact that many of the Proto-Sinaitic signs had no hieroglyphic equivalents. Scholarly hopes of finding the story of the Exodus in these scratchings were scotched. Nevertheless, it is quite possible that a script similar to the Proto-Sinaitic script was used by Moses to write down the Ten Commandments on tablets of stone.

Proto-Canaanite scripts

We still do not know if Gardiner's 1916 guess was correct, plausible though it is. For some decades after Petrie's discoveries in Sinai, the inscriptions were taken to be the 'missing link' between the Egyptian and Phoenician (alphabetic) scripts. But why should lowly miners in out-of-the-way Sinai have created an alphabet? *Prima facie*, they seem to be unlikely inventors. Subsequent discoveries in Lebanon and Israel (*right*) have shown the Sinaitic theory of the alphabet to be a romantic fiction. These suggest that Canaanites were the inventors of the alphabet, which would be reasonable. They were cosmopolitan traders at the crossroads of the Egyptian, Hittite, Babylonian and Cretan empires; they were not wedded to an existing writing system; they needed a script that was easy to learn, quick to write and unambiguous. Although unproven, it is probable that the Canaanites created the first alphabet.

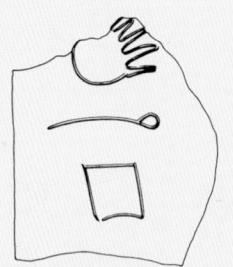

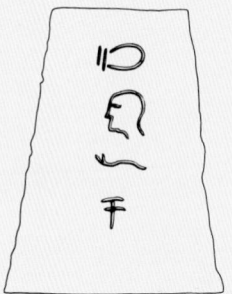

Fragmentary Proto-Canaanite inscriptions from (top) **Shechem,** (middle) **Gezer (on a potsherd),** (bottom) **Lachish (on a dagger). The dates are believed to be 17th and 16th centuries** BC, **i.e. before the Proto-Sinaitic inscriptions. The meanings are unknown.**

An Alphabet in Cuneiform

Literary tablet from Ugarit, northern Syria, written in alphabetic cuneiform, *c.* 14th century BC.

From Ugarit, on the northern coast of Syria at modern Ras Shamra, we have hard evidence of the existence of the alphabet by the 14th century BC, that is well after the date of the Proto-Sinaitic writing. The kingdom of Ugarit was a grand one by Canaanite standards. Its capital covered 52 acres and was heavily fortified. Large donkey caravans converged on the city from Syria, Mesopotamia and Anatolia to exchange goods with merchants from Canaan and Egypt as well as the maritime traders who arrived by ship from Crete and Cyprus and the Aegean. The city functioned as a great bazaar. Its trade can be gauged from the cargo of a shipwreck excavated not long ago off the southern coast of Turkey – copper, tin, tools, chemicals, glass ingots, faience and amber beads, ceramics, ivory, jewellery, luxury goods, semi-precious stones, textiles and timber. No less than ten languages and five different scripts were in use at Ugarit, which walked a political tightrope between the Egyptian and Hittite empires.

The dominant script appears to have been Akkadian cuneiform, at least to begin with. But then someone in Ugarit, or some group of people – perhaps senior merchants? – decided, it appears, that Akkadian cuneiform was too cumbersome and unreliable a system for writing the city's native Semitic tongue. Instead an alphabet was introduced, presumably imported from further south in Canaan (we do not know for sure). Rather than adopting a small set of pictographic or quasi-pictographic signs, however, the people of Ugarit were conservative: they decided to write their new alphabet in cuneiform. They therefore invented a set of simple cuneiform signs, some 30 in all, that bore no resemblance to the signs of Akkadian cuneiform, just as the signs of Old

Bilingual seal of Mursilis II, Hittite king, from the palace, Ugarit.

Left **Bronze statuette of a god, possibly Baal, from Ugarit.**

the signs was probably adopted from that of Proto-Canaanite alphabets (whose order of signs admittedly is unknown). We can guess this from the fact that some of the tablets are abecedaries, that is, they list the signs in the cuneiform script in a fixed order that resembles the modern order we have inherited nearly 3500 years later. Here is an example:

'a b g ḫ d h w z ḥ ṭ y k š l
m ḏ n ẓ s ʿ p ṣ q r ṯ
ġ t 'i 'u s

Below **Silver statuette from Ugarit.**

Another tablet (broken), discovered only in 1955, goes even further. It lists the Ugaritic signs in the same order as before (*below left*) and adds to each one its Akkadian syllabic equivalent (right-hand part of fragment). The tablet is in fact a school tablet: we can imagine some unfortunate child from Ugarit in the last centuries of the 2nd millennium BC labouring over the hundreds of Akkadian signs and wondering why anyone should want to write in Akkadian script when a simple alternative was available.

Persian cuneiform invented under Darius bear no resemblance to those of the much older Babylonian cuneiform. Ugaritic cuneiform would have been gibberish to a Babylonian scribe.

Over 1000 tablets in Ugaritic cuneiform have been discovered since 1929. They consist of administrative texts – commercial correspondence, tax accounts and other governmental business records – written with 30 signs, and literary and religious texts written with only 27 signs. The latter bear striking similarities, in theme and even in phrasing, to stories from parts of the Old Testament. It seems that these biblical stories were written down many centuries before they were written in Hebrew.

Abecedaries

How did the Ugaritic inventor decide on the shapes of the signs and their order? Most likely the simplest signs were applied to the most frequently heard sounds. The order of

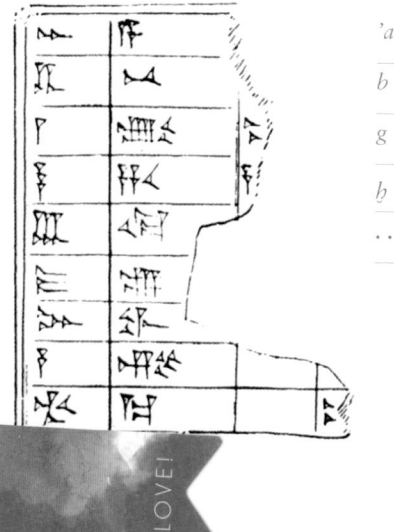

'a   a
b   be
g   ga
ḫ   ḫa
. . . etc.

The Phoenician Letters

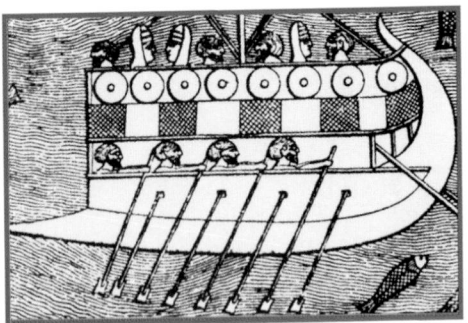

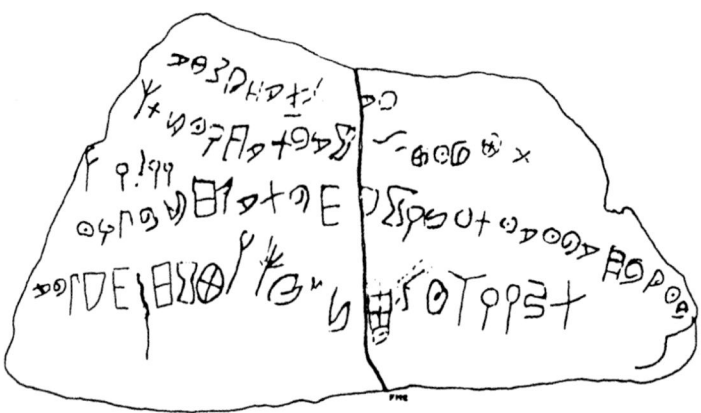

There is no clear line of descent from the Proto-Canaanite inscriptions of the first half of the 2nd millennium BC to the relatively stable alphabetic script written by the Phoenicians from about 1000 BC, the forerunner of the Hebrew script and the Greek alphabet. Ugarit and its cuneiform script seem to have been wiped out in about 1200 BC by the influx of the Sea Peoples. Another experiment in creating a script (*right*) took place on the coast south of Ugarit, at Byblos, some time during the 2nd millennium (the date is very uncertain). The script has been called 'pseudo-hieroglyphic', implying that it was influenced by Egyptian hieroglyphs. While this is quite possible, there is no certainty, and some of the signs resemble Cretan Linear A, an equally likely candidate as an influence. The meaning of the signs is completely opaque; all that can be said for sure is that there are about 120 distinct signs, and hence the script cannot be an alphabet. It seems to have had no effect on the subsequent Phoenician script.

Another early inscription (*top right*) from what is now Israel, dated to about the 12th century BC, suggests that the alphabetic idea was catching on. It contains more than 80 letters in five lines written by an unskilled hand, and appears to be a rather unsuccessful attempt by a semi-literate person at writing an abecedary, that after some letters degenerated into a collection of random signs without meaning.

Above left **Drawing of a relief from the Assyrian palace of Sennacherib, showing the flight of the Phoenicians in their ships, *c.* 700 BC.**

Above **Ostracon from Israel, *c.* 12th century BC.**

Left **'Pseudo-hieroglyphic' script (as yet undeciphered) from Byblos on the Phoenician coast, 2nd millennium BC.**

Opposite page **Phoenician inscriptions, which are found all around the Mediterranean.**
Top **Inscription from Idalion, Cyprus, 391 BC, commemorating the dedication of gold plating by the king of Kition and Idalion.**
Middle **The earliest, such as this sarcophagus inscription of King Ahiram of Byblos, date from the 11th century BC.**
Bottom **The latest, in the Punic script, dates from the 3rd century AD.**

Phoenician	Name	Phonetic value
𐤀	aleph	'
𐤁	beth	*b*
𐤂	gimel	*g*
𐤃	daleth	*d*
𐤄	he	*h*
𐤅	waw	*w*
𐤆	zayin	*z*
𐤇	ḥeth	*ḥ*
𐤈	teth	*ṭ*
𐤉	yod	*y*
𐤊	kaph	*k*
𐤋	lamed	*l*
𐤌	mem	*m*
𐤍	nun	*n*
𐤎	samekh	*s*
𐤏	ayin	'
𐤐	pe	*p*
𐤑	sade	*s*
𐤒	qoph	*q*
𐤓	reš	*r*
𐤔	šin	*sh/s*
𐤕	taw	*t*

The Phoenician alphabet has 22 letters and does not mark vowels.

The Phoenicians

Byblos is the site of the earliest recognizably Phoenician inscriptions. These date from the 11th century BC, and inaugurate a script that continues to be found all around the Mediterranean for the next millennium and more.

The Phoenicians were the ancient world's greatest traders, who set out from their city states, such as Byblos, Sidon and Tyre, explored the Mediterranean and the Atlantic coast and may even have circumnavigated Africa, more than 2000 years before the Portuguese. Among their most important items of merchandise was the purple dye exuded by the 'murex' snail, indeed 'Phoenician' is a Greek word (first used in Homer's *Iliad*), thought to mean 'dealer in purple' – as does 'Canaan'. We do not know a great deal about the Phoenicians, compared with the ancient Egyptians and Greeks, because they left few records and almost no literature, but we can tell from their inscriptions that their alphabet of 22 letters went with them wherever they ventured. The names of these letters were the same as those in use by the Hebrews and today in the Hebrew script. The Phoenicians indicated no vowels, only consonants.

If we apply this venerable alphabet to one of the earliest Phoenician inscriptions – that inscribed on the impressive sarcophagus of King Ahiram of Byblos (*above*) – we get the following somewhat sinister warning (perhaps about the alphabet?): 'Beware! Behold [there is] disaster for you down here.'

What the Greeks Heard

The Greek historian Herodotus called the alphabet 'phoinikeia grammata', 'Phoenician letters', brought to Greece, he said, by the legendary Kadmos. Some 2500 years later, we are not much further in accounting for the origin of the Greek alphabet. Every scholar agrees that the Greeks borrowed the alphabet from the Phoenicians, but most now think this occurred among Greeks living in Phoenicia, from where it spread to the mother country.

We can visualize a Greek sitting with a Phoenician teacher and copying down the signs and sounds, as the Phoenician pronounced each sign. The scope for distortion was considerable, because the 'barbarous' Phoenician letter names would not have rolled naturally off the Greek tongue. Consider how the untrained English ear cannot distinguish between 'rue' (street) and 'roux' (reddish) in French. Every language offers many similar examples. So Phoenician 'aleph' (ox) became 'alpha' in Greek, 'beth' (house) became 'beta', 'gimel' (throw stick) became 'gamma', and so on. In the process, the names became meaningless (as is the word alphabet). The 22 Phoenician consonants were adopted as Greek consonants *and* vowels, and three new signs were added. Although the introduction of vowels seems a major innovation, it seems to have occurred not because the Greek adapter intended it but because he could find no other way of transferring a particular Phoenician consonant into Greek. The consonants are 'weak', sometimes known as semivowels. Thus 'aleph', the glottal stop pronounced like a coughed *ah*, sounded to Greek ears like a funny way of saying *a*.

Phoenician	Name	Phonetic value	Early Greek	Classical Greek	Name
	aleph	'		A	alpha
	beth	b		B	beta
	gimel	g		Γ	gamma
	daleth	d		Δ	delta
	he	h		E	epsilon
	waw	w			digamma
	zayin	z		Z	zeta
	ḥeth	ḥ		H	eta
	teth	ṭ		Θ	theta
	yod	y		I	iota
	kaph	k		K	kappa
	lamed	l		Λ	lambda
	mem	m		M	mu
	nun	n		N	nu
	samekh	s			xi
	ayin	'		O	omicron
	pe	p		Π	pi
	sade	s			san
	qoph	q			qoppa
	reš	r		P	rho
	šin	sh/s		Σ	sigma
	taw	t			tau
				Y	upsilon
				X	chi
				Ω	omega

The Greeks and the Alphabet

There are two major difficulties in deciding the date of invention of the Greek alphabet. First, the earliest known alphabetic Greek inscription dates from only about 730 BC. Second, there are no known practical or business documents for over 200 years after the invention of the Greek alphabet.

Before the decipherment of Linear B in 1952, the Greeks were regarded as illiterate until the arrival of the alphabet. Since the decipherment, it has been conventional to imagine a 'Dark Age' of illiteracy in Greece between the fall of the Homeric Greeks and the rise of the classical Greeks after, say, 800 BC. In other words, Linear B disappeared and with it went Greek knowledge of writing. This is still the orthodox view. Some scholars, however, believe that this 'Dark Age' is a fiction, and that the Greeks had knowledge of alphabetic writing much earlier than the 8th century BC, perhaps as early as 1100 BC. A principal piece of evidence in favour of this theory is that the direction of early Greek inscriptions is unstable: sometimes they run from right to left, sometimes from left to right, sometimes boustrophedon. But the direction of Phoenician writing, itself unstable prior to about 1050 BC, *was* stable, from right to left, probably by 800 BC. So, the argument goes, the Greeks must have borrowed the Phoenician script in the earlier phase of its development, not after it had settled down.

The date of the invention – anywhere between 1100 and 800 BC – is therefore controversial and is likely to be resolved only by the discovery of Greek inscriptions prior to the 8th century BC.

Even more controversial is *why* the alphabetic script suddenly appeared. It is certainly extraordinary that there are no economic documents among the early Greek inscriptions, unlike Linear B inscriptions. Instead the early alphabet users from all parts of Greece display private, almost literary concerns. Could economic inscriptions have existed once and simply perished, being written on impermanent materials? It seems unlikely that no trace would remain, where other documents have survived. One solution to the conundrum, seriously considered by a few scholars, is that the inventor of the alphabet was a brilliant contemporary of Homer who was inspired to find a way of recording the poet's oral epics, *The Iliad* and *The Odyssey*. The vowelless Phoenician system proved useless for the task of writing epic verse, so a new writing system with vowels and rhythmic subtlety was needed. Though there are solid grounds for this theory, it is surely likely that knowledge of such a feat would have been preserved by the Greeks themselves. But – sad to say for romantics – there is no hint in Greek tradition that Homer and the origin of the alphabet are connected.

Greek boustrophedon inscription, an epitaph, *c.* 550 BC. The reversed letters in the first two lines are clearly visible.

The earliest Greek inscription, a vase from Athens, *c.* 730 BC, inscribed to 'him who dances most delicately'; probably it was a prize.

Chapter 10 New Alphabets from Old

Etruscan 'bucchero' jug, 6th century BC, inscribed with the Etruscan alphabet. The Etruscans borrowed the alphabet of the Greeks, altered it, and transmitted it to the Romans. Today most nations use an alphabet.

The Family of Alphabets

From its unclear origins on the eastern shores of the Mediterranean, writing employing the alphabetic principle spread – to the West (via Greek) to modern Europe, to the East (via Aramaic, in all probability) to modern India. Today, as a consequence of the colonial empires, most of the world's peoples except the Chinese and Japanese write in an alphabetic script. Most alphabets use between 20 and 30 basic symbols; the smallest, Rotokas, used in the Solomon Islands, has 11 letters, the largest, Khmer, used in Cambodia, has 74 letters.

The alphabetic link between the Greeks and the Romans was, as we have seen, the Etruscans. They inscribed many objects with the alphabet, such as the 'bucchero' jug opposite, which dates from the 6th century BC. And in Mesopotamia, by the 5th century BC, many cuneiform documents carried a notation of their substance in the Aramaic alphabet, inked onto the tablet with a brush. From the time of Alexander the Great, cuneiform was increasingly superseded by Aramaic; it eventually disappeared around the beginning of the Christian era. In Egypt, fairly soon after that, the Coptic alphabet supplanted Egyptian hieroglyphs.

The time chart below shows how some of the modern alphabetic scripts emerged from the Proto-Sinaitic/Canaanite scripts. It does not include the Indian scripts, since their connection with Aramaic is problematic and, strictly speaking, only partially proven. Nor does it show later alphabets such as the Cyrillic alphabet used in Russia, which was adapted from the Greek alphabet in the 9th century AD, the Korean Hangul alphabet, invented in the 15th century, or the so-called Cherokee alphabet, invented in 1821.

Evolution of the main European alphabetic scripts. (Time-scale approximate. After Healey)

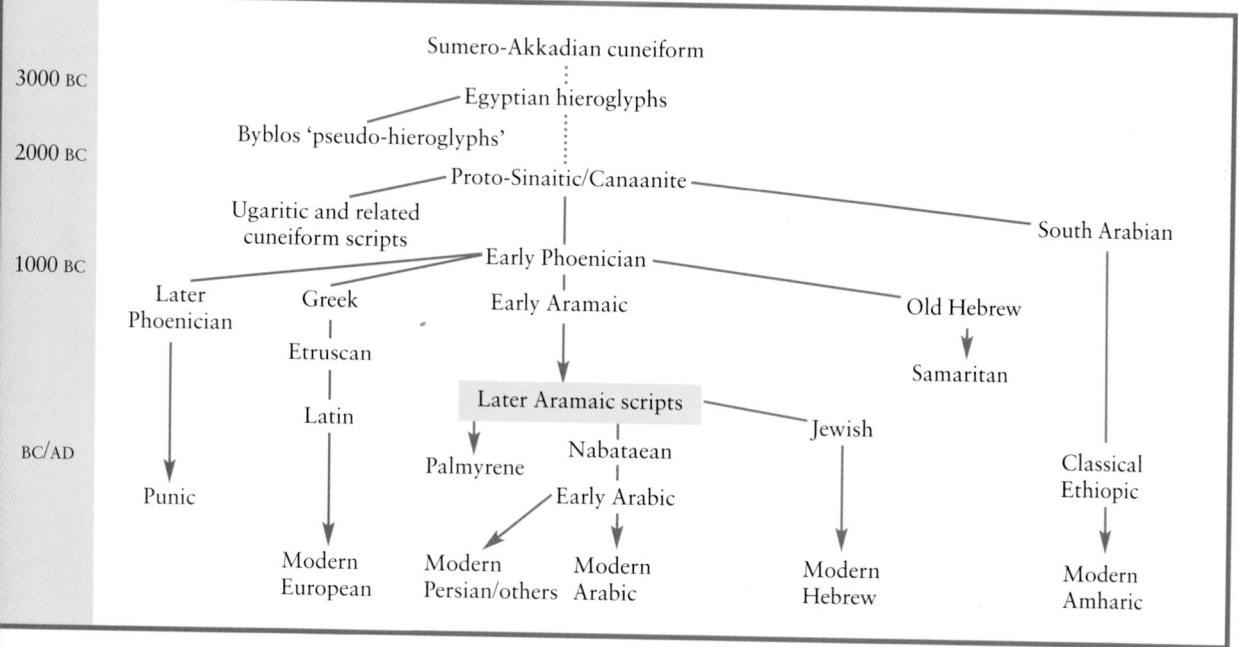

The Greek and Latin Letters

There was more than one alphabet in ancient Greece. The alphabetic signs of classical Greece, which are still in use in Greece today, are known as the Ionian alphabet. They did not become compulsory in Athenian documents until 403–2 BC. Long before that, Greek colonists had taken a somewhat different script, the Euboean alphabet, to Italy. This was taken over by the Etruscans, with some modifications, and later adopted by the Romans.

The reason why modern European and modern Greek letter-forms differ can therefore be traced to the use of the Euboean alphabet in Italy from about 750 BC. For instance, the letters A and B descend from the same signs in both the Euboean and Ionian alphabets, while C and D descend from the Euboean form, which differs from the Ionian forms preserved in the modern Greek Γ and Δ.

As an example of Etruscan and Roman modification, let us take the Euboean Γ. The Etruscans had no distinct /g/ sound, and so they employed the g sign Ϲ for /k/. The old k sign therefore ceased to be of use, being replaced by C (pronounced as in 'cat'). And so the alphabet came to the Romans basically without any K (though the Romans chose to retain K for a very few specific words). But they, unlike the Etruscans, required to represent /g/: since the sign Ϲ was already spoken for (it was representing /k/ in Etruscan and would continue to do so in Latin), the Romans invented a new sign for /g/ by adding a stroke to the existing C, thereby producing G.

The Roman/Latin script was modified slightly in turn, on the way to becoming its

Phoenician	Phoenician name	Modern symbol	Early Greek	Classical Greek	Greek name	Early Latin	Classical Latin
	ʼaleph	ʼ		A	alpha	A	A
	beth	b		B	beta		B
	gimel	g		Γ	gamma		C
	daleth	d		Δ	delta	O	D
	he	h		E	epsilon	Ǝ	E
	waw	w			digamma	Ⅎ	F
							G
	zayin	z		Z	zeta		H
	ḥeth	h		H	eta	日	
	teth	t		Θ	theta		I
	yod	y		I	iota	I	(J)
	kaph	k		K	kappa	ʎ	K
	lamed	l		Λ	lambda		L
	mem	m		M	mu	ᙏ	M
	nun	n		N	nu	Ν	N
	samek	s			xi		O
	ayin	ʻ		O	omicron	O	P
	pe	p		Π	pi		
	sade	s			san		Q
	qoph	o			qoppa		R
	reš	r		P	rho		S
	šin	sh/s		Σ	sigma	ʃ	T
	taw	t			tau		V
				Y	upsilon	V	V
				X	chi		X
				Ω	omega		Y
							Z
PHOENICIAN			**GREEK**			**LATIN**	

odern English equivalent. There were four ounds in Anglo-Saxon for which there were o counterparts in Latin:

(1) /w/ came to be written with a runic ymbol Þ known as wynn. In Middle nglish, this was replaced by 'uu' or 'w'; is rarely found after 1300.

(2) /θ/ and / ð / – as in modern English hin' and 'this' – came to be written by a unic symbol known as thorn, Þ. To this as later added the symbol ð, which was alled eth. In Middle English both letters ere replaced by 'th'. But Þ has survived n the 'Y' of the artificial modern form 'Ye lde English Tea Shoppe'.

(3) /a/ – as in modern English 'hat' – was epresented using the Latin digraph æ, which ame to be called ash, after the name of the unic symbol representing the same sound.

In Middle English this too had fallen out of use, probably as a result of sound changes.

Cyrillic became the script for more than 60 languages. Its inventor was alleged to be St Cyril (*c.* 827–69), who was entrusted with the mission by the Byzantine emperor Constantine at the request of the Slav king of Moravia; the king wanted a script which was independent of the Roman church, and which recognized only Hebrew, Greek and Latin for the translation of the Bible.

This is the legend; in fact Cyril seems to have devised the Glagolitic alphabet – while the Cyrillic script was actually created later. The Cyrillic script had 43 letters, the majority of which appear to have been derived from the Greek scripts of the time. Today's Cyrillic scripts usually have about 30 letters.

Above left **The Book of Kells, before AD 807, kept in Trinity College Library, Dublin. This manuscript of the Gospels is written in the so-called Insular script developed by Irish monks from the uncial script used in official Roman documents of the 3rd century AD onwards (Latin 'litterae unciales' means 'inch-high letters'). Each monastery developed its own characteristic variant of uncials.**

Above right **The Cyrillic script, used to write the Four Gospels for Tsar Ivan Alexandre of Bulgaria, 1355–6. The script is best known today for its use as the Russian alphabet.**

Hebrew and the Aramaic Script

ebrew is well known as the script of orthodox Jewry and a national script of modern Israel. Less well known is the fact that there are two distinct Hebrew scripts. The first, found only in religious literature and among a tiny community of Samaritans, is by far the older, having evolved from the Phoenician script around the 9th century BC and disappeared from secular use with the dispersion of the Jews in the 6th century BC. The second script, sometimes known as the Jewish script or 'square Hebrew', evolved from Aramaic (used by the Jews in their Babylonian captivity), after they returned to the province of Judah. 'Square Hebrew' dates from the late 3rd century AD, and is the script now used in Israel. The original Hebrew script and its later form seem to have influenced one another quite strongly.

Aramaic, which grew out of the Phoenician script, was immensely influential for well over 1000 years. The official script of the later Babylonian, Assyrian and Persian empires (thus displacing cuneiform), it was also the vernacular language of Jesus Christ and the Apostles, and probably the original language of the Gospels (the Dead Sea Scrolls are written partly in Aramaic). It was also the principal language of traders from Egypt and Asia Minor to India. Its extinction came only with the unifying force of Arabic (whose script descended from Aramaic script) and Islam during the 7th century AD.

Right **Writing implements of a Sefardi scribe in Jerusalem, late 19th century. The script is 'square Hebrew'. For centuries it was used only for religious literature, but from the 19th century onwards it began to be used for colloquial writing too. Today it is a national script of Israel.**

One of the Dead Sea Scrolls, 1st century BC to 1st century AD, written in ink on leather. These religious and legal texts were found in caves in Palestine during the mid-20th century. They are written chiefly in the Hebrew and Aramaic languages, using the old Hebrew script and the Jewish script, one of the offshoots of the Aramaic cursive script. The writing is similar enough to modern printed Hebrew to be read with ease.

Letter name	Phonetic value	Phoenician	Modern Hebrew	Modern Arabic
aleph	ʾ		א	ا
beth	b		ב	ب
gimel	g		ג	ج
daleth	d		ד	د
he	h		ה	ﻩ
waw	w		ו	و
zayin	z		ז	ز
ḥeth	ḥ		ח	ح
teth	ṭ		ט	ط
yod	y		י	ي
kaph	k		כ	ك
lamed	l		ל	ل
mem	m		מ	م
nun	n		נ	ن
samekh	s		ס	س
ayin	ʿ		ע	ع
pe	p		פ	ف
sade	ṣ		צ	ص
qoph	q		ק	ق
reš	r		ר	ر
šin	sh/s		ש	ش
taw	t		ת	ت

Modern Hebrew letters evolved from Phoenician letters via the Aramaic script, as did modern Arabic letters. There are a few resemblances to the Phoenician letters, but most of the letters are different. Note that vowels are not directly marked in Hebrew or Arabic. In due course, vowels came to be marked using three basic signs above and below the line. In Arabic, there are also extra consonants, 28 in all (not shown).

Semitic Languages

Both Hebrew and Aramaic are Semitic languages. In principle, Semitic scripts do not mark vowels, only the 22 consonants. Thus the three letters in Hebrew that stand for *ktb* or *ktv* can take the meanings: 'katav' (he wrote), 'kotev' (writes, a writer), 'katuv' (written), 'kitav' (script, document), 'kitovet' (address), 'kitubbah' (marriage contract), 'katvan' (clerk). In practice, various additional signs have been used to aid the reader in pronouncing the vowels. The commonest of these is a system of dots placed above or below a letter, referred to as 'vowel points' or 'matres lectionis', Latin for 'mothers of reading'.

Clumsy as this may appear to be, the Hebrew script (in both its forms) has always exerted a powerful appeal on the Jews. For many centuries after Christ, during the Jewish diaspora, the use of 'square Hebrew' was restricted largely to religious literature.

Then, during the 19th century, it was revived as a colloquial script. The modern Hebrew language is based on this tenaciously surviving script, reversing the normal relationship of a script being based on a language. This creation is, in the words of one scholar, 'unprecedented . . . unique in the history of human speech'.

The Arabic Script

The Arabic script is today one of the great scripts of the world, owing to the fact that it is the sacred script of Islam. The Arabs as a people are identifiable as early as the Assyrian period (in the 9th to 7th centuries BC), but they did not become prominent historically until about the time of Christ. The first independent Arab kingdom known to us is that of the Nabataeans, centred on Petra in modern Jordan. They spoke a form of Arabic but wrote in the Aramaic script, the official administrative script of the Assyrians and Persians. The presence of certain distinctively Arabic forms and words in these Aramaic inscriptions eventually gave way to the writing of the Arabic language in

Nabataean Aramaic script. This was the precursor of the Arabic script, which arose during the first half of the first millennium AD and replaced the Aramaic script. Thus the line of descent was from the Phoenician to the Aramaic to the Nabataean to the Arabic script.

From the beginning of the Islamic period in the early 7th century AD, there appear to have been several forms of the Arabic script. In all of them there are 28 consonants instead of the 22 consonants of Aramaic, in order to represent sounds that are in the Arabic languages but not in the Aramaic language. A new ordering of the consonantal alphabet was also established, largely on the basis of the shapes of the letters (which read from right to left).

Arabic calligraphy. With the coming of Islam, the artistic spirit of the Arabs went into calligraphy and abstract decoration because of the general Muslim reluctance to paint pictures with religious imagery.

Above **Detail from the Koran in Muhaqqaq script from Baghdad, Iraq, 1304.**

Left **Shiah prayer in Thuluth script in the shape of a falcon, by Muhammad Fatiyab, early 19th century, Iran.**

Below **Seljuq gold wine bowl engraved on rim with foliated kufic script, early 11th century, Iran.**

ndian Scripts

The earliest known Indian inscriptions are those of the Emperor Asoka (*c.* 270– *c.* 232 BC). They are rock edicts erected in various parts of northern India, written in two scripts, Kharosthi and Brahmi, the more important of which is Brahmi. No less than about 200 different South and Southeast Asian scripts derive, directly or indirectly, from the Brahmi script: that is nearly all the Indian scripts, leaving aside those imported into India with Islam. They include southern scripts used to write Dravidian languages, as well as the northern scripts used to write Sanskrit and its descendants.

One thing is quite clear about this early period in India: the Indians used their sophisticated knowledge of phonology and grammar to organize their alphabets differently from that of the Aramaic alphabet. The letters are classified in accordance with place of articulation in the mouth: vowels and diphthongs come first, then consonants in the following logical order: gutturals, palatals, retroflexes, dentals, labials, semi-vowels and spirants. But often it was a syllable that was represented by the Indian scripts; consonant signs that express inherent vowels, i.e. syllables, are extremely important in Indian writing systems. Thus the sign for 'b' in Bengali represents the sound *bo* (where the *o* is short).

The origins of the modern Indian scripts are unclear. Some Indian and a few non-Indian scholars have tried o trace a link between the undeciphered cript of the Indus Valley Civilization p. 146–48) and the earliest Buddhist scriptions, but since there is a gap of more an 1500 years between the two, this xplanation is far-fetched. Most scholars – dian and non-Indian – agree that the ramaic script was the parent script of one f the earliest Indian scripts, Kharosthi, even hough hard evidence of the link is lacking.

Left **Bengali script, a modern descendant of Brahmi script, on a film poster designed by Satyajit Ray, 1960. The title is *Devi* (The Goddess). The Bengali script uses a mixture of syllabic letters and vowels arranged in an order based on that determined by Indian phoneticians well over 2000 years ago.**

Below left **One of the earliest inscriptions of India on a fragment of an edict of the Emperor Asoka, inscribed in Brahmi, 3rd century BC.**

Below right **Two descendants of the Brahmi script, used in the south of India on a copper plate describing a grant, AD 769–70. The top lines are in Sanskrit written in Grantha script, the other lines are in Tamil written in Vatteluttu characters, slanting slightly to the left. Vatteluttu is older than the modern Tamil script (not shown here).**

An Alphabet Invented by a King

The Korean alphabet, known as Hangul, is one of the few alphabets that can be exactly dated. The story of its invention and deployment is an appealing and instructive one. For more than a millennium after the Koreans acquired the art of writing, they naturally wrote in Chinese characters. Then, in 1443–4, King Sejong (1397–1450) introduced a script consisting of 28 letters. The new system was announced with the statement that 'His Majesty personally created' it. No doubt this was the best way to ensure the new script's adoption, but it also seems to have been the truth, or at least a close approximation. Sejong was an unusually learned and far-sighted monarch who issued an edict in 1434 calling for his people to search everywhere for 'men of learning and sophistication, without regard to whether they are of noble birth or mean, earnestly encouraging them and urging them to teach people to read, even women and girls.'

The new script met with entrenched resistance from the literati. More than half a millennium later, Hangul has yet to supplant Chinese characters entirely throughout Korea. North Korea, ruled by a dictator, adopted Hangul exclusively in 1949, with notable success; South Korea, by contrast, has tended to use a 'mixed' script, consisting of Hangul and Chinese characters – rather as the Japanese system uses syllabic 'kana' and Chinese characters. South Korean intellectuals are divided about the merits of a Hangul-only script, at least partly because of its exclusive use in North Korea. Nevertheless, South Korea is inching along in the same direction as North Korea, with ever greater use of Hangul-only writing.

It is not exactly clear how Sejong came under the spell of the alphabetic principle. The Koreans were in direct contact with the Mongols, who wrote in two alphabetic scripts, Uighur and Phags-pa, the latter named after a Tibetan lama who developed the script at the request of Kublai Khan on the basis of Tibetan, which was itself based on an Indian model. Indian Buddhist writings transmitted through Chinese were also undoubtedly influential – Sejong was deeply interested in Buddhism. Buddhist religious terms were originally expressed in some Indian alphabetic writing and then rendered clumsily into Chinese syllabic characters (since there were no Chinese equivalents); the awkwardness of this process must have acted as a spur to Sejong in his creation of a new script.

King Sejong's explanation of the Korean alphabetic script Hangul, in a modern facsimile of a blockprint. Hangul is shown side by side with Chinese characters.

Runes

The vast majority of European scripts derive from the Roman letters – which has tended to obscure the existence of one significant European script, the runic script, whose links with the Roman script are less certain. From as far back as the 2nd century AD, runes have been found that were used to record the early stages of Gothic, Danish, Swedish, Norwegian, English, Frisian, Frankish and various tribal tongues of central Germania. These peoples were therefore not illiterate, as sometimes thought, before the period when they became Christian and began to use the Roman alphabet.

There was a range of runic scripts, reflecting the range of languages involved. The total number of known runic inscriptions is probably in the region of 5000, almost all of which are located in Nordic countries. The great majority are in Sweden, where discoveries of rune stones are still frequently made. Norway has over 1000 inscriptions, and Denmark some 700; Iceland has about 60, all from comparatively late times, and there are also runic texts from Greenland and the Faroes. Some of those in Britain, found in the Isle of Man and in the Orkneys, Shetlands, Ireland and Western Isles, are the work of travelling Norsemen; Anglo-Saxon England has, in addition to several issues of coins with runic legends, some 70 inscribed objects; Germany about 60; elsewhere in Europe there is a scattering of runes.

We do not know where and when runes were invented. Finds of early rune-inscribed objects in eastern Europe, at Pietroassa in Rumania, Dahmsdorf in central Germany

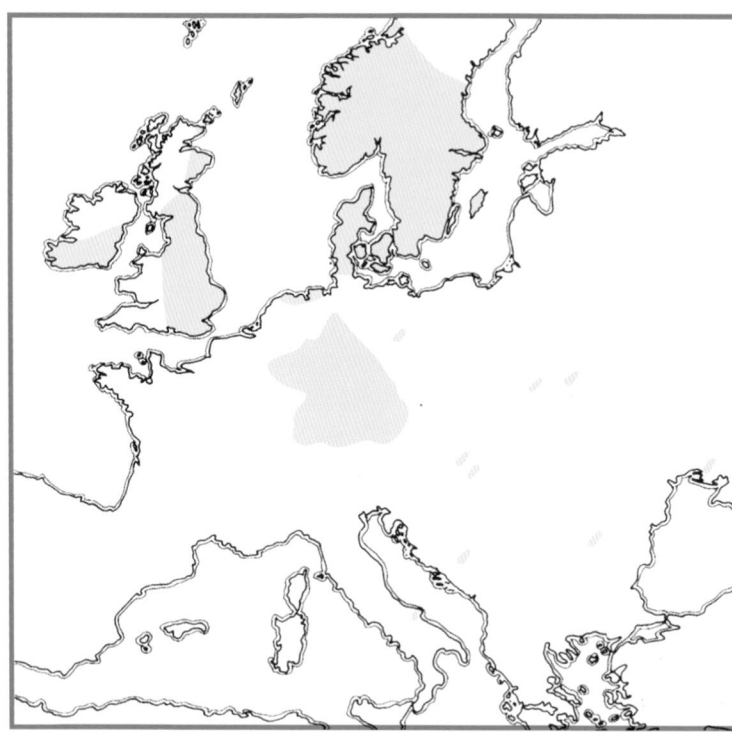

and Kowel in Russia, indicated that runes may have been invented in that general area, perhaps by Goths on the Danube frontier or beside the Vistula. Another hypothesis notes the resemblance between the runes and characters used in the inscriptions of the Alpine valleys of southern Switzerland and northern Italy and goes on to ascribe the invention to romanized Germani from that area. A third hypothesis prefers one of the Germanic tribes of Denmark, perhaps southern Jutland, as the progenitors of runes; many of the earliest inscriptions come from this general area, and early runic texts continue to be found in various regions of Denmark. But on one point all scholars of runes agree: the Roman alphabet exercized influence of some kind on the runic script.

Runes were used for over a thousand years among a wide variety of cultures and traditions. Note, for example, that the individually plotted findspots of runes to the south and east parallel the movements of migrating Goths *c.* AD 200, of Christian Anglo-Saxon pilgrims in the 8th century and of Viking adventurers of the 11th century.

Reading the Runes

ᚠᚢᚦᚨᚱᚲᚷᚹᚺᚾᛁᛃᛇᛈᛉᛊᛏᛒᛖᛗᛚᛜᛟᛞ

f   u   þ   a/æ   r   k   g   w   h   n   i   j   ï   p   z   s   t   b   e   m   l   n   o   e

(th)   *(R)*   *(ng)*

The runic alphabet has 24 letters, arranged in a peculiar order known as the 'futhark' after its first six letters. Here it is written from left to right, but it could be written from right to left equally well in early times, or even boustrophedon. An individual letter could also be reversed on occasions, apparently at whim, and might even be inverted. There was no distinction between capital and lower-case letters.

Some of the runic letters are obviously related to letters of the Roman alphabet, as 'r', 'i' and 'b'. Others could well be adaptations of Roman letters, as 'f', 'u' (Roman V inverted), 'k' (Roman C), 'h', 's', 't', 'l' (Roman L inverted). But other runes, such as those representing *g*, *w*, *j*, *p*, scarcely resemble Roman forms with the same sound value.

The sound values given above are approximate: the sounds of early Germanic languages are not exactly paralleled in modern English. There is a rune, for example, for the spirant sound *th*, as in 'thin' (it was used in early English spelling, as we have seen on p. 171, and called 'thorn'). There is a vowel ᛁ, represented here as *ï*, the pronunciation of which is disputed. Runic script could also distinguish between *ng* in 'ungrateful' (ᛏ + ᚷ) and *ng* as in 'sing', ◇.

But even though runic inscriptions can usually be 'read' – in the same sense as Etruscan inscriptions – their meaning is frequently cryptic, because of our lack of knowledge of the early Germanic languages. Hence the origin of today's expression 'to read the runes' – meaning to make an educated guess on the basis of scanty and ambiguous evidence. As a scholar of runes has remarked, the First Law of Runo-dynamics is 'that for every inscription there shall be as many interpretations as there are scholars working on it.'

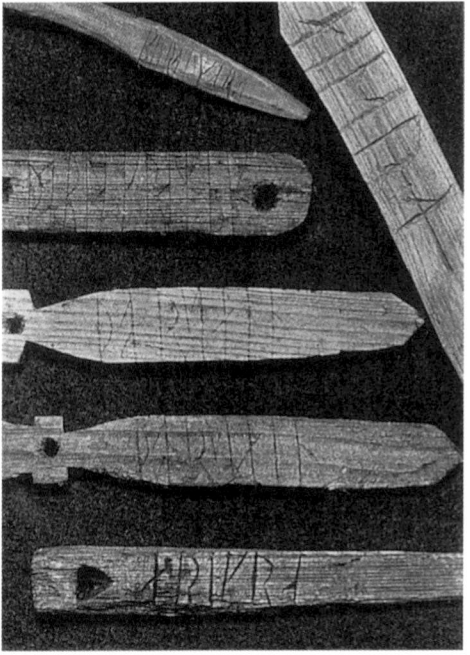

Below **Runic merchants' labels on wood from Bergen, western Norway, 12th century AD. Each gives the owner's name and would have been tied onto or stuck onto goods bought. Wood was an ideal medium, since it could be shaved if a mistake was made and burnt as kindling after use – but its easy decay means that there are no runic inscriptions surviving from early times.**

Right **The Franks Casket, *c.* AD 700. This panel depicts a scene showing Wayland the Smith (left) and the Adoration of Christ with the title 'mægi', i.e. Magi, in a tiny box above it.**

The most famous of the English runic objects is probably the Franks Casket, dating to around AD 700 and named after the man who donated most of it to the British Museum. The front of the box (*below*) has scenes of Wayland the Smith (*left*) and the Adoration of Christ (*right*), above which appears the word 'mægi', 'Magi'. The main inscription can be read clockwise round the box, starting at top left:

TOP LINE:
fisc. flodu | ahof on ferg
RIGHT SIDE:
en berig
BOTTOM LINE (read right to left):
warþ gasric grorn þær he on greut giswom
LEFT SIDE:
hronæsban

The text is a riddle about the origins of the material from which the box is made: 'the fish beat up the seas onto the mountainous cliff; the king of the terror became sad when he swam onto the shingle'. The answer is given in the last word at the left, 'hronæsban' (whale's bone): the box comes from the bone of a beached whale.

We can see that even at the time of their use, runes were considered to be esoteric signs. The brooch shown here was found in Scotland, and belonged to a Celt named *malbri þaastilk*, 'Melbrigda', according to the runes written to the left of the pin: those to the right of the pin, however, are just meaningless pseudo-runic decoration.

In Anglo-Saxon England, there appears to have been a rivalry between the Roman and the runic scripts. Sometimes both scripts were used on the same object, as on the gold ring from Lancashire (*below*). The rivalry had nothing to do with religion – the Christian church had no particular animus against runes – but everything to do with prestige; by the Norman Conquest in 1066, the Roman script had triumphed and in Britain the runic script had almost entirely disappeared from use.

Below **A Celtic-type brooch found at Hunterston, Scotland, with runes to the left of the pin.**

Middle **A gold finger ring of the 9th century from Lancashire, England, with the legend in a mixed runic/Roman script: 'Ædred owns me, Eanred engraved me'.**

The Cherokee 'Alphabet'

Cherokee Alphabet.

D *a*	R *e*	T *i*	Ꮯ *o*	Ꮎ *u*	i *v*
S *ga* Ꮃ *ka*	Ᏺ *ge*	Ᏹ *gi*	A *go*	J *gu*	E *gv*
Ꮚ *ha*	P *he*	Ꮸ *hi*	Ꮂ *ho*	Ꮁ *hu*	Ꮹ *hv*
W *la*	Ꮰ *le*	P *li*	Ꮬ *lo*	M *lu*	Ꮍ *lv*
Ꮉ *ma*	Ꮊ *me*	H *mi*	Ꮋ *mo*	Ꮓ *mu*	
Ꮎ *na* Ꮏ *hna* G *nah*	Ꮥ *ne*	h *ni*	Z *no*	Ꮕ *nu*	Ꮓ *nv*
T *qua*	Ꮳ *que*	Ᏻ *qui*	Ꮖ *quo*	Ꮗ *quu*	Ꮛ *quv*
Ꮜ *sa* Ꮝ *s*	Ꮷ *se*	Ꮎ *si*	Ꮷ *so*	Ꮄ *su*	R *sv*
Ꮣ *da* Ꮤ *ta*	Ꮥ *de* Ꮦ *te*	Ꮧ *di* Ꮨ *ti*	Λ *do*	Ꮪ *du*	Ꮫ *dv*
Ꮬ *dla* Ꮭ *tla*	Ꮮ *tle*	C *tti*	Ꮯ *tlo*	Ꮰ *tlu*	P *tlv*
Ꮳ *tsa*	Ꮴ *tse*	Ꮵ *tsi*	K *tso*	Ꮷ *tsu*	Ꮸ *tsv*
Ꮹ *wa*	Ꮺ *we*	Ꮻ *wi*	Ꮼ *wo*	Ꮽ *wu*	6 *wv*
Ꮾ *ya*	Ꮿ *ye*	Ᏸ *yi*	Ᏹ *yo*	Ᏺ *yu*	B *yv*

lthough the Cherokee script invented by Sequoya in 1821 is traditionally known as an alphabet, it is really a syllabary based largely on assigning syllabic values to the individual letters of the Latin alphabet. Thus J represents the sound *gu*, and M the sound *lu*. The 85 symbols represent 6 vowels, 22 consonants, and some 200 phoneme clusters and syllables.

The 'alphabet' was learned by many Cherokees, first in North Carolina, its place of origin, and later in Oklahoma, where many of the Cherokees had emigrated after 1830. Newspapers and official documents of the Cherokee nation, and other materials, were published in the script, using type designed in Boston in 1827. Soon 90 per cent of Cherokees were literate in the script. However the system later fell into disuse – though recently there have been attempts to revive it.

Initially, Sequoya had tried to make a character for each word, only abandoning this approach after about a year when he had put down several thousand characters. Then he hit upon the idea of dividing words into parts of syllables. Since he lacked confidence in his ability to discriminate sounds, he called upon the help of his wife and children, whose more acute ears helped him finally to arrive at all the sounds of their language. Once he had established these, Sequoya set about devising symbols with the aid of an English spelling book. He compiled 200 symbols, which he then reduced to a total of 85.

Cherokee 'Alphabet'.

Left **Cherokee Sequoya (*c.* 1760–1843) explains his 'alphabet'. The portrait is a contemporary one by Charles Bird King. Sequoya knew no English but he had contact with American settlers and was determined to emulate the achievement of their writing system, so as to create a Cherokee equivalent of the white man's 'talking leaves'.**

The Mystique of the Alphabet

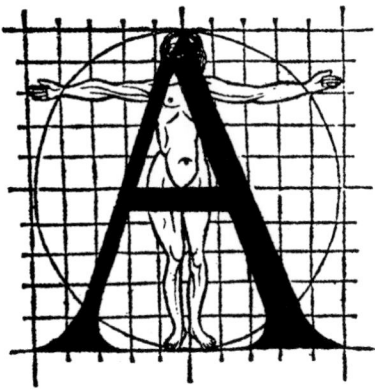 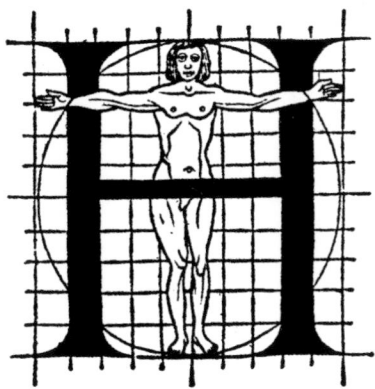 

It is often said that the alphabet was necessary for the growth of democracy, because it enabled very many people to become literate. Others claim that the West's triumph in the modern world, particularly in science, is largely the result of a so-called Alphabet Effect. They contrast the West with China: while both West and East developed science, they note, the West went on to develop the analytical thinking of, say, Newton or Einstein, and left China far behind, because these thinkers were nurtured in the letter-by-letter principle (inherent in the alphabet). Put at its crudest, alphabets are alleged to promote reductionist thinking, Chinese characters holistic thinking.

The first suggestion, about democracy and the alphabet, has a kernel of truth. But did the alphabet help democracy to grow, or did a nascent desire for democracy give rise to the alphabet? (Of course, if one believes that the writing down of Homer was the spur, then the Greek alphabet appears to have had a supremely aristocratic conception!) The ancient Egyptians had access to an alphabet without vowel signs as early as the 3rd millennium BC. Instead of using it,

they chose to write in hieroglyphs using multiple signs: perhaps they felt no urge for democracy in their political system?

The second suggestion, about science, appealing as it is, is a fallacy. It is quite conceivable that the Chinese writing system, by its enormous complexity, retarded the spread of literacy – but it is ludicrous to connect a deep cultural trend, such as a dearth in analytical thinking, with the predominance of logograms over phonograms in Chinese writing. One might as well try to link the fact that Indo-Europeans write epic poetry with the fact that they drink milk – in contrast to the Chinese, who do neither. A distinguished sinologist has ironically dubbed this the Milk Diet Effect. For worthwhile explanations of profound cultural differences, we need to look at cultures in the round, rather than singling out one aspect such as the way a culture writes, however important that may appear. After all, if Newton and Einstein could understand gravity and relativity, they could surely have mastered an education imparted in Chinese characters – or, for that matter, in Egyptian hieroglyphs or Babylonian cuneiform.

Champfleury alphabet, 1529, designed by Geoffroy Tory (*c.* 1480–*c.* 1533). Tory, a pupil of Leonardo da Vinci and Albrecht Dürer, was appointed 'imprimeur du roi' (printer to the king) by the French monarch Francis I. Of the letter A Tory noted that it 'has its legs apart in the manner of a man's legs and feet as he strides along'. The cross-bar of the A 'precisely covers the man's genital organ, to denote that modesty and chastity above all else are required in those who seek access and admission to good letter forms, among which A is the entrance gate and first in order in all ABCs.'

Chapter 11 *Chinese Writing*

Calligraphy class in Canton middle school.

Reading the Bones

If great claims are made for the power of the alphabet, even greater ones attach to Chinese writing. Chinese characters are said to be 'ideographic' – a word carefully avoided in this book in favour of the more specific 'logographic' – that is, characters are thought to be capable of communicating ideas without the intervention of phoneticism or indeed spoken language. Thus it is claimed that Chinese speakers of Mandarin and Cantonese who do not know each other's 'dialect' and cannot talk to each other, can nevertheless communicate in writing through Chinese characters. Some people (both Chinese and westerners) even claim that the same scenario applies to Chinese, Japanese, Korean and (formerly) Vietnamese speakers, whose languages differ greatly but who have shared the use of Chinese characters in their scripts. This, of course, would be quite impossible for equivalent English, French, German and Italian speakers, who also use the same script. The implication is that the Chinese writing system works in a completely separate way from scripts with a large phonographic component. Writing systems, according to advocates of the ideographic principle, come in two fundamental varieties, one ideographic (e.g. Chinese), the other phonographic (e.g. alphabets).

Each of these claims is bogus, as we shall see. Myths have obscured the understanding of Chinese characters for centuries, beginning with their origins, for which we still have virtually no evidence: did the Chinese invent them independently, or were they influenced by diffusion of writing from the Middle East? Only since 1899 has reliable early Chinese writing been discovered. It is in the form of the so-called oracle bones. For many years before 1899, traditional Chinese medicine shops in Peking had sold 'dragon bones', which were in fact old turtle shells and ox scapulae churned up by farmers' ploughs in a village near the town of Anyang in northern Henan province. Signs were frequently found scratched on the surface of these objects; they were usually hacked off with a spade by the farmers before the bones were sold, as being inappropriate to dragon bones. The signs were, however, of great interest to two Chinese scholars in Peking, who recognized that some of the signs were similar to the characters on early bronze inscriptions. They bought up all the inscribed shell and bone fragments they could find in the medicine shops of Peking and published rubbings of the inscriptions.

Subsequent excavations and decipherment during the 20th century showed that the inscriptions were the earliest known examples of Chinese writing. They are records of divinations by the twelve kings of the later Shang dynasty, who ruled from about 1400 to about 1200 B C.

The beginning of Chinese writing. The Shang kings prepared turtle shells and ox scapulae for divination purposes by drilling and chiselling concavities in them in such a way that when heat was applied to the shell by the diviner, a crack would appear shaped either ⌐ or ⌐ (hence the modern character 卜, 'to divine'). The cracks were interpreted to show the reply of the royal ancestors to questions (the prognostication). This rubbing of an oracle bone (below) from the reign of Wu Ding deals with childbirth. The prognostication reads: 'The king, reading the cracks, said: "If it be a 'ding' day childbearing, it will be good. If it be 'geng' day childbearing, it will be extremely auspicious."' The verification reads: 'On the thirty-first day, "jia-yin" (day 51), she gave birth. It was not good. It was a girl.' Many of the signs on the oracle bones are recognizable antecedents of modern Chinese characters.

The Development of Chinese Characters

人 女 子 口 日 月 山 川 水 雨 竹 木 隹
1   2   3   4   5   6   7   8   9   10   11   12   13

How close is the connection between the oracle bone characters three millennia old and today's Chinese characters? A literate Chinese person, untutored in the ancient script, would probably find much of an oracle bone inscription incomprehensible at first glance, but after a little study the connections would begin to emerge. But many of the Shang signs have no modern descendants, just as many modern characters have no Shang ancestors. Of the 4500 Shang signs distinguished to date, some 1000 have been identified, and in many cases their evolution has been traced to a modern character.

Some of these evolved signs are clearly pictographic. But their proportion is much less than often suggested. No one doubts that pictography was important in the origins of Chinese characters, but it was certainly *not* the overriding principle in the formation of the early signs. And even in the cases that are definitely pictographic, the iconicity is fugitive. Above are 13 modern characters with pictographic ancestors. Try to guess what is depicted. You may have a

plausible idea in one or two instances. Now look at the oracle bone forms at the bottom of the page and beneath them the first stage of stylization, the Seal script, still used in the engraving of seals. The Seal script is found in bronze inscriptions (such as the one which appears opposite) from the western Zhou period, 1050–771 BC.

The answers are as follows: (1) man, in the generic sense, (2) woman, (3) child, (4) mouth, (5) sun, (6) moon, (7) mountain, (8) river, (9) water, (10) rain, (11) bamboo, (12) tree, (13) short-tailed bird.

Styles of Chinese Character
The changes in style of writing a given character generally reflect periods in Chinese history. The Shang dynasty was followed by the Zhou dynasty (*c.* 1028–221 BC), in which the Great Seal script flourished. Politically and administratively, however, this was a long period of disunity. Characters were created by writers living in different historical periods and speaking different dialects: the effect was greatly to complicate the use of phoneticism in the Chinese script.

Top row **Oracle bone characters.**
Bottom row **Seal script descendants.**

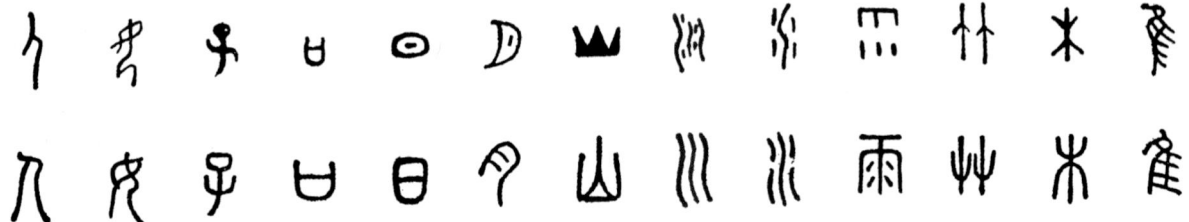

With the establishment of the unified empire of Qin in 221 BC, a spelling reform was introduced along with a simplified Small Seal script. The latter remained in use until the 1950s, when the Communist rulers of China introduced the present still-controversial Simplified script.

Below is the evolution of two characters from Shang to Simplified script. Both are pictographic but in different ways: the first character, 'lái', means 'come' and derives rebus-wise from the homophonous word for 'wheat' (which in its archaic form it depicts), the second character, 'mǎ', means 'horse'.

Over three millennia the number of Chinese characters increased dramatically. In the Shang period, there were some 4500, as we have seen; in the Han dynasty almost 10,000, despite the reform of the Qin dynasty (221–206 BC); by the 12th century there were 23,000; and by the 18th century there were almost 49,000 characters – many of them, to be sure, variants and obsolete forms. The overall appearance of the characters changed considerably over time, and many individual characters suffered attrition in form, all of which greatly muddled the picture of how particular characters have come to have the meanings they have, based on their constituent parts.

Nevertheless, the basic principles on which Chinese characters have been constructed have remained unchanged.

Above **Bronze inscription in the Seal script, from the western Zhou period, *c.* 1028–771 BC.**

	Shang	Great Seal	Small Seal	Scribal	Regular	Simplified
lái come	來	來	來	來	來	来
mǎ horse	馬	馬	馬	馬	馬	马

Left **The evolution of two Chinese characters. The Great Seal script, shown above, was the style of the Zhou dynasty (*c.* 1028–221 BC); the Small Seal script was the style of the Qin dynasty (221–206 BC); the Scribal and Regular scripts were the styles of the Han dynasty (206 BC–AD 220). (From DeFrancis, 1984)**

Classifying Chinese Characters

How can 49,000 characters, or more importantly 10,000 characters, be analysed and classified for the purpose of, say, dictionary making? There is no simple answer. Traditionally, Chinese characters have been divided into five (some would say six) different groups according to the principle of their composition.

We have already come across the first group, which consists of pictograms. The second group represents words not pictorially but with other visually logical forms. For example, the numbers one, two, three are represented by one, two and three lines:

Another example is:

上　　　　下

above　　　below

We might call this group 'simple representational'.

In the third group, which might be called 'compound representational', the logic is more complex: at the level of ideas rather than the visual. A favourite example is the combination of the characters for sun and moon to form 'bright':

日　　月　　明

sun　　moon　　bright

The fourth group involves the rebus principle. We have just seen an example, in which the character for wheat is used for 'come', because the word for wheat, 'lái', is homophonous with the word for 'come'.

Another example is the character for 'elephant' which is also used for 'image', because both words are pronounced *xiàng*.

The final group, often termed 'semantic-phonetic', involves the combination of a character indicating the meaning of a word with a character indicating its pronunciation. Thus the character for female person is combined with the character with the sound value *mǎ* to create a new character meaning mother:

'female person' + *mǎ* = 'mā' (mother)

Note that the phonetic component does not give the pronunciation precisely: the tones differ. The difference is crucial, given that 'mǎ' means 'horse'. It is often imagined that the meaning of 媽 is really derived from the combination of two ideas, in other words,

woman + horse = mother ('female horse')

rather than being derived from the combination of an *idea* with a *phonetic*. But this ideographic notion, appealing as it is (not least to overworked mothers), has no foundation and is a good example of the misunderstandings of Chinese characters that abound. It is *wrong* to think of Chinese characters as 'ideographic' in this sense.

The proportions of characters in the five groups have not remained constant with time. There was a higher proportion of pictographic characters during the Shang dynasty than is now the case. Today the vast majority of characters, over 90 per cent, is of the 'semantic-phonetic' variety.

268 lí-lǐ

黎 lí 为í 众。~民。~

漓(灘) lí 为í ①见
281 页'淋漓'条

缡(褵) lí 为í

篱(籬) lí 为í

醨 lí 为í

梨(棃) lí 为í

犁(犂) lí 为í

黧 lí 为í

黎 lí 为í

蔾(藜) lí 为í

熬 lí 为í

罹 lí 为í

蠡 lí 为í

劙 lí 为í

礼(禮) lǐ 为ǐ

李 lǐ 为ǐ

lǐ 269

里(❹❺裏、裡) lǐ 为ǐ ①市制

俚 lǐ 为ǐ

哩 lí 为í

浬 lǐ 为ǐ

娌 lǐ 为ǐ

理 lǐ 为ǐ

锂 lǐ 为ǐ

鲤 lǐ 为ǐ

逦(邐) lǐ 为ǐ

澧 lǐ 为ǐ

醴 lǐ 为ǐ

鳢 lǐ 为ǐ

Xinhua dictionary, 1990 edition. Chinese dictionaries are ordered by the general meaning of characters rather than by their sound, and by the shape of characters. Dictionaries are therefore cumbersome to use, even for a fluent native speaker.

Chinese Dictionaries

To know that a Chinese word is pronounced and written in a certain way will not enable its meaning to be found in a Chinese dictionary. For the Chinese have not produced a single dictionary with entries arranged in simple alphabetical order – with, say, the character pronounced *xiàng* coming later in the dictionary than the character pronounced *mǎ* ('x' normally coming after 'm'). Instead they have contrived a host of other schemes based on characters' *shape*, rather than pronunciation or meaning.

Some dictionaries arrange the characters by the number of strokes required to draw a particular character, a series of movements drummed into Chinese writers at school. It is common to see a dictionary user counting up the number of strokes in a complex character on his or her fingers. It could easily be 20 or more. Where the number of strokes is miscounted, a time-consuming search is required in the general area of the nearest guess at the stroke number. More popular is the 'radical-stroke' system, employed by the

first Chinese dictionary (2nd century AD) which arranged its 9353 characters under 540 semantic keys or 'radicals', such as 'water', 'vegetation', 'insect' (compare 'female person' in 媽 , 'mother'); the number of keys was later reduced to 214. These were then ordered according to number of strokes – from 1 to 17 – with a fixed order imposed on radicals having the same number of strokes (thus the 'water' radical was always 85th in the list). To use the dictionary, one has to determine under which radical the word in question might be classified – often a tricky decision. One popular dictionary contains a 'List of Characters Having Obscure Radicals' that includes fully *one twelfth* of its 7773 characters.

The radical-stroke system of 214 radicals remained standard until the 1950s. Now, with Simplified characters, dictionaries arrange the radicals under anything from 186 to 250 categories; there is no standard. The resultant chaos – as if, say, different western dictionaries used different A–Z orderings – can easily be imagined.

The Soothill Syllabary

Chinese characters have both a phonetic and a semantic component. The former gives a clue to the pronunciation of the character, the latter to its meaning. Instead of being classified by stroke number or semantic key (p. 187), Chinese characters can also be classified by phonetic key. Native Chinese speakers have generally left this approach to phonetically minded foreigners, who were mainly foreign missionaries. One of them was W. E. Soothill; in the 1880s he classified some 4300 characters on the basis of 895 phonetics.

Part of the Soothill syllabary is printed opposite. Each character in a column contains the phonetic at the top of the column (e.g. 'mǎ'); these internal phonetics have been highlighted. The pronunciation of each character in a column is mostly very similar; but in appearance and stroke number (not to mention meaning), the characters in a column will differ enormously.

If we choose certain phonetic columns and pick out the characters that share the same semantic/radical and place them in rows, we can make a semantic–phonetic grid (*below*). If we follow the column under phonetic 264, 'áo', we can see that the phonetic is a good guide to the pronunciation of four characters which contain it. But if we follow a row, such as semantic 9, 'person', the semantic is clearly *not* a good guide to meaning. Generally, in Chinese characters, phonetics prove better guides to pronunciation than semantics do to meaning – contrary to the predictions of

The Methodist Free Church, Wenchou, where the Reverend W. E. Soothill had his mission. His Chinese congregation can be seen standing in front of the church.

Below and opposite
Chinese characters have both a phonetic and a semantic component. The former gives a clue to the pronunciation of the character, the latter to its meaning.

phonetic / semantic	敖 áo 264	參 cān 282	堯 yáo 391	甫 fǔ 597
9 亻 person	傲 ào: proud	傪 cān: good	僥 jiǎo: lucky	傅 fù: help
64 扌 hand	摮 áo: shake	摻 shān: seize	撓 nǎo: scratch	捕 bǔ: catch
75 木 wood	檄 áo: barge	槮 shēn: beam	橈 náo: oar	楠 fú: trellis
85 氵 water	滶 áo: stream	渗 shèn: leak	澆 jiāo: sprinkle	浦 pǔ: creek

holars who maintain that Chinese is ctually a logographic script in which honography is hardly significant.

In practice, native speakers use both mantic and phonetic clues when reading naracters. Consider these two characters hich share the same phonetic:

A 仃 'dīng' (alone)

B 汀 'tīng' (sandspit)

The pronunciation of this phonetic honetic 2 in the Soothill syllabary) is *dīng*. therefore represents the pronunciation of naracter A exactly and that of character B ith 75 per cent accuracy (three phonemes, *ng* and tone, out of a possible total of ur). The semantic in each case is also elpful, though less than the phonetic: in A 丁 suggests 'man', in B 氵丁 suggests vater'. A Chinese reader could begin the rocess of guessing the characters either ith the phonetic or with the semantic omponents. But in either case, he or she ould need to have *learnt* in advance the gnificance of the three components; their napes alone would not be of any practical ssistance.

The foregoing analysis demonstrates hat, for a native speaker, reading Chinese naracters is part memory feat and part bility to spot interconnections. What it ertainly does not resemble – despite claims the contrary – is the memorization and call of several thousand telephone umbers. Chinese readers are not like hinese telegraph clerks who indeed do onvert each character into a standard four-igit code. (Using this code, 'arriving omorrow noon' would be sent as 2494 1131 022 0582 0451.) However intimidating hinese characters may appear to a reign learner, they are by no means ntirely random.

phonetic 75	phonetic 158	phonetic 255	phonetic 391
皇 huáng	辟 pì	馬 mǎ	堯 yáo
喤 huáng	僻 pì	瑪 mǎ	嶢 yáo
徨 huáng	譬 pì	碼 mǎ	巕 yáo
惶 huáng	闢 pì	螞 mǎ	僥 jiǎo
湟 huáng	嬖 pì	鎷 mǎ	澆 jiǎo
煌 huáng	避 pì	媽 mā	翹 qiáo
鰉 huáng	壁 pì	犸 mà	磽 qiáo
蝗 huáng	璧 pì	禡 mà	蹺 qiāo
鍠 huáng	劈 pì	罵 mà	嘵 xiāo
隍 huáng	癖 pǐ	獁 mà	驍 xiāo
遑 huáng	臂 pèi	嘛 ma	曉 xiǎo
篁 huáng	擘 pò		燒 shāo
凰 huáng	孽 niè		譊 náo
堭 huáng			橈 náo
艎 huáng			鐃 náo
			撓 nǎo
			髐 náo
			嬈 ráo
			蕘 ráo
			蟯 ráo
			饒 ráo
			繞 rào

The Chinese Language

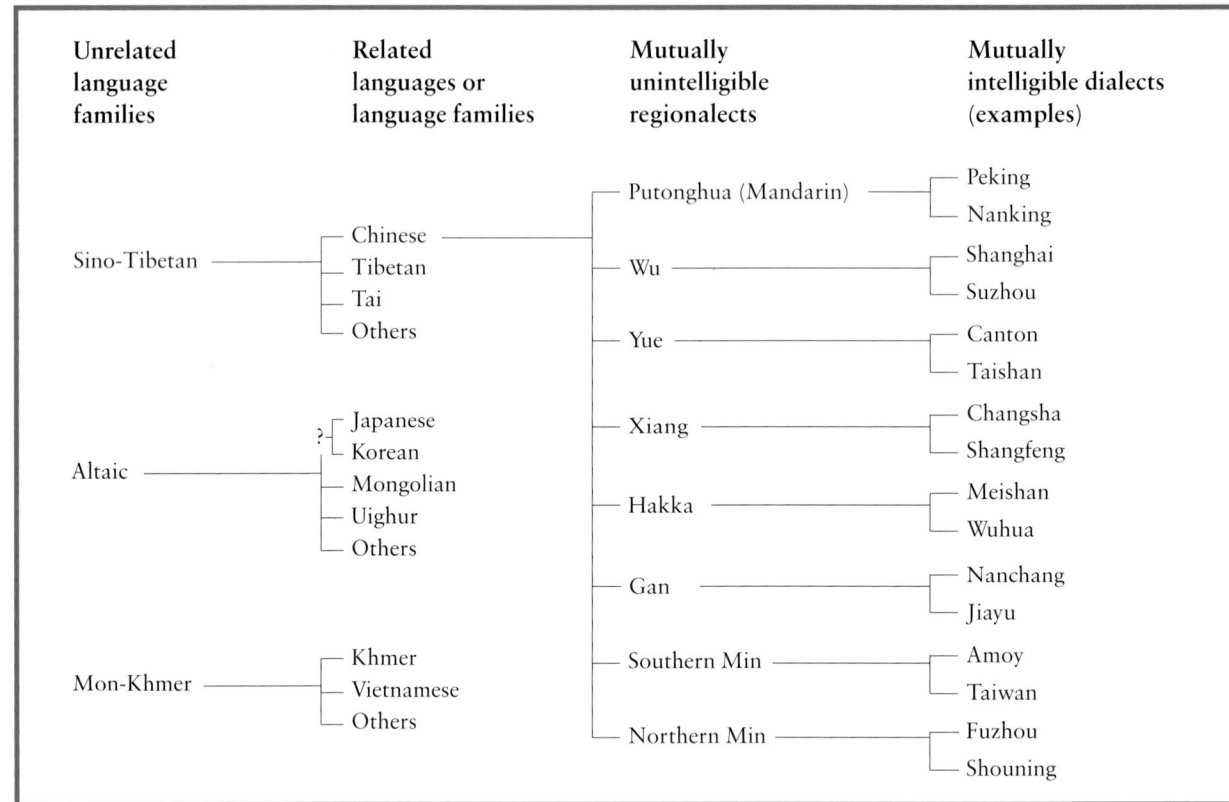

Unrelated language families	Related languages or language families	Mutually unintelligible regionalects	Mutually intelligible dialects (examples)
Sino-Tibetan	Chinese, Tibetan, Tai, Others	Putonghua (Mandarin)	Peking, Nanking
		Wu	Shanghai, Suzhou
		Yue	Canton, Taishan
Altaic	Japanese ?, Korean, Mongolian, Uighur, Others	Xiang	Changsha, Shangfeng
		Hakka	Meishan, Wuhua
		Gan	Nanchang, Jiayu
Mon-Khmer	Khmer, Vietnamese, Others	Southern Min	Amoy, Taiwan
		Northern Min	Fuzhou, Shouning

In 1569, a Dominican friar in China became the first foreigner to suggest that those Chinese who could not understand each other's speech could nevertheless communicate in writing. The idea is still widely held. But it is not true.

What the outside world calls the Chinese language is in fact made up of eight regional languages ('topolects' or 'regionalects') that are mutually unintelligible, and tens, if not hundreds, of true dialects. Over 70 per cent of Chinese do however speak a single language, Mandarin, also known as Putonghua ('common speech'). Modern *written* Chinese is based on Mandarin or Putonghua. It is the dominance of

Mandarin speakers in China, both in classical times and today, that has fuelled the myth of the universal intelligibility of Chinese characters.

The languages of East Asia are shown above in family-tree form. It is immediately obvious that Chinese, Japanese/Korean and Vietnamese belong to three different families, despite sharing the use of Chinese characters in their scripts. Chinese belongs to the Sino-Tibetan family, which may be loosely compared with the Indo-European family; the various Chinese regionalects such as Yue (Cantonese) and Wu (spoken in the Shanghai region) are then analogous to English, Dutch and German in the

Germanic group or French, Spanish and Italian in the Romance group; while the dialects within Mandarin such as are spoken in Beijing and Nanking are comparable to the British, American and Australian dialects of English or the Neapolitan, Roman and Tuscan dialects of Italian. And just as French and English speakers cannot understand each others' literature without learning each others' language (despite sharing the same Roman script), so Cantonese speakers cannot understand modern written Chinese properly without learning how to speak Mandarin: Cantonese is nearer to Mandarin than, say, Spanish is to French, but the differences in grammar, vocabulary and pronunciation are still major ones.

Tones

There are six tones in Cantonese and only four tones in Mandarin: high level, high rising, low dipping and high falling. (Japanese has no tones of the Chinese kind.) Tones in Chinese disambiguate the large number of what would otherwise be homophones; when, as often happens, foreigners ignore tones, they naturally conclude that Chinese is an even more 'difficult' language than it really is. For instance, 'ma', without indication of tone, can mean 'mother', 'hemp', 'horse' and 'scold'; 'shuxue' can mean 'mathematics' and 'blood transfusion'; 'guojiang' can mean 'you flatter me' and 'fruit paste'. With tone indication the meanings are clearly distinguished.

Left and below Family tree of East Asian languages and map showing the regionalects and dialects of China. More than 70 per cent of Chinese speak Mandarin, while 5 per cent speak Cantonese (Yue). (From DeFrancis, 1984)

Below Chinese is a tonal language. Mandarin has four tones: (top to bottom) **high level, high rising, low dipping and high falling.**

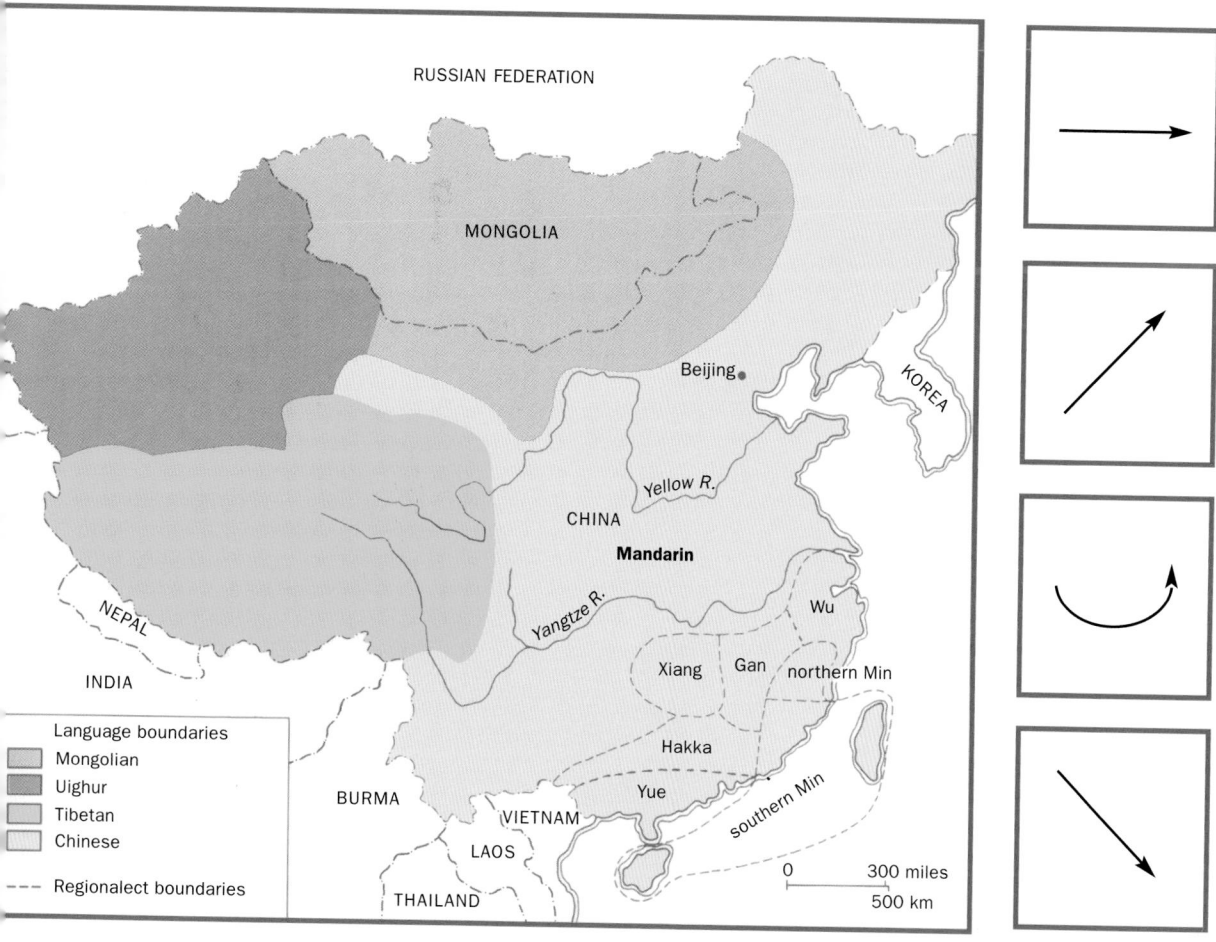

Chinese Calligraphy

'Calligraphy' means originally 'beautiful writing'. It has been practised in all cultures and all periods, from the ancient Egyptian Book of the Dead, through illuminated medieval western and Arabic manuscripts, to today's elaborate wedding invitations. But in China calligraphy has always been more than simply refinement or elaboration of writing; it has been synonymous with writing. The Chinese do not speak of 'fine handwriting', but simply of 'the art of writing', 'shufa'. In classical China, writing ('shu') was an art on a par with painting, poetry and music, sometimes even above them.

The reason is, of course, the unique variety of forms in the Chinese script, as compared to alphabetic scripts. The Chinese writer was naturally challenged to use his brush to express this variety aesthetically, while remaining legible – a crucial requirement. The Chinese calligrapher aims to endow the Chinese characters with life, to animate them without distorting their fundamental shapes. In doing so, his artistic personality enters into the forms in a way that is not true of western calligraphy, which is on the whole impersonal. The names of the greatest Chinese calligraphers are well known in China, unlike those of calligraphers in the West.

In the recent words of a foreign student of Chinese calligraphy – which are perhaps a little exaggerated in their claims – 'the brush is not a rough tool like the pen, but an instrument which registers every move of the hand, however slight or sudden, with the exactness of a seismograph. The Chinese calligrapher uses it to record forces arising from the depths of his being: while western calligraphy produces arrested forms, Chinese calligraphy is in essence an art of movement.'

Equipment of the Chinese calligrapher. Apart from brushes and paper, the writer requires an inkstone, an inkstick and water for adding to the powdered ink. This 6-inch-high (15-cm) inkstone (left) shows a tortoise rising from the water, symbolizing the emergence of the primordial signs.
The hairs of Chinese brushes (below), which are generally inserted into bamboo handles, are of goat, hare or marten, the hairs of wild martens shot in autumn being especially prized for their brisk reaction to changes of pressure, which imparts a spiritedness to the writing of Chinese characters.

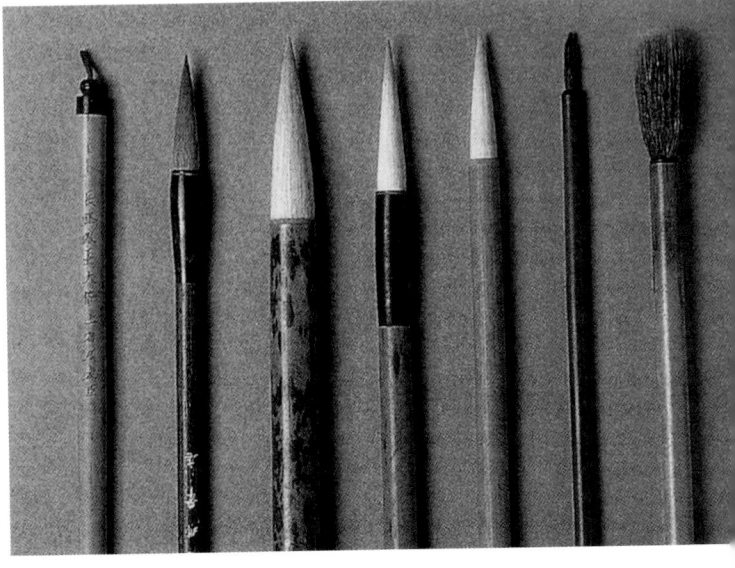

Chen Hongshou, *The Four Joys of Nan Sheng-lu* (1649). The scholar prepares to write. His paperweight is a carved lion; before him is a bowl of water with a ladling spoon, inkstick and inkstone with ink ground in it; on his left is a jug of wine, a cup and a citron in a bowl.

Forming Characters: Craft and Art

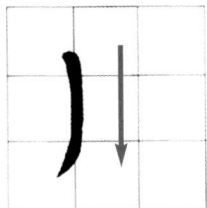 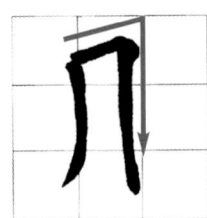  

The number of strokes needed to write a Chinese character is, as we saw (p. 187), an important guiding principle of Chinese dictionaries. Above, for instance, are the four strokes in the character 'dan' (cinnabar).

Chinese children learn the technique early, beginning with the simplest characters and moving progressively to more and more complex ones. Following the teacher, a class of young children traces the characters rhythmically in the air with broad gestures of arm and hand. As the children trace, they name each element – bar, leg, dot and so on – and at the end they pronounce the character. Then, when the gestures have been learnt, the children write the character down, again broadly, rhythmically and collectively. In due course they learn to write the character small and on their own. Here is part of an immature exercise book by a five- or six-year-old schoolboy:

From schoolboy exercises to the work of a master calligrapher requires many years of practice, devotion and study of earlier masters of the art. The vitality of a master's work is partly a product of technique and partly the expression of personal sensibility.

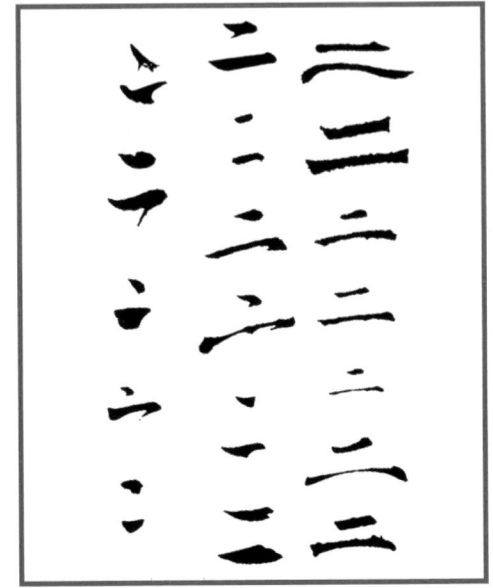

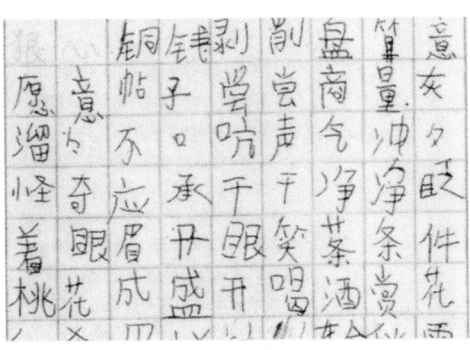

Vital techniques in Chinese calligraphy. The four characters on the first line are correctly drawn but lacking in life. By offsetting the lines, the calligrapher can create the four lively (and superior) variants beneath. The characters are: (1) 'qe' (pieces), (2) 'ren' (man), (3) 'mu' (tree) (4) 'he' (to join).

Variant forms of the character 'er' (two). For a Chinese reader, legibility is maintained, while the art in calligraphy is given full play.

The character 'shou', (longevity), written in Small Seal script by Wu Changshuo (1844–1927) in 1923, his 80th year. Many great pieces of calligraphy, particularly from earlier periods, have four or five or even more autographs appended to them by later calligraphers who thereby express their joy at the original master's achievement.

Pinyin: Romanizing Chinese

In 1936, the leader of the Communist rebels in China, Mao Zedong, told the American journalist Edgar Snow: 'We believe Latinization is a good instrument with which to overcome illiteracy. Chinese characters are so difficult to learn that even the best system of rudimentary characters, or simplified teaching, does not equip the people with a really efficient and rich vocabulary. Sooner or later, we believe, we will have to abandon characters altogether if we are to create a new social culture in which the masses fully participate.'

In practice, Mao encountered so much opposition from the literati that a compromise was struck. In 1955, the characters were simplified by eliminating certain variants and reducing the number of strokes in many of those remaining. In 1958, the government introduced romanized Chinese script, known as Pinyin ('spell sound'), as the official system for writing the sounds of Chinese and for transcribing Chinese characters. Pinyin was adopted for, among other things, the spelling of Chinese names outside China (hence Peking became Beijing, Canton Guangzhou, and so on).

During the Cultural Revolution in the 1960s, Pinyin went into eclipse: xenophobic Red Guards, supporters of character simplification, tore down street signs written in Pinyin as evidence of China kow-towing to foreigners. Today, the Chinese probably have the worst of both worlds: chaos in the character script and an uncertain status for the romanized script. According to John DeFrancis, a leading western exponent of Pinyin, 'A whole generation, both of people and of time, has been uselessly sacrificed in a timid, bumbling, and predictably unsuccessful attempt to achieve mass literacy through the simplification of characters.'

Schoolchildren learn both characters and Pinyin (first introduced in 1958). Evidence suggests that children learn Pinyin much more quickly than characters. 'Digraphia' (the use of two scripts) probably represents the future of Chinese writing.

Simplified Characters

Character simplification sounds like a good idea. Reducing the number and complexity of essential characters should make the

Chinese script easier to learn, should it not? The government thought that illiterates could begin by learning, say, 1000 or 1500 of these Simplified characters, particularly characters linked to local conditions in the village or factory. It was hoped this would give the peasants and workers a core vocabulary. Later, perhaps, some of them could go on to learn the full script.

These beliefs proved unfounded. It was one thing for Mao Zedong and other leaders familiar with the full script to save time in writing by using the Simplified characters, quite another for illiterate peasants, workers and low-level party bureaucrats to learn the script from scratch. Confusion was the result. In 1982, for instance, the following five (Simplified) characters, written by government workers, appeared on electric power poles in a street in Tianjin:

马
车
弊
奋
斗

The *People's Daily* carried a photograph and remarked that people were baffled by the characters. The first two characters spell 'mǎchē' (horse cart), the third does not exist, and the last two are 'fèndòu' (struggle). The explanation appears to be that the writers had miswritten the third character, which should have been 带 'dài' (carry), and that the last two characters are misspellings for 粪兜 'fèndōu' (manure bag). The enigmatic message was supposed to be an exhortation to cart drivers to carry manure bags so that their horses would not litter the street.

It is hardly surprising that writing reform is controversial in China. Not only is the

Chinese script beautiful, mysterious and unique, it is older than any other living script. An educated Chinese person is bound to feel that the script is part of his or her identity. Nevertheless, Mao Zedong and many other senior reformers of Chinese writing were probably right: the Chinese script is an insurmountable obstacle to progress in China. It is for this reason that Chinese reformers, eschewing talk of abandoning characters totally, are now emphasizing a policy of 'digraphia', the use of two scripts, Pinyin *and* characters, each to be used in the areas for which it is best adapted. (Pinyin, for example, is best suited for inputting Chinese into computers.)

Chinese typewriter. There are over 2000 characters in such a machine; the total available font could be as high as 10,000 characters. When the typist presses a key, an arm picks up the required character and strikes it against the paper. The arm moves either horizontally or vertically. Trained operators type at 20–30 characters per minute; casual users can manage only two or three. The use of these unwieldy contraptions – which show the complexity of the Chinese script more vividly than almost anything else – is now almost zero with the advent of computers.

Below **Map of Beijing labelled in Chinese characters and Pinyin. Chinese official policy now supports both systems. Mao was an accomplished calligrapher who nevertheless believed that China should sweep away its script in favour of the romanized script. In 1956, praising the efforts of script reformer Wu Yuzhang, Mao told the party leaders: 'If the Latin alphabet had been invented by the Chinese, probably there would not be any problem. The problem arises from the fact that the foreigners did the inventing and the Chinese did the copying ... All good things from abroad, things that are useful to us, we should study and take over entirely, digesting them and transforming them into our things.'**

Chapter 12   *Japanese Writing*

The earliest work of Japanese literature. *Kojiki*, an ancient history of Japan, was completed in AD 712; this copy was printed from woodblocks in 1803. The main text is written in Chinese characters (kanji), but beside these characters are smaller Japanese phonetic signs (kana), indicating the Japanese pronunciation of the character. To this day, Japanese writing consists of two systems of signs, kanji and kana, mixed together.

Learning Kanji

Chinese is about as different from Japanese as any language could be, both in phonological system, grammatical categories, and syntactic structures', according to an American student of Japanese. Nevertheless, the Japanese based their writing system on Chinese characters, which they referred to as 'kanji', their approximation of the Mandarin term 'hanzi' (Chinese characters). In borrowing the characters, the Japanese of course altered their original Chinese pronunciation in particular ways corresponding to the sounds of the Japanese language.

Eventually the Japanese invented a fairly small set of supplementary symbols – which are actually simplified versions of the kanji, phonetic in nature and known as 'kana' – in order to make clear how kanji used for writing Japanese were to be pronounced and how to transcribe native words. It would have been simpler, one might reasonably think, if the Japanese had used *only* these invented symbols and had abandoned the Chinese characters altogether – but this would have entailed the rejection of a writing system of enormous prestige. Just as a knowledge of Latin was until recently *sine qua non* of the educated European – as was a knowledge of Sumerian for those educated in Akkadian in the second millennium BC – so a familiarity with Chinese has always been considered essential by the Japanese literati.

Today an ordinary educated Japanese person is supposed to know nearly 2000 kanji; those of a literary turn of mind may command some 5000 kanji or more. This has been true only since the Second World War, however, as a result of the mass education policy introduced during the American Occupation. Not surprisingly, many Japanese found the demands of such learning extremely stressful. It is probably no coincidence that there was a peak in suicides among juveniles in the period 1955–58, when the first wholly post-war educated students were leaving school. Since then, the necessity of learning kanji has acted as a unifying force in Japanese society, helping to reinforce both the myth that the Japanese are somehow unique and the already mentioned 'ideographic' myth (that Chinese characters do not involve phonography). The experience of becoming literate in Japanese is something like learning the answers to thousands of 'trivia' questions, but without the consolation that it is only a game. Careers, income and status depend on mastering kanji. 'No wonder', says a second American student of the language and script, 'Japanese are convinced that kanji are wordless molecules of meaning!'

Pronouncing Kanji

On top of having to learn the shapes of the kanji, the Japanese must also learn their sounds. These fall into two basic categories, either of which may apply depending on context. For the foreigner who is learning Japanese, this can be perplexing: how does one tell which of the two or more readings of a kanji is the correct one? It is rather like knowing that the usual English pronunciation of '2' in '2 + 3' is *two*, but in '$x^2 + 3$' it is *squared*.

Kanji lesson in modern Japanese crammer. Primary school children are supposed to learn 960 kanji; another 1000 or so are in theory acquired during secondary school (and university education). Children generally (but not always) begin with the simpler 'kun' reading of a kanji, that is the native Japanese pronunciation, and leave the 'on' reading (the Chinese-derived pronunciation) until later.

Below **Not all kanji have both a 'kun' and an 'on' reading. This depends on whether Japanese does or does not have a close translation equivalent of the corresponding Chinese word. Some single 'on' words have been borrowed into Japanese but more often, 'on' readings occur in groups forming longer words. Below are five examples of kanji that take a 'kun' reading when standing alone and an 'on' reading when combined with other kanji.**

The two categories are known as the 'kun' reading and the 'on' reading (also known as the Sino-Japanese reading). Broadly speaking, the first is a native Japanese gloss, the second a pronunciation derived from Chinese. The 'kun' reading of the kanji for ocean is 'umi', while the 'on' reading is 'kai'. The pronunciation of the character 海 in Mandarin is *hǎi*. The 'on' reading is known to be derived from an earlier Chinese pronunciation which was used at the time when the kanji was borrowed into Japanese (about the 7th century AD).

	水	下	海	面	星
'kun' reading	mizu	shita	umi	omote	hoshi
meaning	water	below	ocean	face	star

	水面	下水	海水	水面下	水星
'on' reading	suimen	ge sui	kai sui	sui men ka	sui sei
meaning	water surface	sewage	sea water	underwater	Mercury

Two Japanese Syllabaries: Hiragana and Katakana

Japanese phonetic script dates from a period soon after the borrowing of Chinese characters to write Japanese words. The Japanese took various kanji and simplified them to produce two syllabaries, known today as 'hiragana' ('easy kana') and 'katakana' ('side kana'). Each consists of some 46 signs augmented by two special diacritics (not shown) and by a technique of symbol combination for representing complex syllables, seen below. Note that curved lines are relatively common in hiragana, while straight lines tend to be characteristic of katakana.

Why *two* syllabaries? Originally hiragana was used for informal writing and katakana for more formal works such as official documents, histories and lexical works.

Below **Japanese kana, syllabic letters. The upper rows (black) are hiragana; the lower rows (red) are katakana.**

a	ka	sa	ta	na	ha	ma	ya	ra	wa	
あ	か	さ	た	な	は	ま	や	ら	わ	
ア	カ	サ	タ	ナ	ハ	マ	ヤ	ラ	ワ	

i	ki	shi	chi	ni	hi	mi		ri		
い	き	し	ち	に	ひ	み		り		
イ	キ	ツ	チ	ニ	ヒ	ミ		リ		

u	ku	su	tsu	nu	fu	mu	yu	ru		
う	く	す	つ	ぬ	ふ	む	ゆ	る		
ウ	ク	ス	ツ	ヌ	フ	ム	ユ	ル		

e	kesu	se	te	ne	he	me		re		
え	け	せ	て	ね	へ	め		れ		
エ	ケ	セ	テ	ネ	ヘ	メ		レ		

o	ko	so	to	no	ho	mo	yo	ro	(w)o	n
お	こ	そ	と	の	ほ	も	よ	ろ	を	ん
オ	コ	ソ	ト	ノ	ホ	モ	ヨ	ロ	ヲ	ン

Today hiragana is the more frequently employed script, and katakana serves roughly the same function as italic type in alphabetic scripts. Foreign names and foreign terms recently borrowed into Japanese are nearly always written in katakana. For instance, in this cinema advertisement:

Here the American name Clint Eastwood has been spelt in katakana as follows: *Kurinto Isutouddu*, there being no *l* sound in Japanese. The consequent misspelling in English clearly reflects this fact (though ironically the Japanese pronunciation of the *r* sound is quite close to some *l* sounds in British English).

And how do the Japanese decide whether to use kana or kanji in a sentence? There is a fair amount of fluctuation and overlap between the two. However, as a very general guide, kana serve to represent inflectional affixes, grammatical particles, many adverbs and the vast majority of words of European origin, while kanji are employed to write the majority of nouns – both native Japanese and Sino-Japanese ones, other than those of western origin – and many verb and adjective bases.

The advertisement above, for an ordinary Japanese hotel, illustrates the distinction. The katakana in the top line and in the bottom two lines (there are no hiragana) stand out from the kanji by virtue of being simpler. The top line is the name of the hotel, *Oriento Hoteru* (Orient Hotel). The bottom two lines to the right of the kanji

read: *kādokīshisutemu* (card key system)/ *bā*, *furansu resutoran* (bar, French restaurant).

The rest of the advertisement is a mixture of kanji, 'romaji' (roman letters, e.g. TV), numerals and pictograms/logograms. Consider the line beneath the name of the hotel, which is actually its address (〒 872, means simply Postcode 872):

	山	口	県	中	川	市	森	田	町 2-16
'kun' reading	yama	guchi	(agata)	naka	gawa	ichi	mori	ta	machi
'on' reading	san	kō/ku	ken	chū	sen	shi	shin	den	chō

The various correct readings in this context ('kun' and 'on') have been highlighted. The full address (read from right to left) is:

2–16, Morita Cho, Nakagawa Shi, Yamaguchi Ken, [postcode] 872
which means:
Number 16, 2nd Street, Morita Ward, Nakagawa City, Yamaguchi Prefecture, [postcode] 872.

The rest of the advertisement concerns distance (15 minutes by car from Japan Rail, JR, i.e. Nakagawa Station), price (starting at 11,800 Yen), parking (for 20 vehicles), style (metal frame block with 15 storeys, 200 rooms, 40 Japanese-style and 160 western-style, all with TV, telephone and airconditioning), and location (in town centre).

Kana versus Kanji

All Japanese sentences can in principle be written entirely in kana. In fact one of the greatest works in Japanese literature – Murasaki Shikibu's *The Tale of Genji* (early 11th century) – was written in hiragana (though her original manuscript no longer exists). Kana for centuries was the main style of writing used by women. Today most Japanese Braille is written in kana, without using any kanji; and the result is that the Japanese blind are able to read more easily than many of the Japanese sighted!

Why then do the Japanese as a whole not convert to writing in kana alone? Why do they persist with the awkward intricacies of the mixed kana and kanji script? Several factors contribute to their determination, to which we shall shortly return. Here we shall mention only one: homophony. All languages have it: examples are 'to', 'too', 'two' in English or 'cou', 'coup', 'coût' in French.

In Japanese, however, the homophony is on a grand scale. Consider the meanings of the various Sino-Japanese words listed on the right which all have the pronunciation *kanshō*.

If these many kanji compounds were to be replaced with a few kana spelling *kanshō*, the ambiguity might be a serious handicap in communication. There are numerous comparable potentially ambiguous examples of homophony in Japanese. Admittedly they are not all as wide-ranging, and would in many cases be clarified by the context of a word in a sentence; nevertheless homophony is widely thought to be a major barrier to kana-only writing.

Kanji		Meaning
奸	商傷	vice merchant
感	傷	sentimental
干	渉	interference
完	勝	victory
湔	症	irritable
感	賞	to praise
勧	賞	to encourage
勧	奨	encouragement
鑑	賞	to appreciate
観	賞	to admire
観	照	contemplation
観	象	to observe the weather
環	礁	atoll
緩	衝	buffer/bumper
官	省	government office
簡	捷	to expedite
管	掌	to manage

Homophony in Japanese. These 17 different kanji are all pronounced *kanshō*. (Nine further kanji have been omitted.) If they were to be written as one kana, serious confusion would result. The context of a word would not always be sufficient to enable the reader to select which meaning the writer had in mind.

'The letter in the wind', woodblock by Torii Kiyohiro, 1751–64. A woman's paper handkerchiefs are carried away by the wind, along with a love letter she has been concealing. The writing is a mixture of kana and kanji; the 'haiku' (a kind of Japanese poem) written 'in the air' appears to be bawdy verse with several double-entendres. Prints of this kind – revealing parts of the female body normally kept covered – were known as 'abunae' (dangerous pictures). In earlier periods of Japanese history, such as that of Murasaki, writer of *The Tale of Genji*, women wrote almost entirely in kana rather than kanji, which were used by men and regarded as more prestigious. By the 18th century (the time of the artist, Kiyohiro), this taboo had broken down.

The Most Complicated Writing in the World

In 1928, Sir George Sansom, an authority on Japan, remarked of its writing system that 'There is no doubt it provides for me a fascinating field of study, but as a practical instrument it is surely without inferiors.' A modern authority, Marshall Unger, added recently: 'In a broad sense, over the centuries, Japanese script has "worked". Japanese culture has not flourished *because of* the complexities of its writing system, but it has undeniably flourished in spite of them.'

Imagine, for instance, that you need to spell your name and address over the telephone. It is easy enough with an alphabet, well-nigh impossible with certain kanji that distinguish personal and place names which sound alike. How do you describe each of some 2000 symbols? You have to speak of, say, 'three-stroke *kawa*' (*sanbongawa*) – as opposed to all other kanji that can be read *kawa*; or *yoko-ichi*, the kanji read *ichi* that is written with a single horizontal stroke. But this method of naming kanji is of limited usefulness, because kanji shapes vary so widely and nonuniformly. Thus, in face-to-face conversations, in the absence of pencil and paper, the Japanese resort to pantomime: they use the right index finger as a 'pencil' to 'write' the kanji in the air or on the palm of the left hand. But often this too fails, and a person must use an appropriate common word as a label for the kanji. For example, of the dozens of kanji that can be read *tō*, only one can also stand for the noun 'higashi' (east); this character is then readily labelled *higashi to iu ji*, 'the character *higashi*'. When, however, a kanji has only one

reading, and you wish to describe it, you have a problem. To identify the kanji that stands for *tō* in 'satō' (sugar) you cannot do much more than say something like, 'It's the one used in the last syllable of the word for sugar.' If that does not trigger the memory of the person you are talking to, you must go back to the shape: 'It's the kanji with the "rice" radical on the left, and the *tang* of "Tang Dynasty" on the right.'

This print by Torii Kiyonobu (1664–1729) shows a street bookseller in the early 18th century. On the top of her pile of books is Murasaki's *The Tale of Genji*. Beneath that are books on music; the inscription on the box is an advertisement. The bookseller holds a writing brush in one hand and a guide to letter-writing in the other.

Romaji: the Romanization of Japanese

During the 1980s, the Roman alphabet began to invade Japanese writing through advertising. Words which before would have been written in katakana in magazines and newspapers and on television and billboards suddenly began to be written in Roman letters, even in the middle of a sentence otherwise written in kana and kanji. Could the alphabet eventually take over, driving out the centuries-old kanji, or is the gradual absorption of alphabetic letters just another example of the Japanese ability to extract from a foreign culture what is of benefit to them? Can *three* different systems of writing coexist?

There can be no doubt that the alphabet has acquired prestige in Japan, as once the Chinese characters did. This is not just a love of novelty, but seems to reflect a disenchantment with the rigours of kanji culture (also seen in the move away from demanding reading towards comics containing relatively few kanji). As the head of product development at Sony remarked in 1984, 'With the word "love" in Roman letters, we can work that into a graphic design and it carries a kind of cuteness and charm. But the Chinese ideogram for "love", we couldn't put that on a kid's school bag. It would carry a feeling of intrinsic difficulty, create resistance instead of sales appeal.'

Brand names of imported goods, spelt in Roman letters, may often be difficult to express in Japanese. But some Japanese companies, both large and small, feel that printing their Japanese brand name in Roman letters gives them a fresh, prestigious corporate identity.

Roman letters have been glamorous in Japan since the 1980s.

Kanji, Kana and Romaji

This breakfast cereal packet of 1985 is an amusing example of the Japanese script at its most 'mixed'. The basic message of the advertisement is that if a man does not receive a good breakfast before facing the working day, he will not prosper in his job. (Hence the male figure wilting as he hangs onto a strap while commuting to work.) The slogan across the top (1) is written in kanji and hiragana, and reads:

chō shoku nuki wa shusse ga osoi!?
No breakfast, slow promotion!?

The large characters in the top right-hand corner (4) are pure kanji and read (in parody of the well-known masthead of the newspaper *Asahi Shinbun*):

chōshoku shinbun
Breakfast Newspaper

Beneath them the brand name Kellogg's (5) appears in Roman letters – but in the middle of the 'newspaper' Kellogg's has been spelt in katakana as *keroggu* (3), with the final apostrophe 's', since it is a particle, spelt in hiragana (the curled symbol 'no' here expresses possession). Roman capital letters ABCD have been used to signify vitamins, and the come-on slogan 'BIG CHANCE' is also in Roman letters – but the offer, a 'stoneware morning set', is spelt out in Japanese script (2), katakana again: *sutōnuea mōningusetto*. The main text, which is addressed to both children and anxious wives/mothers, is of course in kanji and kana without extraneous English words.

Opinions differ among the Japanese about their hybrid modern writing system.

(After Crystal)

The majority do not see romaji as a threat to kana and kanji – rather as having a kind of charm – but there are some who regard the influx of romaji as a sign of the degeneration of Japanese culture.

The Future of Writing in Japan

R eform of the Japanese script was under serious discussion as far back as the 1880s, long before the expansion of mass education in Japan after the Second World War. It made little progress in the face of conservatism. In 1938, for instance, a committee cautiously recommended that there be two categories of kanji: one for use in school textbooks and for general use, the other for special texts such as imperial rescripts. This reform was not implemented.

Then, during the war, the army took a hand. It was experiencing dangerous incidents as a result of conscript soldiers who were unable to read all the characters describing the parts of weapons. By 1940, the army had limited the number of kanji for weapons parts to 1235 and was considering the feasibility of cutting this number in half. Yet, at the same time, the military reports in civilian newspapers and magazines were being made deliberately obscure by employing rare kanji, in the propagandistic conviction that such writing would impress and overawe the general public.

After the war, some reform of the script did take place, but the commitment fell foul of politics, despite the enormously increased numbers of Japanese who were now expected to master large numbers of kanji. The ability to do this had always been seen as (to use an appropriate pun) character forming; in post-war Japan, one had to learn at least 1900–2000 kanji in school. There was no serious attempt, unlike in China with the introduction of Pinyin, to alleviate the burden of kanji. China had only kanji, whereas Japan already had a phonetic system in operation, in the form of the kana syllabaries; perhaps this fact contributed to the difference in government policies.

Only in the 1980s was attention to the script revived. It came from the growing need to employ the Japanese script in electronic data processing. Computers were becoming popular in Japan, though nothing like as fast as in the West. (It was the preference for hand-written documents that led Japan to develop the use of fax; even today far more official and commercial Japanese correspondence is hand-written than in the West.) Kanji impose some awkward obstacles in the way of computerization.

Street sign in Tokyo. The top two lines in yellow are in hiragana; the bottom line (in white) is in kanji.

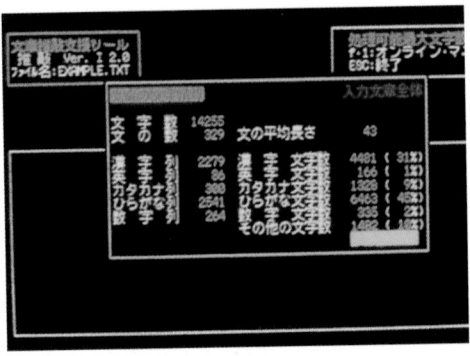

The Computerization of Kanji

The difficulties come with both output and input. To take output first, the printing of kanji is much more demanding of computer memory than the printing of alphabetic scripts. Memory sufficient for outputting alphabets is insufficient for kanji. A typical grid of 16 by 16 pixels distorts some kanji significantly; as shown on the right, at least 24 by 24 pixels are required to achieve a legible resolution on screen.

With an increase in memory, these problems are solved. Much more problematic is input. How is a computer keyboard for inputting at least 2000 kanji to be designed? – certainly not like that of the Chinese typewriter we saw earlier. How is an inherently illogical system (kanji) to be turned into a system that a computer can understand, and organized in such a way that an operator can work fast, rather than constantly pausing to scroll through a large number of possible kanji until exactly the right one is found? Can the input of kanji into computers ever hope to approach speeds comparable with that of input of alphabetic scripts?

J. Marshall Unger, who has studied the problem from a knowledge of the Japanese language and script, thinks the answer is, at bottom, no. He lists nine incompatibilities between kanji and computers in the form of a table, laid out below. Unger concludes that, 'To whatever extent one can legitimately call the historical use of kanji a success, it is because the vagaries and fluidity of kanji are well suited to the way people think and work.' In other words, kanji and computers are mismatched because the human mind is not fundamentally a computer.

Those who feel that it is, who believe in Artificial Intelligence, have suggested that computers can eventually be made to recognize and process hand-written kanji – with enough effort by computer scientists. Many Japanese have gratefully accepted these assurances, and have devoted time and money to developing such computers. To date there has been limited success. It looks likely that the need for computerization will one day lead to the abandonment of kanji in electronic data processing, if not in other areas of Japanese life.

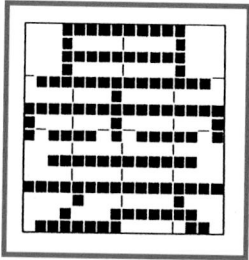
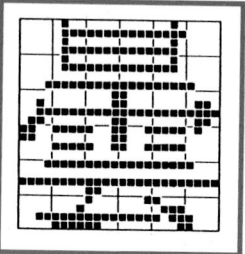

Kanji for 'cloudy'.
Top **16 by 16 pixel grid;**
middle **24 by 24 pixel grid;**
bottom **as the character should look.**

When kanji are used to represent Japanese-language data on computers, they are:			
	wasteful	imprecise	unwieldy
because sets of kanji are	1 large	2 open	3 ill-ordered
because readings of kanji are	4 redundant	5 ambiguous	6 artificial
because kanji shapes are	7 complex	8 abstract	9 homogeneous

Chapter 13

From Hieroglyphs to Alphabets
– and Back?

'Far from being worth a thousand words, a picture often requires a thousand words to explain it.'

John DeFrancis,
Visible Speech, 1989

In the mid-1970s, with ever-increasing international travel, the American Institute of Graphic Arts co-operated with the United States Department of Transportation to design a set of symbols for airports and other travel facilities that would be clear both to travellers in a hurry and those without a command of English. They came up with 34 symbols, shown opposite (the meanings are given on p. 226).

The design committee made a significant observation. They wrote: 'We are convinced that the effectiveness of symbols is strictly limited. They are most effective when they represent a service or concession that can be represented by an object, such as a bus or car glass. They are much less effective when used to represent a process or activity, such as Ticket Purchase, because the [latter] are complex interactions that vary considerably from mode to mode and even from carrier to carrier.' The designers concluded that symbols should not be used alone, they must be incorporated as part of 'an intelligent total sign system', involving both symbols and alphabetic messages. To do otherwise would be to sow 'confusion' among air travellers.

Some scholars of writing systems today disagree with this assessment of the potential of symbols for communication. They are willing to call modern hieroglyphs such as airport signs, road signs and the signs used in instruction manuals for electronic goods, 'writing' – along with musical notation, mathematical notation, circuit diagrams, Amerindian pictograms and the earliest clay tablets from Sumer (all of which we have termed proto-writing).

In theory, they argue, with enough imagination and ingenuity, a system of signs could be expanded into a 'universal' writing system which would be purely logographic, independent of any language and capable of expressing the entire range of thought that can be expressed in speech.

For these scholars do not hold with the belief that full writing is based on speech. They claim, on the contrary, that alphabetic writing has influenced speech, hence the fact (for example) that children think there are more sounds in 'pitch' than 'rich', even though the two sign sequences *tch* and *ch* are phonologically equivalent. These scholars do not accept the 'triumph of the alphabet'. Indeed they see no theoretical need for the phonetic principle in writing or reading. They point to the Chinese characters (less so the Japanese script) and claim them as evidence that pure logography is at least a possibility. Their basic contention is that there are two kinds of possible writing system, phonographic and logographic, which are of equal validity. This book, by contrast, maintains that the phonographic principle is primary in practical writing sytems, though logography can and always does supplement it; and that all full writing systems are differing mixtures of phonography and logography.

Logographic Utopia

The desire to believe in logographic writing is deep rooted and complex. Horapollo was a believer, as was Athanasius Kircher, both of whom claimed to 'read' Egyptian hieroglyphs non-phonographically. So was Leibniz, who in 1698 wrote: 'As regards

'Universal' symbols.
Signs for the 1972 Munich
Olympics (below) and logos
for Coca-Cola (left) from the
1980s indicate the power
of both pictograms and
phonograms in modern
graphic communication.
The Coca-Cola logos are
written in the following
languages (from the top,
left to right): Spanish, Thai,
Turkish, Japanese, French,
Chinese, Hebrew, Arabic,
Greek, Russian, Dutch,
Korean.

signs, I see . . . clearly that it is to the interest of the Republic of Letters and especially of students, that learned men should reach agreement on signs.'

There is today a general (if obscure) wish to view logographic writing as 'holistic', rather than 'reductionist' like alphabetic writing; as the writing of the colonized rather than the colonizer, the virtues of which have been overlooked; and as being capable of expressing thoughts more subtly, humanly and mercurially than phonographic symbols, which are seen as artificial, even inherently authoritarian. Pure logography thus becomes a kind of Utopia, in which language barriers no longer exist and we all fraternally communicate through universal symbols. (Ironically, the existence of *two* fundamental writing systems is regarded by its advocates as better than

    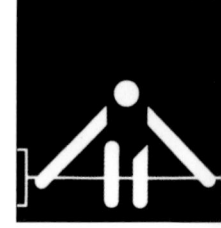

nothing   spoilt   very good   danger

unsafe place   man with gun   bad dog   dishonest man

in   out   stop   go

kind-hearted woman   you can camp here   tell pitiful story   if you are sick, you will be cared for

Gypsy and hobo signs. Intriguing as these are, they do not suggest that a full writing system could be developed without using phonography, as some scholars believe.

unified mass of hybrid writing systems, all of one 'mixed' variety.) Overall the belief in ɔgography, for all its vaunted modernity – ɔr would-be 'post-modernity' – is really a ɪatter-day version of the ancient belief in the ɪnysterious and spiritual East. In the ɪepresentative view of a European expert ɪn Chinese calligraphy, the alphabet is 'like ɪurrency, which reduces all the products of ɪature and human industry to the common ɪenominator of their exchange value [and] ɪontracts the infinite wealth of physical ɪeality to combinations of a few signs devoid ɪf any intrinsic value ... Chinese writing, [by ɪontrast], ... leads one not so much to look ɪehind the visible signs for abstract entities ɪs to study the relations, configurations and ɪecurrences of phenomena which are signs and of signs which are phenomena ... It sets the mind thinking along lines which are different from ours but just as rewarding.'

This is seductive, like the folkloric idea of the Great Wall of China – which in fact never at any time existed as a single, monolithic structure spanning northern China from the sea to the desert. The logographic principle accords with the way most of us feel that we think better than the alphabetic principle, which is inevitably associated with the reductionist idea that our brains are just extraordinarily sophisticated digital computers. The logographic principle reminds us of E. M. Forster's famous injunction 'only connect!', whereas the alphabetic principle might be summarized as 'only dissect'.

The increasing visual bias of our public culture reinforces the seductiveness. In the industrialized world we are surrounded by powerful imagery. We depend on the word, whether spoken or printed, much less than previous generations. Cinema, not literature, was the art form of the 20th century. Cinema's capacity to engage mass audiences worldwide subliminally suggests that a language of images is feasible and natural. We tend to forget how important words actually are to movies.

There is a parallel between the development of cinema and of writing systems. In order to tell a story, most silent movies were periodically compelled to insert caption cards, printed or hand-written; the images alone could not cope. And of course once 'talkies' were introduced, the silent cinema quickly perished. Even the greatest film artists did not feel a need to eschew sound in the interests of cinematic purity. Jean Renoir wrote of sound: 'I didn't know how to see until about 1930 when the obligation of writing dialogue brought me down to earth, and established a real contact between the people I had to make talk and myself.' As for the audience, it immediately embraced talkies. Today, to watch a silent film – even one of the most imaginative – is to feel that something is missing. The same is true, *a fortiori*, of our reaction to one of the early Sumerian tablets from Uruk or a series of unknown pictograms such as those on page 210. They lack a dimension. The introduction of sound revolutionized cinema; the introduction of phonography turned proto-writing into full writing.

The Evolution of Writing

If this is a valid parallel, in what sense can we speak of modern writing having 'evolved' from ancient writing? Until the last few decades it was universally agreed that

over centuries western civilization had tried to make writing a closer and closer representation of speech. The alphabet was naturally regarded as the pinnacle of this conscious search; the Chinese script, conversely, was generally thought of as hopelessly defective. The corollary was the belief that as the alphabet spread through the world, so eventually would mass literacy and democracy. Scholars – at least western scholars – thus had a clear conception of writing progressing from cumbersome

We live in an age of image-based communication, epitomized by cinema, the 20th-century art form. But we tend to forget how important words are to movies. In *Schindler's List* (1994), words form the crux of the film: they are literally a matter of life and death.

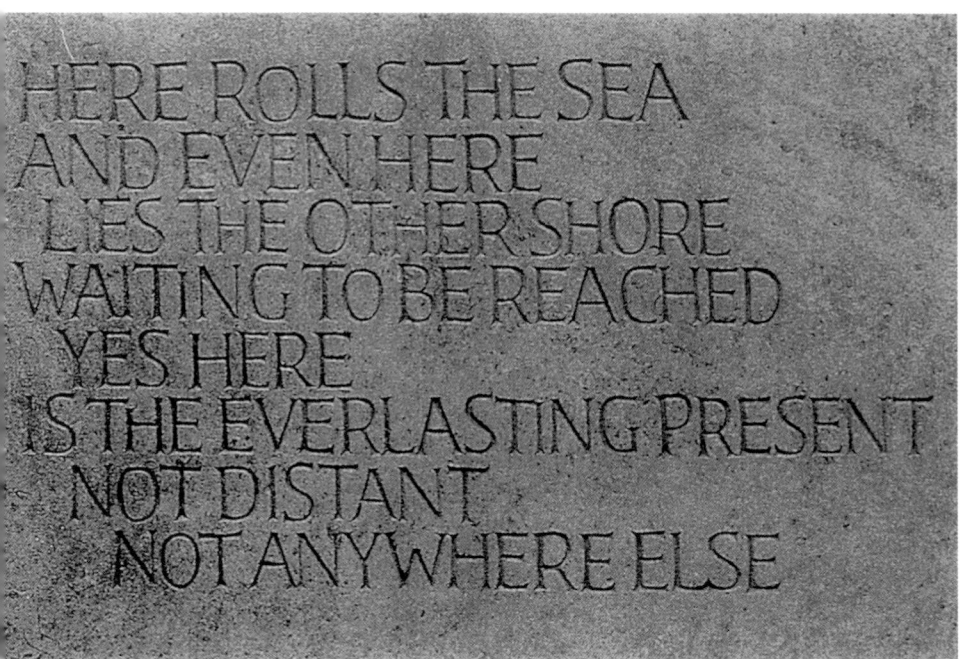

HERE ROLLS THE SEA
AND EVEN HERE
LIES THE OTHER SHORE
WAITING TO BE REACHED
YES HERE
IS THE EVERLASTING PRESENT
NOT DISTANT
NOT ANYWHERE ELSE

The power and mystery of alphabetic letters. This inscription, cut in limestone by Ralph Beyer in the 1980s, is from *Sadhana: The Realisation of Life* by Rabindranath Tagore (1913).

cient scripts with multiple signs to simple d superior modern alphabets.

Few are now as confident. The periority of the alphabet is no longer taken r granted. More fundamentally, the pposed pattern of a deepening perception phonetic efficiency producing an creasing simplicity of script, is not borne t by the evidence. The ancient Egyptians, we have seen, had an 'alphabet' of 24 signs arly 5000 years ago, but chose not to use it. he Maya could have used far more purely honetic spellings, if they had wished, stead of elaborate logographic and mixed gographic/phonographic equivalents. And e Japanese, rather than using more and ore frequently their simple syllabic kana, ose to import more and more kanji Chinese characters), of which there were one time almost 50,000.

It is tempting to draw another parallel, is time between the evolution of writing stems and the evolution of life on earth. rom simple beginnings – pictograms and rotozoa – there developed complexity.

Sometimes, this ramified, leading to unwieldy excesses – cuneiform or Chinese characters, and dinosaurs; but it also led to highly successful forms – the alphabet, and *homo sapiens*. In both processes of evolution, extinctions periodically occurred.

No doubt one cannot read too much into this comparison. It is difficult enough to assess the contemporary relationship between the alphabet, literacy and democracy, which seems on the face of it more probable. Surely, one might think, if a script is easy to learn, then more people will grasp it than if it is difficult to learn; and if they then come to understand public affairs better than they did before, they will be more likely to take part in them and indeed to demand a part in them. Certainly, government educational policies in today's democracies stress the importance of high levels of literacy and reinforce the common assumption that to be illiterate is to be backward. But that said, many other factors come into play in considering literacy, besides the ability to read and write;

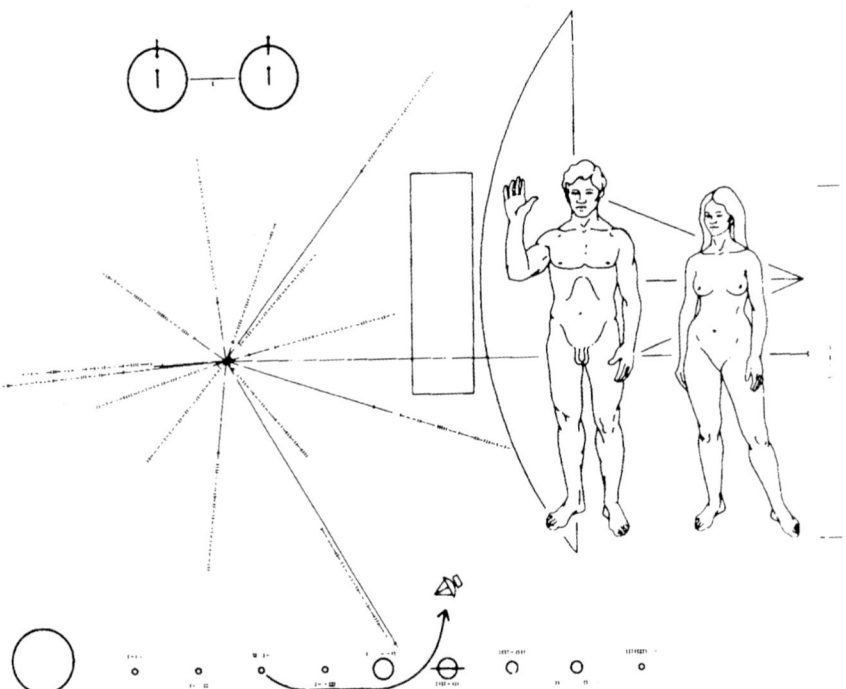

Space Age and Ice Age proto-writing. Many thousands of years separate the creators of these two 'pictograms', but it is difficult to avoid the feeling that the unknown Ice Age artist, working on the wall of a French cave, had a mind as modern as that of Carl Sagan, the astronomer, who designed this 6-inch by 9-inch (15 by 23 cm) gold-anodized aluminium plate to be attached to the antenna of the spacecraft *Pioneer 10*, before it was launched into deep space in 1972. We cannot elucidate the full meaning of the ox and come to know whether the prehistoric cave painters had some conception of a writing system – nor we do know their level of sophistication in spoken communication. Sagan, by contrast, has given a written explanation of every part of this plaque. 'It is written in the only language we share with the recipients: Science.' (continued opposite)

economic, political, social and cultural conditions must also be favourable if literacy and democracy are to take root and grow. We cannot explain the absence of radical societal change in ancient Egypt or its presence in ancient Greece in terms of hieroglyphs versus the alphabet, just as today we obviously cannot attribute Japan's high rate of literacy to its possession of the most complicated writing in the world.

The Hieroglyphic Legacy

The person unfamiliar with Far Eastern scripts must surely be amazed that anyone could use Japanese kanji or Chinese characters with ease, even on the briefest and friendliest acquaintance such as offered in this book. And the same goes for the scripts of the ancient Egyptians, Mesopotamians and Maya. So is that the chief interest of the ancient scripts for those of us outside a tiny esoteric circle of scholars – a sense of wonder at human linguistic ingenuity? Leaving aside the aesthetic appeal of many ancient writings, the cultural information they contain about the ancient world, and the intellectual challenge they furnish to decipherers, are these deceased scripts simply curiosities, to be regarded like Ptolemaic epicycles, the phlogiston theory and Chinese footbinding?

It seems unlikely that alphabet users have anything to learn from the ancient world that will be of *direct* use in improving their own scripts.

anything, China, Japan and other Far Eastern nations that employ Chinese characters, are likely to turn increasingly to phonetically based scripts, such as kana and pinyin; in other words, the alphabetic principle will eventually spread even into these last logographic bastions. This, after all, is what has happened to every other nation in history. In China, it is what Mao Zedong, Zhou En Lai and some other leaders desired, even though they were thwarted by more conservative minds. Any writing reform must needs take a long time and be a chaotic process – somewhat in the way that Latin took centuries to disappear from educated written discourse in Europe. In the English-speaking world, even the smallest spelling and grammatical changes may provoke extreme feelings. Imagine the reaction to any official move to introduce a wholesale change of script in Britain or America, such as that advocated by George Bernard Shaw (p. 40)!

No, the legacy of the hieroglyphs is perhaps a more subtle one, which touches on the relative status of speech and writing, phonography and logography. In the final analysis, Egyptian hieroglyphs, Mesopotamian cuneiform, Mayan glyphs and other complex scripts are fascinating because they make us ponder afresh the processes of reading, writing, speaking and thinking. And the living, functioning presence of the equally formidable Chinese and Japanese scripts serves to remind us of how little of these processes we understand. We can probe the chemical composition of stars in far-off galaxies and analyse the neural chemistry of our brains. But in the realm of the mind and consciousness our understanding is primitive. As yet no one can give much account of what is taking place in your head as you read this sentence. Detailed, sympathetic study of ancient writing systems in comparison with our own may provide us with some helpful clues.

(continued) **At the bottom of the plaque is a certain energy transition in the hydrogen atom. Hydrogen being the most abundant element in our galaxy, and physics being assumed to obey the same laws throughout our galaxy, this part of the message should communicate to an advanced civilization coming across *Pioneer 10* tens or hundreds of thousands of years from now. The extraterrestrials should be able to calculate that the plaque belongs to a very small volume of the Milky Way Galaxy and a single year in the history of that galaxy (1970). The sun and planets shown along the bottom of the plaque should allow the exact location to be pinpointed; and the drawing of the spacecraft leaving the solar system will surely be understood. But what will the unknown beings read into the human figures, which to us are the most obvious part of the message? They are likely to prove much more elusive than the meaning of the Ice Age ox is to us. 'The human beings', says Sagan, 'are the most mysterious part of the message.'**

POSTSCRIPT: Writing in the New Millennium

As the 6th millennium of recorded civilization opened, Mesopotamia was again at the centre of historical events. Where once, at the birth of writing, the statecraft of absolute rulers like Hammurabi and Darius was recorded in Sumerian, Babylonian, Assyrian and Old Persian cuneiform on clay and stone, now the Iraq Wars against Saddam Hussein generated millions of mainly alphabetic words on paper and on the internet written in a babel of world languages.

But although the technologies of today's writing are immeasurably different from those of the 3rd millennium BC, its linguistic principles have not changed very much since the composition of the Sumerian epic of Gilgamesh. Even the printed book, despite many ominous predictions of its digital doom, shows few credible signs of going the way of the clay tablet and the papyrus roll. Indeed, ironically, books have been one of the items most successfully traded on the World Wide Web from its earliest days. Speaking for myself, as the literary editor of a higher education newspaper during the internet revolution, I was constantly amazed by the ever-increasing stream of ever-expanding textbooks sent for review, even as their authors and publishers poured resources into companion compact discs and websites for those titles.

Nevertheless, the seismic impact of electronic writing and archiving on information distribution (including of course my own research) has further polarized the debate about the correct definition of 'writing'. While some people persist in thinking that the digital explosion has made little or no difference to what happens in their minds when they actually read, write and think, others just as stoutly maintain that the digitization of writing is radically altering our absorption of knowledge and will soon usher in the long-awaited 'universal' communication system imagined by Leibniz three centuries ago. Moreover, this latter faith in the increasing intelligence of computers chimes with many scholars' growing respect for the intelligence behind ancient scripts. Down with the monolithic 'triumph of the alphabet', they say, and up with Chinese characters, Egyptian hieroglyphs and Mayan glyphs, with their hybrid mixtures of pictographic, logographic and phonetic signs. This conviction has in turn encouraged a belief in the need to see each writing system as enmeshed within a whole culture, instead of viewing it simply as a technical solution to a problem of efficient visual representation of the culture's language. While I personally do not share the belief in the hidden power of digitization, and remain sceptical about the expressive virtues of logography, the holistic view of writing systems strikes me as a healthy development that reflects the real relationship between writing and society in all its subtlety and complexity.

At the same time, the hoary questions about writing endure, taking new forms. Where, when, how and why did it begin?

Opposite **Egyptian bone tags from tomb U-j at Abydos, *c.* 3200 BC. This is the oldest group of inscribed artifacts so far known in Egypt. Some scholars believe that the pictograms on the tags were precursors of the later hieroglyphic writing system. (See p. 223.)**

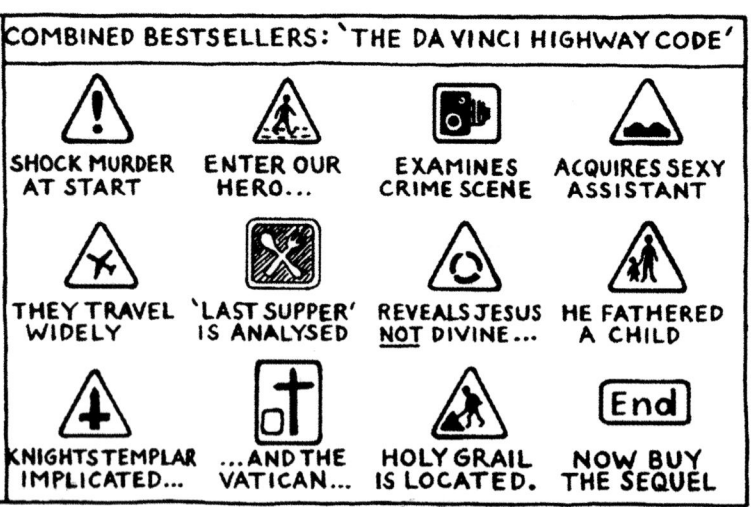

COMBINED BESTSELLERS: 'THE DA VINCI HIGHWAY CODE'

SHOCK MURDER AT START — ENTER OUR HERO... — EXAMINES CRIME SCENE — ACQUIRES SEXY ASSISTANT — THEY TRAVEL WIDELY — 'LAST SUPPER' IS ANALYSED — REVEALS JESUS NOT DIVINE... — HE FATHERED A CHILD — KNIGHTS TEMPLAR IMPLICATED... — ...AND THE VATICAN... — HOLY GRAIL IS LOCATED. — NOW BUY THE SEQUEL

Writing and culture. The visual jokes in these pictograms and their ironic captions – drawn by the cartoonist Mike Barfield in 2004 – are comprehensible by anyone who can read English. But to appreciate the humour fully, the reader needs diverse background knowledge. Ancient inscriptions require similarly complex and subtle interpretation – a tough challenge for 21st-century scholars unaware of all of the inscriptions' original cultural references.

Was it invented in one place, Mesopotamia, or did it emerge independently in several places, notably Mesopotamia, Egypt, the Indus Valley, China and Mesoamerica, at widely differing times? And what was the origin of the alphabet? New archaeological discoveries at the turn of the millennium, in Egypt, China and Central Asia, have shed light on these issues, as we shall see.

Attempts to decipher the undeciphered scripts continue too. The unique Phaistos disc of Crete remains a magnet for decipherers, however misguided. In 1999, two more books announced (totally different!) decipherments of the mysterious disc, one of which, *The Bronze Age Computer Disc*, trumpeted that it is a highly sophisticated calendar, in which the division of the two sides into 30 and 31 sections reflects the numbers of days in the months. At the same time, more plausible decipherments of other scripts captured headlines, notably two claims to have penetrated the Easter Island script and the Isthmian script of Mexico, neither of which eventually met with general scholarly acceptance. In the end, nothing could compare with the drama of the Mayan decipherment story, which by the turn of the century had entered a more mature stage of consolidation, like that of the Egyptian hieroglyphic decipherment after the death of Champollion. Still, there have been solid advances in understanding a number of the remaining enigmatic scripts, especially the Proto-Elamite script of Iran and the Indus Valley script of Pakistan/India. Both are at last being published in accessible, accurate corpuses – thanks to the painstaking work of Robert Englund (Proto-Elamite) and Asko Parpola (the Indus Valley script) – which can be manipulated on a computer. No one should hold their breath, but if some lucky new excavations should uncover a considerable cache of new inscriptions, as is certainly possible judging from past experience with Linear B and the Etruscan script, then these major undeciphered scripts may yet be read much more fully than at present. (In 2006 a stone celt apparently bearing four signs in the Indus script was accidentally discovered by a school teacher digging a pit in his back-yard in southern Tamil Nadu, far from the Indus Valley – lending futher support to the theory that the Indus language is Dravidian.)

New Discoveries, Old Conundrums

Yet another sensational discovery in Etruscan occurred recently. In 1999, the Italian authorities revealed that a bronze tablet with about 200 Etruscan words on it – the third-longest known Etruscan text – had been found in the area of Cortona, near Lake Trasimeno, and named the *Tabula Cortonensis*. The circumstances of the find, apparently on a building site with other bronze objects, were not entirely clear, and traces of a steel brush were found on the tablet's surface, suggesting that someone had tried to find out if the metal was gold. An anonymous telephone call warned that the objects were not from the claimed find spot. A piece of the tablet was also missing, but despite the authorities' sifting the earth at the building site, nothing turned up; furthermore, a soil analysis showed that the soil at the site and that inside the bronze objects did not coincide. It was the hope of verifying whether the tablet really was from Cortona and of locating the missing fragment that delayed the public announcement of the find for over six years.

Seven of the eight pieces of the tablet remain, which could be fitted together with only small gaps. That it was broken in antiquity could be proved from a scientific analysis of the lines of fracture; maybe someone had intended to melt it down and reuse the bronze. Its size, 11.2 x 18 in (28.5 x 45.8 cm), is roughly that of two sheets of office paper. A handle at the top suggests that the tablet once hung in a public place, such as an archive. Its date of manufacture lies between 225 and 150 BC.

The characters, which run from right to left, as usual with Etruscan inscriptions (but of course opposite to the Greek alphabet), have been beautifully inscribed on both sides of the tablet, either from a mould using the *cire perdue* (lost wax) technique or, more probably, by direct engraving on the bronze. They cover all of the first side but only eight lines of the second side. Important observations were feasible without actually reading the

The Tabula Cortonensis, the third-longest Etruscan inscription, 3rd or 2nd century BC.

inscription. For a start, it is clear that one scribe wrote both sides of the tablet, except for the last six lines of the first side, which are engraved more deeply and therefore with an accentuated curvature. (Why there were two scribes, we can only guess.) Secondly, there are four unusual marks, ⌐, on the first side that look remarkably like the 'insert paragraph' marks of a modern proof-reader: which is exactly what their function appears to have been (highlighted). Finally, we can note that the sign standing for *e*, ∃, which the Etruscans borrowed from ∃, the Greek epsilon, appears in *two* versions in the Tabula Cortonensis, facing in opposite directions ∃ and Ɛ. This variant, which is known from other inscriptions to be local to the Cortona area, is virtual proof that the tablet is from Cortona; an inference reinforced by the occurrence of the name Velara, spelt with the local form of the epsilon, twice on the tablet (highlighted): AꟼA⅃Ɛꟼ – Velara is an ancestral (or family) name characteristic of Cortona.

The tablet was quickly read by applying the Etruscan alphabet. Word divisions were easily recognized from the dots inscribed in the bronze and from the familiarity of many of the sign groups as proper names and other known words, such as 'cel' (earth, land), 'vina' (vineyard) [related to Latin 'vinum' (wine)], 'puia' (wife), 'clan' (son), 'rasna' (Etruscans, people) and the numerals 'zal' (2), 'sa' (4) and 'sar' (10). But there were so many names (more than two-thirds of the words) and a relatively high proportion of unknown words among the remaining words, that it was not possible to translate the document, though we can be sure of its general content. According to Luciano Agostiniani, who published the Tabula

Cortonensis in 2000, what can be stated almost for certain is that the tablet is a record of a contract between the Cusu family, to which Petru Scevas belongs, and 15 other people, witnessed by a third group of names, including some of their children and grandchildren. It relates to a sale, or lease, of land including a vineyard,

First side of the Tabula Cortonensis. Four paragraph marks and two instances of the name VELARA are highlighted in the drawing.

the plain of Lake Trasimeno, a place apparently spelt 'celtinêitiss tarsiminass':

᛭ＭＡＨＩＨＨＺ۹Ａ۴·Ｍ۲Ｉㆍ۴Ｉ۳ＨＩ۴۴Ǝ᛭

The first part of the word, 'celtinêi' is known to be related to 'cel' (earth, land), 'tiss' is likely to mean 'lake': a reasonable deduction, which added a new word to our Etruscan vocabulary.

Ground-breaking recent discoveries of inscriptions in Egypt fall into two groups. The first relates to the origin of the hieroglyphs in the late 4th millennium, while the second concerns the origin of the alphabet in the early 2nd millennium.

At Abydos, German excavators led by Günter Dreyer and Ulrich Hartung opened a royal tomb known as U-j and discovered the oldest group of inscribed artifacts so far known in Egypt, dating to about 3200 BC or perhaps a little earlier, in other words definitely pre-dynastic. Some are ceramic jars, more than 100 of them, bearing large single or paired signs on their walls. However the second type of artifact, the more intriguing of the two, consists of nearly 200 small bone and ivory tags (see p. 218), just over half an inch (1.5 cm) in height on average, drilled in one corner, which look as if they were once attached to bales of cloth or other valuable grave goods that have vanished with tomb robbers. Inscribed on the tags are numerals – in groups of up to twelve single digits, plus the sign for 100 and the sign for 100 + 1 – and pictographic signs, although puzzlingly the numerals and the pictograms hardly occur together on the same tag. At least some of the pictograms, but certainly not the majority, strongly resemble the later hieroglyphs, in particular some birds, a stretch of water (the uniconsonantal sign for š – see p. 97) and possibly a cobra.

In Dreyer's view, which he published in 1998, the tags suggest the existence of a writing system with logographic and phonetic elements that would give rise to the familiar hieroglyphs within a few hundred years, what's more a system inspired by economics, not politics or religion – as with the inventories written on the earliest clay tablets of Mesopotamia – but belonging to so early a date that the invention of writing in Egypt may even have predated that in Mesopotamia. However all this is speculative, except perhaps for the element of accountancy and the date, which is based on radiocarbon dating (though even the date is not secure – Dreyer prefers one somewhat earlier than 3200 BC). On the evidence, there is simply no way to be sure of the precise usage and meaning of this limited repertoire of primitive signs, or of how they may have been connected with the later hieroglyphs; and there is nothing in the signs that requires a phonetic reading based on the Egyptian language. Dreyer's fellow Egyptologist John Baines, though sympathetic to his vision, comments that, 'The discovery of tomb U-j has taken the understanding of early Egypt and its writing forward enormously, but unless significantly more material is found, I doubt whether it will be possible to establish a generally agreed interpretation of its inscriptions.'

Around the same time, two American archaeologists, John Coleman Darnell and his wife Deborah, made a discovery in the Egyptian desert at Wadi el-Hol, west of Thebes, while they were surveying ancient travel routes. In 1999, they announced they had found what appeared to be alphabetic writing dating from c. 1900–1800 BC, a date considerably earlier than the earliest alphabetic inscriptions from Lebanon and Israel.

The two short inscriptions are written in a Semitic script and, according to the experts, the letters were most probably developed in a fashion similar to a semi-cursive form of the Egyptian script. The writer is thought to have been a scribe travelling with a group of mercenaries (there were many such mercenaries working for the pharaohs). If this theory turns out to be correct, then it looks as if the alphabetic idea was, after all, inspired by the Egyptian hieroglyphs but invented in Egypt, rather than Palestine – which would make the Darnells' theory into a revised version of the theory first suggested by Sir Alan Gardiner in 1916 in his decipherment of the Proto-Sinaitic signs (see p. 161). Yet the new evidence is by no means conclusive, and the search for more inscriptions continues. The riddle of the alphabet's origin(s) has not yet been solved.

In China, the growth of archaeology in the late 20th century produced a steady flow of inscribed artifacts dating back as early as the 7th millennium BC, some five thousand years before 1200 BC, the long-

Probable alphabetic inscription from Wadi el-Hol, Egypt, c. 1900–1800 BC. The only signs that can be read, tentatively, are the two nearest to the bottom of the photograph, which may represent 'el' (god) in ancient Semitic. The early date of the inscription implies that the alphabet originated in Egypt, not Palestine.

accepted date of the oracle-bone inscriptions of the Shang civilization.

A number of scholars, the majority of them Chinese, have attempted to establish a link between these Neolithic pot marks and the simplest oracle-bone signs (crosses, arrows, parallel lines and other simple shapes), and have then claimed the highest antiquity for Chinese writing. But such claims are unprovable, since they rest only on graphic similarities and, as we know from other scripts, such comparisons are shaky at best and at worst deeply misleading. However, what does seem reasonable is that the sophisticated oracle-bone writing system did not develop suddenly and *ex nihilo*. It seems very likely that a writing system existed in China before 1200 BC. But did it develop by borrowing from outside China, or instead evolve indigenously in a pre-Shang culture that is still awaiting excavation? Sinologists differ strongly on this. Robert Bagley, for example, thinks that the Shang writing probably developed independently and slowly out of earlier Chinese cultures, only now being excavated and understood, while Françoise Bottéro favours Chinese borrowing of writing with rapid invention of the characters, probably under the original influence of Mesopotamian writing.

Could the discovery of a solitary seal from Central Asia, announced in 2001, offer a clue to the solution of this Chinese puzzle? The seal was found in Turkmenistan, on the northern borders of Iran and Afghanistan, by an American archaeologist Fredrik Hiebert, and belongs to the Bronze Age 'Oxus civilization', until recently little known except to a handful of Soviet archaeologists. Radiocarbon dating puts its date in the mid 3rd millennium BC, so it is more than four

thousand years old, comparable in age to the famous Indus Valley seals. Its signs look sophisticated and a bit Chinese, but since no other sample has been found by the excavators, it is far too soon to declare that the seal is definitely writing. Yet at the very least, this find reminds us there may have been communication between Asian cultures even at this early period, as with the much later Silk Road. To be highly speculative for a moment, is the Turkmenistan seal a link in a chain that propagated the idea of writing across the Old World from the Near East to the Far East in the 3rd/2nd millennium BC? The story of writing continues to tantalize us.

Pottery signs from Yangshao culture, China 5000–4000 BC. Some Chinese scholars see resemblances between these signs and the signs of the much later writing system of the Shang civilization.

Seal from Anau, Turkmenistan, mid 3rd millennium BC. So far unique – unlike the Indus Valley seals of the same period – the signs on this seal may or may not have formed part of an extinct writing system in Central Asia.

Answers

94 The basket with a handle on the far right of the smaller picture is the wrong way round. Compare the one on the left.

97 The hieroglyphs may be transcribed as follows: (1) Mary, (2) Charles, (3) Elizabeth, (4) William, (5) Patricia, (6) Alexander, (7) Cleopatra.

210 The signs have the following meanings:
first row telephone, post, currency exchange, first aid, lost and found;
second row baggage lockers, lift, men's toilets, women's toilets, toilets;
third row information, hotel information, taxi, bus, ground transportation;
fourth row rail transportation, air transportation, heliport, water transportation;
fifth row car rental, restaurant, coffee shop, bar, shops;
sixth row ticket purchase, baggage check-in, baggage claim, customs, immigration;
seventh row smoking, no smoking, parking, no parking, no entry.

Further Reading

This is not a scholarly bibliography but rather a small selection of books and articles directly relevant to each chapter of this book. Only books that deal substantially with writing are included; most general studies of ancient civilizations are excluded. The date given is usually the date of first publication in English.

Introduction/General Works
Most of these books contain extensive bibliographies.

Baines, John, John Bennet and Stephen D. Houston (eds), *The Disappearance of Writing Systems: Perspectives on Literacy and Communication*, 2008

Daniels, Peter and William Bright (eds), *The World's Writing Systems*, 1996

DeFrancis, John, *Visible Speech: The Diverse Oneness of Writing Systems*, 1989

[Galeries Nationales du Grand Palais], *Naissance de l'écriture: cuneiformes et hiéroglyphes*, 1982 (exhibition catalogue)

Gaur, Albertine, *A History of Writing*, 3rd edition, 1992

Harris, Roy, *The Origin of Writing*, 1986

Houston, Stephen D. (ed.), *The First Writing: Script Invention as History and Process*, 2004
—— (ed.), *The Shape of Script: How and Why Writing Systems Change*, 2012

Pope, Maurice, *The Story of Decipherment: From Egyptian Hieroglyphs to Maya Script*, revised edition, 1999

Postgate, Nicholas, Tao Wang and Toby Wilkinson, 'The evidence for early writing: utilitarian or ceremonial?', *Antiquity*, 69, 1995

Sampson, Geoffrey, *Writing Systems*, 1985

[Trustees of the British Museum: no editor, six authors with an introduction by J. T. Hooker] *Reading the Past: Ancient Writing from Cuneiform to the Alphabet*, 1990 (includes 'Cuneiform', 'Egyptian Hieroglyphs', 'Linear B and Related Scripts', 'The Early Alphabet', 'Greek Inscriptions' and 'Etruscan')

Woodard, Roger D. (ed.), *The Cambridge Encyclopedia of the World's Ancient Languages*, 2004

World Archaeology, February 1986 (special issue on early writing systems)

Reading the Rosetta Stone
Boas, George (trans.), *The Hieroglyphs of Horapollo*, 2nd edition, 1993

Champollion, Jean-François, *Egyptian Diaries*, 2001 (in English translation)

Iversen, Erik, *The Myth of Egypt and Its Hieroglyphs in European Tradition*, 2nd edition, 1993

Parkinson, Richard, *Cracking Codes: The Rosetta Stone and Decipherment*, 1999
—— *The Rosetta Stone*, 2005

Ray, John, *The Rosetta Stone and the Rebirth of Ancient Egypt*, 2007

Robinson, Andrew, *The Last Man Who Knew Everything: Thomas Young*, 2006

Sound, Symbol and Script
Bissex, Glenda L., *Gnys at Work*, 1980

Crystal, David, *The Cambridge Encyclopedia of Language*, 1987

Kolers, Paul, 'Some formal characteristics of pictograms', *American Scientist*, 57, 1969

McCarthy, Lenore, 'A child learns the alphabet', *Visible Language*, Summer 1977

Pinker, Steven, *The Language Instinct: The New Science of Language and Mind*, 1994

Saussure, Ferdinand de, *Course in General Linguistics*, (Roy Harris trans.), 1983

Proto-Writing
Bahn, Paul and Jean Vertut, *Images of the Ice Age*, 1988

Englund, Robert K., 'The origins of script', *Science*, 11 June 1993 (review of Schmandt-Besserat, *Before Writing, 1* – see below)

Marshack, Alexander, *The Roots of Civilization*, 2nd edition, 1991

Nissen, Hans J., Peter Damerow and Robert K. Englund, *Archaic Bookkeeping: Writing and Techniques of Economic Administration in the Ancient Near East*, 1993

Quilter, Jeffrey and Gary Urton (eds), *Narrative Threads: Accounting and Recounting in Andean Khipu*, 2002 (study of *quipu*)

Schmandt-Besserat, Denise, *Before Writing, 1: From Counting to Cuneiform*, 1992

Cuneiform
Bermant, Chaim and Michael Weitzman, *Ebla: A Revelation in Archaeology*, 1979

Collon, Dominique, *Near Eastern Seals*, 1990

Cooper, Jerrold, 'Bilingual Babel: cuneiform texts in two or more languages from ancient Mesopotamia and beyond', *Visible Language*, 27, 1993
—— 'Babylonian beginnings: the origin of the cuneiform writing system in comparative perspective', 2004, in Houston (ed.), *The First Writing* – see Introduction

Larsen, Mogens Trolle, *The Conquest of Assyria*, 1996

Postgate, J. N., *Early Mesopotamia*, 1992

Potts, D. T., *The Archaeology of Elam*, 1999

Powell, Marvin A., 'Three problems in the history of cuneiform writing: origins, direction of script, literacy', *Visible Language*, Autumn 1981

Walker, C. B. F., *Cuneiform*, 1987

Egyptian Hieroglyphs
Arnett, William S., *The Predynastic Origin of Egyptian Hieroglyphs*, 1982

Baines, John, 'Literacy and ancient Egyptian society', *Man*, 18, 1983

Davies, W. V., *Egyptian Hieroglyphs*, 1987

Faulkner, Raymond O. (trans.), *The Ancient Egyptian Book of the Dead*, revised edition, 1985

Gardiner, Alan H., *Egyptian Grammar*, 3rd edition, 1957

Reeves, Nicholas, *The Complete Tutankhamun*, 1990

Robinson, Andrew, *Cracking the Egyptian Code: The Revolutionary Life of Jean-François Champollion*, 2012

Wilkinson, Richard H., *Reading Egyptian Art: A Hieroglyphic Guide to Ancient Egyptian Painting and Sculpture*, 1992

Zauzich, Karl-Theodor, *Discovering Egyptian Hieroglyphs: A Practical Guide*, 1992

Linear B
Chadwick, John, 'Linear B', in *Current Trends in Linguistics*, 2, (Thomas A. Sebeok ed.), 1973
—— *Linear B and Related Scripts*, 1987
—— *The Decipherment of Linear B*, 2nd edition with a new postscript, 1992

Evans, Arthur, *The Palace of Minos at Knossos*, 4, 1935

Kober, Alice E., 'The Minoan scripts: fact and theory', *American Journal of Archaeology*, 52, 1948

Robinson, Andrew, *The Man Who Deciphered Linear B: The Story of Michael Ventris*, 2002

Ventris, Michael, 'Deciphering Europe's earliest scripts', *Listener*, 10 July 1952
—— 'King Nestor's four-handled cups: Greek inventories in the Minoan script', *Archaeology*, Spring 1954

— *Work Notes on Minoan Language Research and Other Unedited Papers*, (Anna Sacconi ed.), 1988

entris, Michael and John Chadwick, *Documents in Mycenaean Greek*, 2nd edition, 1973

Mayan Glyphs

oe, Michael D., *Breaking the Maya Code*, revised edition, 1999

— *The Maya*, 7th edition, 2005

oe, Michael D. and Mark Van Stone, *Reading the Maya Glyphs*, 2001

Houston, Stephen D., *Maya Glyphs*, 1989

— 'Writing in early Mesoamerica', 2004, in Houston (ed.), *The First Writing* – see Introduction

norosov, Yuri V., 'The problem of the study of the Maya hieroglyphic writing', *American Antiquity*, 23, 1958

Martin, Simon and Nikolai Grube, *Chronicle of the Maya Kings and Queens*, 2000

Miller, Mary-Ellen, *The Murals of Bonampak*, 1986

obertson, Merle Greene, *The Sculpture of Palenque, 1: The Temple of the Inscriptions*, 1983

chele, Linda and Peter Mathews, *The Code of Kings: The Language of Seven Sacred Maya Temples and Tombs*, 1998

tephens, John L., *Incidents of Travel in Yucatan, 1 and 2*, 1841

tuart, David, 'The Rio Azul cacao pot', *Antiquity*, 62, 1988

Thompson, J. E. S., *Maya Hieroglyphic Writing*, 1950

— *A Commentary on the Dresden Codex*, 1972

Undeciphered Scripts

onfante, Giuliano and Larissa Bonfante, *The Etruscan language: An Introduction*, revised edition, 2002

utinov, N. A. and Y. V. Knorosov, 'Preliminary report on the study of the written language of Easter Island', *Journal of the Polynesian Society*, 66, 1957

Chadwick, John, *Linear B and Related Scripts*, 1987 (covers Linear A and the Phaistos disc)

Duhoux, Yves, *Le Disque de Phaestos*, 1977

ischer, Steven Roger, *Rongorongo: The Easter Island Script*, 1997

Hood, M. S. F., 'The Tartaria tablets', *Antiquity*, 41, 1967

amberg-Karlovsky, C. C., 'The Proto-Elamites on the Iranian plateau', *Antiquity*, 52, 1978

age, R. I., *Runes*, 1987

arpola, Asko, *Deciphering the Indus Script*, 1994

Robinson, Andrew, *Lost Languages: The Enigma of the World's Undeciphered Scripts*, 2009 (covers the Meroitic, Etruscan, Linear A, Proto-Elamite, Rongorongo, Zapotec, Isthmian and Indus Valley scripts, and the Phaistos disc)

Ventris, Michael, 'A note on decipherment methods', *Antiquity*, 27, 1953

The First Alphabet

Cambridge Archaeological Journal, 2, 1992 (feature devoted to Powell, *Homer and the Origin of the Greek Alphabet* – see below)

Cook, B. F., *Greek Inscriptions*, 1987

Gardiner, Alan H., 'The Egyptian origin of the Semitic alphabet', *Journal of Egyptian Archaeology*, 3, 1916

Hawkins, David, 'The origin and dissemination of writing in western Asia', in *The Origins of Civilization*, (P. R. S. Moorey ed.), 1979

Jeffery, L. H., *The Local Scripts of Archaic Greece*, 2nd edition, 1990

Moscati, Sabatino, *The Phoenicians*, 1988

Naveh, Joseph, *Early History of the Alphabet*, 1982

Powell, Barry B., *Homer and the Origin of the Greek Alphabet*, 1991

Sassoon, John, 'Who on earth invented the alphabet?', *Visible Language*, Spring 1990

New Alphabets from Old

Diringer, David, *The Alphabet: A Key to the History of Mankind, 1 and 2*, 3rd edition, 1968

Gardner, William, *Alphabet at Work*, 1982

Healey, John F., *The Early Alphabet*, 1990

Jean, Georges, *Writing: The Story of Alphabets and Scripts*, 1992

Logan, Robert K., *The Alphabet Effect*, 1986

Sacks, David, *The Alphabet: Unraveling the Mystery of the Alphabet from A to Z*, 2003

Safadi, Y. H., *Islamic Calligraphy*, 1978

Chinese Writing

Billeter, Jean-François, *The Chinese Art of Writing*, 1990

DeFrancis, John, *The Chinese Language: Fact and Fantasy*, 1984

DeFrancis, John and J. Marshall Unger, 'Rejoinder to Geoffrey Sampson, "Chinese script and the diversity of writing systems"', *Linguistics*, 32, 1994

Hessler, Peter, 'Oracle bones', *New Yorker*, 16 and 23 February 2004

Moore, Oliver, *Chinese*, 2000

Tsien, Tsuen-Hsuin, *Written on Bamboo and Silk*, 2nd edition, 2004

Ye, Chiang, *Chinese Calligraphy*, 3rd edition, 1973

Japanese Writing

Gottlieb, Nanette, *Word-Processing Technology in Japan: Kanji and the Keyboard*, 2000

Saint-Jacques, Bernard, 'The Roman alphabet in the Japanese writing system', *Visible Language*, Winter 1987

Seeley, Christopher, *A History of Writing in Japan*, 1991

Unger, J. Marshall, *The Fifth Generation Fallacy: Why Japan Is Betting Its Future on Artificial Intelligence*, 1987

— *Ideogram: Chinese Characters and the Myth of Disembodied Meaning*, 2004

From Hieroglyphs to Alphabets – and Back?

American Institute of Graphic Arts, 'The development of passenger/pedestrian oriented signals for use in transportation-related facilities', *Visible Language*, Spring 1975

Boone, Elizabeth Hill, 'Beyond writing', 2004, in Houston (ed.), *The First Writing* – see Introduction

Hollis, Richard, *Graphic Design: A Concise History*, 1994

Mead, Margaret and Rudolf Modley, 'Communication among all people, everywhere', *Natural History*, 77, 1968

Sagan, Carl, *The Cosmic Connection*, 1972

Taylor, Insup and David R. Olson (eds), *Scripts and Literacy: Reading and Learning to Read Alphabets, Syllabaries and Characters*, 1995

Postscript: Writing in the New Millennium

Agostiniani, Luciano and Francesco Nicosia, *Tabula Cortonensis*, 2000 (in Italian)

Bagley, Robert W., 'Anyang writing and the origin of the Chinese writing system', 2004, in Houston (ed.), *The First Writing* – see Introduction

Baines, John, 'The earliest Egyptian writing: development, context, purpose', 2004, in Houston (ed.), *The First Writing* – see Introduction

Bottéro, Françoise, 'Writing on shell and bone in Shang China', 2004, in Houston (ed.), *The First Writing* – see Introduction

Englund, Robert K., 'The state of decipherment of proto-Elamite', 2004, in Houston (ed.), *The First Writing* – see Introduction

Hiebert, Fredrik T., 'The context of the Anau seal', *Sino-Platonic Papers*, 124, 2002 (published by the University of Pennsylvania)

Li Xueqin, Garman Harbottle, Juzhong Zhang and Changsui Wang, 'The earliest writing? Sign use in the seventh millennium BC at Jiahu, Henan Province, China', *Antiquity*, 77, 2003

Parpola, Asko, 'Study of the Indus script', *Transactions of the International Conference of Eastern Studies*, 50, 2005 (proceedings of a conference in Tokyo)

Subramanian, T. S., 'Significance of Mayiladuthurai find', *The Hindu* (newspaper), 1 May 2006

List of Illustrations

Unless specified otherwise, illustrations on the following pages are by Tracy Wellman: 22, 29, 30, 31, 32, 33, 35, 40, 48, 64, 65, 75, 79, 86, 87, 96, 97, 100, 101, 104, 105, 110, 111, 114, 115, 116, 127 (adapted from Schele and Freidel, *A Forest of Kings*, 1990), 147, 148, 149, 161, 163, 178.

Illustrations on the following pages are reproduced courtesy of Michael Coe: 124–25, 126, 128–29, 130–31, 134–35, 136 (below), 137, 143 (below).

Illustrations on the following pages are reproduced courtesy of H. Nissen: 62–7, 87, 89. All maps are by Annick Petersen.

Introduction

6 Wallpainting from Karashahr, China, 10th century. Copyright British Museum. 8 Ramesses II planning the Battle of Kadesh, 1285 BC. Illustration of a relief at Karnak from I. Rosellini, *Monumenti*, 1832–44. 9 Oracle bone, China, *c*.1500 BC. Copyright British Museum. Stone seal, Mohenjo-daro, *c*. 2000 BC. Photo Enja Lahdenperä for the University of Helsinki, © National Museum of India. 10 Relief with scribes recording the dead. Assyrian, 8th century BC. Copyright British Museum. 11 Section of the Dresden Codex from E. Förstemann, *Die Maya-Handschrift der Königlichen Bibliothek Öffentlichen zu Dresden*, 1892. 12 Angels recording the deeds of men. Illumination from al-Qazwini, *The Wonders of Creation*, Iraq, 1280. Bayerische Staatsbibliothek, Munich. 13 Kemal Atatürk teaching the Roman script. Photo Ministry of Information, Istanbul. 14 Cultural Revolution, China, mid-1960s. Photo *China Pictorial*. 17 Three signs (below) designed for Stansted airport, 1990–91. Pentagram.

Part I

18 Vase showing the life of the Sun-god. Yaloch, Guatemala. Painting by Annie C. Hunter, courtesy University Museum, Philadelphia. Box from Tutankhamun's tomb. Thebes, 14th century BC. Egyptian Museum, Cairo. Ägyptisches Museen Staatliche Museum Preussischer Kulturbesitz, Berlin. Photo Margarete Büsing.

Chapter 1

20 The Rosetta Stone. Egyptian, *c*. 196 BC. Copyright British Museum. 21 Woodcut from C. Giehlow, *Die Hieroglyphenkunde*, 1915. Woodcut from *De Sacris Aegyptiorum notis*, 1574. Woodcut from *Hori Apollinis Selecta hieroglyphica*, 1599. Vulture. Painted Egyptian relief. Photo Jean Vertut. 22 Obelisk in Piazza della Minerva, Rome. Egyptian, 6th century BC. © Photo Peter Clayton. The Minervan obelisk. Engraving from A. Kircher, *Obeliscus Aegyptiacus*, 1666. Sceptre sign. Drawing from the coffin of Sebko. Egyptian, Middle Kingdom. Sceptre sign interpreted as a stork. Woodcut from P. Valerianus, *Hieroglyphica*, 1556. 23 Pastoral letter on an ostracon. Thebes, 6th century AD. Copyright British Museum. 24 Dominique Vivant Denon on a bronze medallet, 1808. Collection Peter Clayton. © Photo Peter Clayton. 24–5 Thebes. Engraving from *Description de l'Egypte*, vol. III, 1823. 26 Thomas Young. Engraving after Thomas Lawrence. © Photo Peter Clayton. 27 Page from Thomas Young's diary. By permission of the British Library. 28 The Philae obelisk, Kingston Lacey. Photo Emily Lane. Four cartouches. Engravings from J.-F. Champollion, *Précis du Système Hiéroglyphique des Anciens Egyptiens*, 1828. 29 J.-F. Champollion from *Académie des Inscriptions*, vol. 25, 1921–22. 30 Cleopatra and her son Caesarion. Relief, 1st century AD, on the temple of Hathor, Dendera. © Photo Peter Clayton. Champollion's name in demotic from J.-F. Champollion, *Lettre à M. Dacier* in *Académie des Inscriptions*, vol. 25, 1921–22. 31 'Tableau des Signes Phonétiques', October 1822. Facsimile in J.-F. Champollion, *Lettre à M. Dacier* in *Académie des Inscriptions*, vol. 25, 1921–22. 32 The Temple of Abu Simbel, inaugurated 1256 BC. © Photo Peter Clayton. 33 Six cartouches of Ramesses II. Engraving from J.-F. Champollion, *Précis du Système Hiéroglyphique des Anciens Egyptiens*, 1828. 34 Lid of

Tutankhamun's alabaster box. Thebes, 14th century BC. Egyptian Museum, Cairo. Miniature coffin for Tutankhamun's intestines. Thebes, 14th century BC. Egyptian Museum, Cairo. Photo The Griffith Institute, Ashmolean Museum, Oxford. 35 Lid of a box with Tutankhamun's name. Thebes, 14th century BC. Egyptian Museum, Cairo. Photo The Griffith Institute, Ashmolean Museum, Oxford.

Chapter 2

36 Table of scripts after DeFrancis, *Visible Speech*, 1989. 37 Masthead of *Le Maître Phonétique*, 1914. 38 American deaf signing from Scott K. Liddell, *American Sign Language Syntax*, Mouton de Gruyter, The Hague 1980. 40 George Bernard Shaw. Photo Irish Tourist Board. 41 Sign in Soho, London. Photo Rob Campbell. Extract from physics text courtesy F. N. H. Robinson. 42 Rebus from G. Palatino, *Libro Nuovo*, *c*. 1540. Rebus letter by Lewis Carroll, *c*. 1869, from Evelyn M. Hatch, *A Selection from the letters of Lewis Carroll to his Child-Friends*, 1933. Sumerian tablet, *c*. 3000 BC. Illustration from A. A. Vaiman, *Über die protosumerische Schrift. Acta Antiqua Academiae Scientiarum Hungaricae 22*, 1974. 43 Samuel Pepys. Engraving from S. Pepys, *Memoires Relating to the State of the Royal Navy* 1690. Last page of Samuel Pepys's diary, 1669. The Master and Fellows of Magdalene College, Cambridge. 45 Advertisement from *l-orizzont*. It-Tlietla 20 September 1994. Osmanian alphabet from David Diringer, *The Alphabet*, London 1968. 46 Inscription from statue of Darius. Susa, 6th–5th century BC. Archaeological Museum Tehran. 47 Sumerian-Akkadian tablet, *c*. 1750 BC. Illustration from M. Civil and R. Biggs, *Notes sur des textes sumériens archaïques, Revue d'Assyriologue*, 60, 1966. Crowd with banners on the Mount of Olives, Jerusalem, 1918. Photo Imperial War Museum. Commemorative rubbing by Mao Zedong, *c*. 1953, from DeFrancis, *The Chinese Language*, 1984. 48 Planting rice in China. Photo from Gerhard Kiesling and Bernt von Kügelgen, *China*, Verlag Neues Leben 1957. 49 Woman praying before the character 'fo'. © Wang Miao/ANA, Paris. 50 12 signs (above) from DeFrancis, *The Chinese Language*, 1984. 18 signs from *Reading the Past*, British Museum Press, 1990. Copyright British Museum. 51 M. C. Escher, *Metamorphosis III* (detail). Woodcut, 1967–68. © 1995 M. C. Escher/Cordon Art-Baarn-Holland. All rights reserved.

Chapter 3

52 Hand print and dots in a cave, Pech Merle. Photo Jean Vertut. 53 Bison with marks. Marsoulas, France. Drawing by H. Breuil, from *Four Hundred Centuries of Cave Art*, Montignac 1952. Engraved horse. Les Trois Frères, France. Drawing after H. Breuil. 54 Customs officers. Engraving after a 15th century window in Tournai Cathedral. The Mansell Collection. Eagle bone from Le Placard, W. France, *c*. 13,500 BC. © Alexander Marshack, *The Roots of Civilization*, Moyer Bell Limited, 1991. Tally stick of 1739. Engraving. The Mansell Collection. Tally stick from the British Exchequer. Courtesy of the Governor and Company of the Bank of England. 55 Kupe, Torres Strait Islands. Copyright British Museum. Inca clerk with quipu. Engraving from G. Poma, *Nueva Crónica*, 1613. Quipu, Peru. Copyright British Museum. 56 Pictorial roster of 84 families in the band of Big Road, Oglala Sioux, Dakota. Drawing, before 1883. National Anthropological Archives. The Smithsonian Institution, Washington. Letter from a Cheyenne father. Illustration from G. Mallery, *Picture Writing of the American Indians*, 1893. 57 Yukaghir Love Letter. Illustration after Shargorodskii, 1895. 59 Clay tokens. Susa, *c*. 3300 BC. Photo courtesy Musée du Louvre, Paris. Leonard Woolley digging at Ur, 1920s. Photo British Museum. 60 Bulla with six tokens. Late Uruk. Musée du Louvre, Paris. © Photo R.M.N. 61 Bulla with seven tokens. Late Uruk. Musée du Louvre, Paris. © Photo R.M.N. Bulla with cuneiform inscription. Nuzi, *c*. 1500 BC. Courtesy Ernst Lacheman. Bulla and X-ray. Susa, Late Uruk. Photo courtesy Musée du Louvre, Paris. 62 Clay tablet. Late Uruk. Staatliche Museen zu Berlin – Preussischer Kulturbesitz Vorderasiatisches Museum. 63 Tablet relating to administration of barley. Uruk. Photo courtesy of Christie's, London.

Black obelisk. Assyrian, 9th century BC. Copyright British Museum. Relief with weighing scene. Kalhu, 9th century BC. Copyright British ..useum. **66** Administrative tablet. Archaic script phase III. From the ..enmeyer collection: State of Berlin. Photo M. Nissen.

..rt II
. Boundary stone. Babylonian, *c.* 1120 BC. Copyright British Museum. ..xt from the Book of the Dead inscribed on a scarab of Web-Seny, 18th ..nasty (1570–1293 BC). Courtesy of the Royal Scottish Museum. Mace ..ad. Babylonian, *c.* 2250 BC. Copyright British Museum.

..apter 4
. Impression of a seal of Ur-Nammu (2112–2095 BC). Copyright British ..useum. Darius hunting lions. Impression of a seal. Iraq, *c.* 500 BC. ..pyright British Museum. **72** Stairway of the Palace of Darius, Persepolis. ..oto courtesy of the Oriental Institute, University of Chicago. Religious ..remony at Persepolis. Engraving from T. Hyde, *Historia Religionis*, 1700. . Carsten Niebuhr. Engraving. Photo Det Kongelige Bibliotek, ..penhagen. Inscription from Persepolis. Engraving from C. Niebuhr, *..isebeschreibung nach Arabien*, 1774. **74** Decipherment by Georg ..otefend. Engraving from A. H. L. Heeren, *Ideen über die Politik*, 1815. ..rtrait of George Grotefend from E. A. Wallis Budge, *The Rise and ..ogress of Assyriology*, 1925. **76** The rock at Behistun. Engraving from ..Flandrin and P. Coste, *Voyage en Perse*, 1851. **77** Portrait of Henry ..wlinson. Mezzotint after Henry Wyndham Philips, 1850. The ..scriptions and relief at Behistun. Lithograph after Rawlinson, from *The ..rsian cuneiform inscription at Behistun*, 1846. **78** Clay cylinder of Tiglath-..eser I (1120–1074 BC). Assyrian. Copyright British Museum. **80** Statue of ..dea. Sumerian, *c.* 2100 BC. Musée du Louvre, Paris. Brick inscription of ..-Nammu (2112–2095 BC). Sumerian. Copyright British Museum. ..pression of a cylinder seal inscribed to Ibni-Amurru. Babylonian, 18th ..ntury BC. Copyright British Museum. Impression of a cylinder seal with ..-abi. Ur, *c.* 2600 BC. Copyright British Museum. **81** Gold plaque of Darius ..m Persepolis, 6th century BC. Archaeological Museum, Tehran. Cone ..scription of Ur-Bau (2155–2142 BC), Lagash. Copyright British Museum. ..–83 School tablet. Old Babylonian period. Copyright British Museum. . Writing in cuneiform. Photos courtesy Marvin A. Powell. **84** Two tablets, ..3000 BC and *c.* 2100 BC. Copyright British Museum. **85** Tablet, *c.* 600 BC. ..pyright British Museum. Stele of Hammurabi. Susa, *c.* 1760 BC. Musée ..I Louvre, Paris. © Photo R.M.N. **86** Tablet with multiplication table. Old ..bylonian. Copyright British Museum. **87** Tablet recording the distribution ..seed grain. Old Sumerian. Photo courtesy Musée du Louvre, Paris. . Tablet concerning field ownership from Shuruppak, *c.* 2600 BC. Staatliche ..useen zu Berlin – Preussischer Kulturbesitz Vorderasiatisches Museum. Photo ..Stenzel. **90** Tablets in the library at Ebla, *c.* 2300 BC. Photo Paolo Matthiae. . The Tarkondemos seal. Copyright British Museum. 'Squeeze' of a ..ttite inscription from Carchemish from D. G. Hogarth, *Carchemish*, 1914.

..hapter 5
.. Narmer palette. Egyptian, *c.* 3200 BC. Egyptian Museum, Cairo. Part of ..letter in hieratic script with comparative hieroglyphs. All rights reserved, ..e Metropolitan Museum of Art, New York. **94–95** False door of Khut-en-..ah. Egyptian, *c.* 2000 BC. Staatliche Museen Preussischer Kulturbesitz ..gyptisches Museum, Berlin. **98** Wooden mirror case from Tutankhamun's ..mb. Thebes, 14th century BC. Egyptian Museum, Cairo. Boltin Picture ..brary. **99** Relief from the temple of Amun-Re, Karnak, 1965–20 BC. . Photo Peter Clayton. **100** Thoth from the funerary papyrus of Sety I. ..emphis, *c.* 1310 BC. Copyright British Museum. **102–103** Section from the ..nerary papyrus of Pawiaenadja, 1000–800 BC. Staatliche Museen zu Berlin ..Preussischer Kulturbesitz Ägyptisches Museum und Papyrussammlung. ..hoto Dr G. Murza. **105** Tile inlaid with the name of Ramesses II, *c.* 1250 ..C. Staatliche Sammlung Ägyptischer Kunst, Munich. **106** Egyptian scribe.

Saqqara, 5th century BC. Musée du Louvre, Paris. Signs for a scribe from G. Möller, *Zeitschrift des Deutschen Vereins für Buchwesen und Schrifttum*, II, 1919. **107** Hesire. Relief carving from Saqqara, *c.* 2700–2650 BC. Egyptian Museum, Cairo. Hirmer Fotoarchiv. Tutankhamun's writing implements. Thebes, 14th century BC. Egyptian Museum, Cairo. Photo The Griffith Institute, Ashmolean Museum, Oxford. Writing implements. Staatliche Museen zu Berlin – Preussischer Kulturbesitz Ägyptisches Museum und Papyrussammlung.

Chapter 6
108 Arthur Evans. Painting by W. B. Richmond, 1907. © Ashmolean Museum, Oxford. **109** 'The Room of the Throne' from A. Evans, *Palace at Minos*, vol. IV, 1935. Photo of Linear B tablet published by A. Evans in *American British School in Athens*, VII, 1900. **111** Gold double-axe. Minoan, *c.* 1500 BC. Iraklion Archaeological Museum. Hirmer Fotoarchiv. **112** Cypriot inscription. Copyright British Museum. **113** Horse tablet from Chadwick, *The Decipherment of Linear B*, 1958. Sanctuary of Aphrodite, Paphos, Cyprus. Photo courtesy Professor Franz Georg Maier. **115** Michael Ventris in 1937. Photo R. & H. Chapman, Buckingham. Grid from Michael Ventris, *Work Notes on Minoan Language Research and Other Unedited Papers*, ed. Anna Sacconi, 1988. **117** Grid from Michael Ventris, *Work Notes on Minoan Language Research and Other Unedited Papers*, ed. Anna Sacconi, 1988. **118** Linear B tablet. Pylos, 13th century BC. **119** Sign drawings by Ventris from *Archaeology*, Spring 1954. Ventris at work. Photo by Tom Blau. Camera Press London.

Chapter 7
120 Section of the Dresden Codex from E. Förstemann, *Die Maya-Handschrift der Königlichen Öffentlichen Bibliothek zu Dresden*, 1892. **121** Eric Thompson. Photo courtesy George Stuart and the National Geographic Society. Photo Otis Imboden. **123** Copán in the late 8th century AD by T. Proskouriakoff. Courtesy Peabody Museum, Harvard University. Drawing by Barbara Fash, from William Fash, *Scribes, Warriors and Kings*, 1991. **124** Drawing below right from David Kelley, *Deciphering the Maya Script*, University of Texas Press, 1976. **125** Rabbit drawing a codex. Drawing by Diana Griffiths Peck. **128** Section of the Dresden Codex from E. Förstemann, *Die Maya-Handschrift der Königlichen Öffentlichen Bibliothek zu Dresden*, 1892. **129** Statuette of the young maize god. Copán. Courtesy American Museum of Natural History, New York. **131** The 'Church'. Chichén Itzá. Photo Irmgard Groth. Portrait of Fray Diego de Landa from *Relación de las Cosas de Yucatán*, 1941. **132** Yuri Valentinovich Knorosov. Photo Michael Coe. **133** Section of the Dresden Codex from E. Förstemann, *Die Maya-Handschrift der Königlichen Öffentlichen Bibliothek zu Dresden*, 1892. **134** Lintel with bloodletting scene. Yaxchilán, AD 770. Copyright British Museum. 3 drawings (above) from Stephen D. Houston, *Maya Glyphs*, British Museum Press, 1989. **136–7** Cylinder vase. Nakbé Region, Guatemala, *c.* 672–830. © Justin Kerr. **138** Mosaic mask. Temple of Inscriptions, Palenque, AD 683. Merle Greene Robertson copyright 1976. **139** Lid of Pacal's sarcophagus. Temple of Inscriptions, Palenque, AD 683. Merle Greene Robertson copyright 1976. **140–141** Glyphs from the edge of Pacal's sarcophagus. Temple of Inscriptions, Palenque, AD 683. Drawings and photographs Merle Greene Robertson copyright 1976. Pacal's name in glyphs drawn by John Montgomery. **142** Mural. Room 2, Bonampak, late 8th century AD. Drawing by Antonio Tejeda. Courtesy Peabody Museum, Harvard University. Reproduced in Mary Miller, *The Murals of Bonampak*, Princeton University Press, 1986. **143** Cacao pot, Rio Azul. Courtesy George Stuart. Photo by George Molley. Glyph drawings by David Stuart.

Chapter 8
144 Zebu seal. Mohenjo-daro, 2500–2000 BC. Photo Erja Lahdenperä for the University of Helsinki. © National Museum of India. **146** Priest-king. Mohenjo-daro, *c.* 2000–1750 BC. Museum of Pakistan, Karachi. **147** Seals

from Mohenjo-daro. Photos Erja Lahdenperä for the University of Helsinki. © Archaeological Survey of India. **148** Drawing (right) from *World Archaeology*, February 1986. **149** Cretan seals from A. Evans, *The Palace at Minos*, vol. IV, 1935. **150** Phaistos disc. Crete, not later than *c.* 1700 BC. Iraklion Archaeological Museum. **151** Proto-Elamite tablet. Musée du Louvre, Paris. Tablet with biscript dedication. Susa, *c.* 2200 BC. Musée du Louvre, Paris. **153** Gold tablets. Pyrgi, *c.* 500 BC. Museo di Villa Giulia, Rome. Photo Scala. **154** Mirror. Etruscan, 3rd century BC. Etruscan gems. Hercle, *c.* 400 BC; Achle, 500–400 BC. Drawings from *Reading the Past*, 1990. Copyright British Museum. Sarcophagus of Seianti Hanunia Tlesnasa. Chiusi, *c.* 150 BC. Copyright British Museum. **155** Rongorongo board. Easter Island. Copyright British Museum.

Part III
156 Base of Trajan's Column, Rome. Photo J. C. N. Coulston.

Chapter 9
158 Souk in Aleppo. Photo Michael Jenner. **159** Illustrations from Rudyard Kipling, *Just So Stories*, 1902. **160** Sandstone sphinx. Serabit el-Khadim, Sinai, 15th century BC. Copyright British Museum. Inscriptions from William Foxwell Albright's *The Proto-Sinaitic Inscriptions and their Decipherment, Harvard Theological Studies*, vol. 22, 1966. Copyright 1966 by the President and Fellows of Harvard College. Reprinted by permission. **162** Literary tablet. Ugarit, *c.* 14th century BC. Copyright British Museum. Bilingual seal of Mursilis III. Ugarit. Hirmer Fotoarchiv. **163** Bronze statuette of a god. Ugarit. Copyright British Museum. Silver statuette. Ugarit, 15th–13th century BC. Aleppo Museum. School tablet. Drawing by C. Virolleaud in *Le Palais Royal d'Ugarit*, vol. II, 1957. **164** Phoenician ship on wall relief from the Palace of Sencherib (705–681 BC), Nineveh. Engraving in A. H. Layard, *Monuments of Nineveh*, 1849. Ostracon from Izbet Sartah. Drawing from F. M. Cross, *Bulletin of the American School of Oriental Research*, no. 238, 1980. Inscription from Byblos. Illustration from M. Dunand, *Byblia Grammata*, 1945. **165** Phoenician inscription on stone (above). Idalion, 391 BC. Copyright British Museum. Inscription (middle) from Donner and Röllig, *Kanaanische und Aramäische Inschriften III*, 1969. Inscription (below) from M. Lidzbarski, *Ephemeris für semitische Epigraphik III*, 1915. **167** Greek inscription on a limestone base, 6th century BC. All rights reserved, the Metropolitan Museum of Art, Rogers Fund, 1916 (16.174.6). Attic jug with inscription, 8th century BC. National Museum, Athens. Photo DAI, Athens.

Chapter 10
168 Bucchero-ware jug in the shape of a cock. Viterbo, 7th–6th century BC. The Metropolitan Museum of Art, Fletcher Fund, 1924. **171** Page from the Book of Kells, before AD 807. Courtesy of the Board of Trinity College, Dublin. Page from the Gospels of Tsar Ivan Alexandre. Bulgaria, 1355–56. By permission of the British Library. **172** Dead Sea Scroll. Title page of the Manual of Discipline, mid-1st century AD. Palestine Archaeological Museum. **173** Scribal implements, 19th century. Courtesy of the Isaac Kaplan Old Yishuv Court Museum, Jerusalem. **174** Detail from the Koran. Iraq, 1304. Shi'ah prayer. Calligraphy by Muhammad Fatiyab, early 19th century. Musée de l'histoire naturelle, Paris. Wine-bowl with kufic script. Seljuq, early 11th century. Copyright British Museum. **175** Film poster by Satyajit Ray, 1960. Courtesy Satyajit Ray. Fragment of pillar with the edict of Ashoka. Central India, 3rd century BC. Copyright British Museum. Part of so-called Velvikudi grant. Copper plate, Madakulam, 769–70 AD. By permission of the British Library. **176** Explanation of Hangul by King Sejong. Modern facsimile. By permission of the British Library. **178** Runic merchants' labels. Bergen, 12th century AD. University Museum of National Antiquities, Oslo, Norway. **179** Hunterston brooch. Early 8th century. © Trustees of the National Museums of Scotland 1995. Ring. Lancashire, 9th century. Copyright British Museum. Panel from the Franks Casket. Ivory

box, *c.* AD 700. Copyright British Museum. **180** Portrait of Sequoya by Charles Bird King, early 19th century. Library of Congress Washington. Cherokee alphabet of 1821. By courtesy of the American Tourist Board. **181** Letters from Geoffroy Tory, *Champ-fleury auquel est contenu l'art et science de la vraie proportion des lettres*, 1529.

Chapter 11
182 Student in a calligraphy class in Canton Middle School. Photo Rupert Harrison. Camera Press London. **183** Oracle bone rubbing from reign of Wu Ting, *c.* 1200–1180 BC. **184** Illustrations from J. F. Billeter, *The Chinese Art of Writing*, Editions d'Art Albert Skira S.A. Geneva, 1990. **185** Rubbing from an inscribed bronze vessel. Chinese, Western Zhou period, 1050–771 BC. Copyright British Museum. Characters from DeFrancis, *The Chinese Language*, 1984. **187** Pages from the Xinhua Dictionary, 1990. **188** Photo from W. E. Soothill, *A Mission in China*, 1907. **192** Inkstone. Hopei province. Private collection. Chinese calligraphy brushes. Private collection. From J. F. Billeter, *The Chinese Art of Writing*, Editions d'Art Albert Skira S.A. Geneva, 1990. **193** Chen Hongshou, 'The Four Joys of Nan Sheng-lu' © Foto Wettstein & Kauf, Museum Rietberg, Zurich. **194** From J. F. Billeter, *The Chinese Art of Writing*, Editions d'Art Albert Skira S.A. Geneva, 1990. **195** The character 'shou' by Wu Changshuo, 1923. From J. F. Billeter, *The Chinese Art of Writing*, Editions d'Art Albert Skira S.A. Geneva, 1990. **196** A children's class in China. © Sally and Richard Greenhill, London. **197** A Chinese typewriter. Photo B. Lang. Detail from map of Beijing. © RV Reise- und Verkehrsverlag. © Cartography: Geo Data.

Chapter 12
198 Page from *Kojiki, Ancient history of Japan*, completed in AD 712. Copy printed in 1803. By permission of the British Library. **200** Japanese crammer. Photo Jung Kwan Chi. Camera Press London. **204–5** 'The letter the wind.' Japanese woodblock by Torii Kiyohiro, 1751–64. Copyright British Museum. Bookseller. Japanese woodblock, Torii Kiyonobu. 18th century. Copyright British Museum. Japanese Cornflakes packet, 1985. Kellogg Company of Great Britain Limited. **208** Street sign. Japanese National Tourist Organisation. Kanji from J. Marshall Unger, *The Fifth Generation Fallacy*, Oxford University Press, New York, 1987.

Chapter 13
210 Signage developed by the Institute of Graphic Arts for U. S. Department of Transportation. **212** Coca-Cola logos. Photo courtesy of Coca-Cola Great Britain and Ireland. Coca-Cola and Coke are registered trademarks which identify the same product of the Coca-Cola Company. Symbols for the 1972 Olympics by Otl Aicher. **213** Gypsy and hobo signs from Albertine Gaur, *A History of Writing*, British Library, revised edition 1993. **214** Poster for *Schindler's List* © 1993 Universal City Studios, Inc. & Amblin Entertainment, Inc. **215** Inscription by Ralph Beyer, 1980s. Courtesy of Ralph Beyer. **216** Diagram engraved on a plate sent into space on *Pioneer 10*, 1972. Photo NASA. Cave painting of an ox, Font de Gaume. Drawing by H. Breuil, from *Four Hundred Centuries of Cave Art*, Montignac 1952.

Postscript: Writing in the New Millennium
218 Bone tags from tomb U-j, Abydos, Egypt, *c.* 3200 BC. Courtesy Deutsches Archäologisches Institut, Cairo. **220** 'The Da Vinci Highway Code' cartoon, 2004. Reproduced by kind permission of Private Eye/Mike Barfield. **221** Tabula Cortonensis, 3rd or 2nd century BC. Florence, Museo Archeologico. **222** Tabula Cortonensis, drawing of side A. Luciano Agostiniani and Francesco Nicosia. **224** Egyptian inscription from Wadi el Hol, Egypt, *c.* 1900–1800 BC. Digital image from a photograph by Bruce Zuckerman and Marilyn Lundberg, West Semitic Research. Courtesy Department of Antiquities, Egypt. **225** Chinese pottery signs from Yangshao culture, *c.* 5000–4000 BC. *Antiquity* 1995. Seal from Turkmenistan, late 3rd millennium BC. Fred Hiebert.